Praise for *Truth and Truthfulness*

"Bernard Williams' last book is the most interesting set of reflections on the values of truth and truth-telling in living memory. His grasp of philosophical arguments is astonishing. . . . The book manages to be both learned and passionate without being pretentious. And of course witty; . . . Williams' analytic expertise is combined with an acute sensibility to historical facts, or claims to fact, about the history of practices of telling the truth about the past, or about oneself. He writes about what Western civilisations do and have done in trying to find out and to tell the truth. The book presents what are argued to be human universals about the values of truth, as opposed to the historical circumstances in which particular ways of finding out come into being."
—*Canadian Journal of Philosophy*

"Anyone who wants to understand the relations between the relatively arcane issues concerning truth debated by philosophy professors, and the larger question of what self-image we human beings should have, would do well to read Williams's new book. It is a major work."
—Richard Rorty, *London Review of Books*

"This brilliant and disturbing book is in part an attempt to reanimate the humanities, or at least save them from the kind of self-destruction which results from claiming that whether they actually say anything true is irrelevant and unimportant. . . . This is a fascinating and riveting work, and it shows, in a way in which no other recent work of philosophy has done, that the subject can be both important and comprehensible—and that is a very considerable achievement indeed."
—Alasdair Palmer, *Sunday Telegraph*

"*Truth and Truthfulness* is subtle, agile, diligent in its treatment of detail, yet always with an eye on the 'big questions.' . . . It is suffused by a sly Oxonian sense of humour and a keen feeling for the pleasures of philosophical argument. Yet this playfulness does not detract from its underlying seriousness of purpose: this is a defence of the value of truth against those modern sceptics who deny its existence."
—Edward Skidelsky, *New Statesman*

"Elegance and subtlety are the hallmarks of Bernard Williams's philosophical style, both in the quality of the thought and the manner of his prose. His contributions have enriched philosophical debate for decades, and as this rich and absorbing book about truth and the vocations of truth shows, they continue to do so."
—A. C. Grayling, *Literary Review*

BERNARD WILLIAMS

❖ ❖

Truth & Truthfulness

AN ESSAY IN GENEALOGY

PRINCETON UNIVERSITY PRESS · PRINCETON AND OXFORD

Copyright © 2002 by Princeton University Press
Published by Princeton University Press, 41 William Street,
Princeton, New Jersey 08540
In the United Kingdom: Princeton University Press,
3 Market Place, Woodstock, Oxfordshire OX20 1SY

Fourth printing, and first paperback printing, 2004
Paperback ISBN 0-691-11791-8

The Library of Congress has cataloged the cloth edition of this book as follows

Williams, Bernard Arthur Owen.
Truth and truthfulness : an essay in genealogy / Bernard Williams.
p. cm.
Includes bibliographical references and index.
ISBN 0-691-10276-7 (cloth : alk. paper)
1. Truth. 2. Truthfulness and falsehood. I. Title.
BD171 .W528 2002
121—dc21   2002023663

ISBN-13: 978-0-691-11791-1

ISBN-10: 0-691-11791-8

British Library Cataloging-in-Publication Data is available

This book has been composed in Janson Typeface
Printed on acid-free paper. ∞
pup.princeton.edu
Printed in the United States of America

9   10   8

❖ FOR ❖

REBECCA, JACOB, JONATHAN,

AND SAM

I have always had a high regard for those who defend grammar or logic.

One realizes fifty years later that they have warded off great dangers.

—PROUST *(M. de Charlus)*

Lack of an historical sense is the hereditary defect of philosophers

... So what is needed from now on is *historical philosophizing,*

and with it the virtue of modesty.

—NIETZSCHE

Contents

❖   ❖   ❖   ❖   ❖

TRUTH & TRUTHFULNESS

1

❖ ❖ ❖ ❖ ❖

THE PROBLEM

1. *Truthfulness and Truth*

Two currents of ideas are very prominent in modern thought and culture. On the one hand, there is an intense commitment to truthfulness—or, at any rate, a pervasive suspiciousness, a readiness against being fooled, an eagerness to see through appearances to the real structures and motives that lie behind them. Always familiar in politics, it stretches to historical understanding, to the social sciences, and even to interpretations of discoveries and research in the natural sciences.

Together with this demand for truthfulness, however, or (to put it less positively) this reflex against deceptiveness, there is an equally pervasive suspicion about truth itself: whether there is such a thing; if there is, whether it can be more than relative or subjective or something of that kind; altogether, whether we should bother about it, in carrying on our activities or in giving an account of them. These two things, the devotion to truthfulness and the suspicion directed to the idea of truth, are connected to one other. The desire for truthfulness drives a process of criticism which weakens the assurance that there is any secure or unqualifiedly stateable truth. Suspicion fastens, for instance, on history. Accounts which have been offered as telling the truth about the past often turn out to be biassed, ideological, or self-serving. But attempts to replace these distortions with "the truth" may once more encounter the same kind of objection, and then the question arises, whether any historical account can aim to be, simply, true: whether objective truth, or truth at all, can honestly (or, as we naturally put it, truthfully) be regarded as the aim of our inquiries into the past. Similar arguments, if not quite the same, have run their course in other fields. But if truth cannot be the aim of our inquiries, then it must surely be more honest or truthful to stop pretending that it is, and to accept that . . . : and then there follows some description of our situation which does without the idea of truth, such as that we are engaged in a battle of rhetorics.

We can see how the demand for truthfulness and the rejection of truth can go together. However, this does not mean that they can happily co-exist or that the situation is stable. If you do not really believe in the existence of truth, what is the passion for truthfulness a passion for? Or—as we might also put it—in pursuing truthfulness, what are you supposedly being true to? This is not an abstract difficulty or just a paradox. It has consequences for real politics, and it signals a danger that our intellectual activities, particularly in the humanities, may tear themselves to pieces.

The tension between the pursuit of truthfulness and the doubt that there is (really) any truth to be found comes out in a significant difficulty, that the attack on some specific form of truth, such as the case I have mentioned, historical truth, itself depends on some claims or other which themselves have to be taken to be true.[1] Indeed, in the case of history, those other claims will be claims *of the same sort*. Those who say that all historical accounts are ideological constructs (which is one version of the idea that there is really no historical truth) rely on some story which must itself claim historical truth. They show that supposedly "objective" historians have tendentiously told their stories from some particular perspective; they describe, for example, the biasses that have gone into constructing various histories of the United States.[2] Such an account, as a particular piece of history, may very well be true, but truth is a virtue that is embarrassingly unhelpful to a critic who wants not just to unmask past historians of America but to tell us that at the end of the line there is no historical truth. It is remarkable how complacent some "deconstructive" histories are about the status of the history that they deploy themselves. A further turn is to be found in some "unmasking" accounts of natural science, which aim to show that its pretensions to deliver the truth are unfounded, because of social forces that control its activities. Unlike the case of history, these do not use truths of the same kind; they do not apply science to the criticism of science. They apply the social sciences, and typically depend on the remarkable assumption that the sociology of knowledge is in a better position to deliver truth about science than science is to deliver truth about the world.[3]

The point that the undermining of some history needs other history is correct and not to be forgotten, but it cannot by itself remove the tensions and put an end to the problem. Such arguments may merely be added to the problem and, as has often happened in recent years, accelerate a deconstructive vortex. Of course all such discussions have their time, and the intense criticism in this spirit that was for a while directed to such things as literary interpretation and the possibility of objective history may now, to some extent, be passing. But this does not mean that the real problems have gone away. Indeed, the real problems have been there, as Nietzsche understood, before the label of "post-modernism" made them a matter of public debate, and they remain there now. Moreover, there is a danger that the decline of the more dramatic confrontations may do no more than register an inert cynicism, the kind of calm that in personal relations can follow a series of hysterical rows. If the passion for truthfulness is merely controlled and stilled without being satisfied, it will kill the activities it is supposed to support. This may be one of the reasons why, at the present time, the study of the humanities runs a risk of sliding from professional seriousness, through professionalization, to a finally disenchanted careerism.

My question is: how can we address this situation? Can the notions of truth and truthfulness be intellectually stabilized, in such a way that what we understand about truth and our chances of arriving at it can be made to fit with our need for truthfulness? I believe this to be a basic problem for present-day philosophy.

The tensions in our present culture that are generated by this problem, the tensions (as I summarily put it) between truth and truthfulness, break out in several styles of conflict. One is that between two views of the Enlightenment. It is a familiar theme of contemporary criticism, one that has been inherited from some members of the Frankfurt School,[4] that the Enlightenment has generated unprecedented systems of oppression, because of its belief in an externalized, objective, truth about individuals and society. This represents the Enlightenment in terms of the tyranny of theory, where theory is in turn identified with the external "panoptical" view of everything, including ourselves. Now there is in any case a question whether the Enlightenment's models of scientific understanding do lead to the denial of political freedom and, if they do, by what social and intellectual routes. I shall argue that there are, equally, positive relations between the concepts of scientific truth and political freedom. But, even apart from that question, there is a another current in the Enlightenment, which is that of critique, a critique that has indeed been a main expression of the spirit of political and social truthfulness. It is in this respect, I believe, that the Enlightenment has been a particular associate of liberalism. In the course of the book, I shall try to explore some associations between liberal critique, on the one hand, and truthfulness on the other—truthfulness, moreover, in its association with truth. Some writers have tried to detach the spirit of liberal critique from the concept of truth, but I shall claim that this is a fundamental mistake. An influential figure in this company is Richard Rorty,[5] and I shall refer to his formulations in various connections. The position he calls "liberal irony" has particularly attracted attention by not wanting to affirm its own truth, but that is not the most important issue it raises. The most significant question is not about the truth-status of political or moral outlooks themselves. It is about the importance that those outlooks attach to other kinds of truth, and to truthfulness.

The tensions in our culture between truth and truthfulness are also expressed in a familiar contrast between two different ways of doing philosophy. I do not mean by this the supposed distinction between "analytic" and "continental" styles in philosophy: besides being, on any showing, dramatically misnamed, this does not represent any one contrast at all. On the questions that concern me here, there is a different distinction. On one side, there is a style of thought that extravagantly, challengingly, or—as its opponents would say—irresponsibly denies the possibility of truth altogether, waves its importance aside, or claims that all truth is "relative" or suffers from some other such disadvantage. To help the argument along, I need a general term to pick out those who adopt this kind of outlook. The term will necessarily be vague: several different views fall within the outlook, and some writers who have the outlook do not distinguish too carefully the particular view they hold. In earlier drafts of this book I called them sceptics about truth, but that was misleading, because "scepticism" brings with it from the philosophical tradition too heavy a suggestion that the problems concern our *knowledge* of the truth, where it is agreed that there is something that we can know or fail to know; whereas the people in question here are more disposed to dismiss the idea of truth as the object of our inquiries altogether, or to suggest that if truth is supposed to be the object of inquiry, then there is no such thing and that what passes itself off as inquiry is really something else. They might be called "subverters," but this has the disadvantage that it is what many of them would be too pleased to call themselves. I shall call them simply "deniers," where that means that they deny something about truth (for instance, at the limit, its existence) which is usually taken to be significant in our lives. What exactly various of them deny will be a central question in the book.

On the other hand, against the deniers, we get reminders from the philosophy of language, particularly in the "analytic" mode, that these reckless claims are plainly false and are not believed by the people who make them, who know perfectly well, for instance, that it is true that it is Tuesday night and that they are in the United States. Moreover, the claims could not be true, since no-one can learn or speak a language unless a large class of statements in that language is recognized to be true. These lines of argument are quite correct, so far as they go, and they will play a part in my discussion. But how far do they get us? This second party—call it the party of common sense—having rehabilitated truth in some of its everyday roles, usually assumes that there is not much to be said about the rest of the deniers' critique. But there may well be much of the critique that the reply leaves untouched: the suspicions about historical narrative, about social representations, about self-understanding, about psychological and political interpretation—all of this may remain as worrying as the deniers suggest.

The commonsense party's attitude to the deniers is based on a misunderstanding. It thinks that since the notion of truth is indeed fundamental, the fact that the deniers are muddled about elementary applications of that notion undermines what they say about everything else. Some deniers have indeed been attached to confused formulations in the philosophy of language, in part derived from a mangling of Saussure, to the general effect that language consists of "arbitrary signs" which "get their meaning" from their relations to other signs, and since this is so, it cannot relate to a non-linguistic world. This is a tissue of mistakes. If *dog* is an "arbitrary" sign for a dog, it is at any rate a sign for a dog, and that must mean that it can refer to a dog: and a dog is a dog, not a word. I shall not go on about this kind of thing. There are more interesting ideas to consider among the deniers' materials. Deniers do not get their views just from simple mistakes about language and truth. Rather, they believe that there is something to worry about in important areas of our thought and in traditional interpretations of those areas; they sense that it has something to do with truth; and (no doubt driven by the familiar desire to say something at once hugely general, deeply important, and reassuringly simple) they extend their worry to the notion of truth itself.

The collective result of these various misunderstandings is that the deniers and the party of common sense, with their respective styles of philosophy, pass each other by.[6] We need to understand that there is indeed an essential role for the notion of truth in our understanding of language and of each other. We need to ask how that role may be related to larger structures of thought which are essential to our personal, social, and political self-understanding. How far are the narratives that support our understandings of ourselves and of each other, and of the societies in which we live, capable of truth? Is truth what they need to have? Or can they be truthful without being true? In facing these questions, we had better be open to the idea that these larger structures can be the object of serious suspicion.

I shall be concerned throughout with what may summarily be called "the value of truth." In a very strict sense, to speak of "the value of truth" is no doubt a category mistake: truth, as a property of propositions or sentences, is not the sort of thing that can have a value. The commonsense party will deny that there is a value of truth in this strict sense, and this is easily accepted. The phrase "the value of truth" should be taken as shorthand for the value of various states and activities associated with the truth. Much of the discussion will be directed to the value of what I shall call the "virtues of truth," qualities of people that are displayed in wanting to know the truth, in finding it out, and in telling it to other people.[7] The deniers, on the other hand, claim that in this deeper sense there is no value of truth: they think that the value of these states or activities, if they have any, is not to be explained in terms of the truth, and it is this I reject. For instance, they may say that even if some people think it very important in itself to find out the truth, there is not really any value in having true beliefs beyond the pragmatic value of having beliefs that lead one toward the helpful and away from the dangerous. Some who hold just this much may be very moderate deniers; so far as the everyday concept of truth is concerned, they may even belong to the commonsense party. But I shall claim that they as much as the more radical deniers need to take seriously the idea that to the extent that we lose a sense of the value of truth, we shall certainly lose something and may well lose everything.

2. Authority

The tensions that break out if one surrenders serious conceptions of truth and truthfulness are also expressed in the conflicts, familiar in the past two decades, about authority in the academy. They were well illustrated in David Mamet's play *Oleanna*.[8] The play has mainly been understood as a piece about sexual harassment and gender relations, and it was in that connection that it created a commotion when it was first staged. But it is also about something else, closely related but importantly different. A complaint constantly made by the female character is that she made sacrifices to come to college, in order to learn something, to be told things that she did not know, but that she has been offered only a feeble permissiveness. She complains that her teacher (whose subject seems to be something like the sociology of education) does not control or direct her enough: he does not tell her what to believe, or even, perhaps, what to ask. He does not exercise authority. At the same time, she complains that he exercises power over her. This might seem to be a muddle on her part, or the playwright's, but it is not. The male character has power over her (he can decide what grade she gets), but just because he lacks authority, this power is mere power, in part gender power. His decision to change her grade is not the sexual harassment that she and her newfound feminist companions later make it out to be, but he has left a space in which almost anything could be understood in that way.

There are some very reductive criticisms of traditional academic authority that do seem to leave us in this position. If the canon of works or writers or philosophies to be studied, and the methods of interpreting them, and the historical narratives that explain those things, are all equally and simultaneously denounced as ideological impositions, we are indeed left with a space structured only by power. This is bad news from several points of view. One is that it leaves the critics themselves with no authority, since they need to tell a tale (a lot of detailed tales, in fact) to justify *that* tale: this is the point that, for instance, the denunciation of history needs history. They also need a tale to explain why they are in a position to tell it. Even if they fall back, rather pitifully, on a claim to authority just from minority status, a tale is needed to explain the relevance of that.

But if no authority, then only power. And—a second piece of bad news—the utterly reductive story will not leave the critics themselves with enough, or any, power. It is always a mistake for a minority or the disadvantaged party to reduce things to the bottom line, for on the bottom line they are simply a minority. Or at least that is so if their reduction of things to the bottom line is actually taken seriously, as in academia it rarely is. (The hard-pressed chairman of an English department once confessed to me that, faced with a group of faculty accusing him of being an agent of the hegemonic power structure, he would have liked to say, "You're right, and you're fired.") Even if they can gather enough power (significantly helped by those who do not think it just a matter of power but feel guilty, uneasy, old-fashioned, and so on) to have wide influence on humanities departments, they do not have enough power to sustain humanities departments when it is felt by a wider world that the humanities are boring, tiresome, and useless. Even if they had enough power to win over some academies, they would not have enough power to sustain that sort of academy. Real power is political, economic, social power, and while it is crucially influenced by ideas, it will be so only if those ideas have some authority.

A third piece of bad news is that the extremity of the entirely reductive or nihilist position (or, rather, the impression that this is the position, since hardly anyone holds it) serves to suppress discussion, not only of how much there may be in the criticisms, but of how we can think about intellectual authority. Here it is worth mentioning a very ancient device of deflationary rhetoric—it goes back certainly to the Greek sophists—which is stock-in-trade with this kind of denier. It consists in taking some respected distinctions between the "higher" and the "lower," such as those between reason and persuasion, argument and force, truthfulness and manipulation, and denying the higher element while affirming the lower: everything, including argument and truthfulness, is force, persuasion, and manipulation (really). This trope has its uses. It can perhaps persuade people to take a more realistic view of the "higher" elements; it may help them to detect misleading idealizations of them. But, besides the fact that it soon becomes immensely boring, it has the disadvantage that it does not help one to understand those idealizations, or, still less, to resituate the original opposition in a new space, so that the real differences can emerge between the force which is argument and the force which is not—differences such as that between listening and being hit, a contrast that may vanish in the seminar but which reappears sharply when you are hit.

Everyone should agree with the commonsense party (indeed everyone to this extent does really agree with them) that there are many everyday truths. This is a very vague notion for now; a more detailed account of ideas related to it will come later.[9] They include not merely statements about limited arrays of what J. L. Austin called "middle-sized dry goods," but many psychological statements—for instance, about what someone is doing—and many statements about the past. (In these connections there is the important notion of a mini-narrative, which may itself express knowledge of what someone is doing.) Everyday truths stand in contrast to such things as interpretative historical narratives and complex psychological interpretations (it is significant, as we shall see, how styles of such interpretation themselves have a history).

In referring to "everyday truths" I do not mean (and this point is central to the philosophical construction that I attempt in later chapters) that they are picked out by being certain or incontestable. When someone claims that a proposition of this kind is true, there are well-known ways of contesting the claim, for instance, by explaining how the person could have come to believe the proposition without its being true: the material of these resources itself to a considerable extent consists of everyday truths. What is incontestable is that on very many occasions propositions of these kinds are true and can be known to be true. Everyday truths can readily and reasonably be counted as facts, and when Nietzsche said, in contradiction to many other things he said, "[F]acts are precisely what there are not, only interpretations," he was wrong.[10]

Everyday truths are important, and their importance should be stressed, for several reasons. One is a central concern of this book: their role in an account of truth and meaning, and in constructing a philosophical anthropology. Second, everyone knows that there are everyday truths, and what many of them are. Philosophy here, on lines variously laid down by Hume, Wittgenstein, Stanley Cavell, needs to recall us to the everyday. All these writers, however, want to recall us to the everyday from the personal alienation of a fantastic philosophical scepticism which claims to doubt that there is an external world, or past time, or other minds. For our present concerns, the recall to the everyday (to the kinds of everyday truths that everyone recognizes) is from a politicized state of denial which is not so much an alienation from the shared world as a condition of sharing in an alienated world.

That state of denial, and the politics that goes with it, offer a real risk of the humanities' being alienated from the rest of society, at least if the humanities are supposed to be regarded as a passionate and intelligent study. (There is no lack of interest in kitsch or heritage humanities, which of course makes the threat more serious.) Busy people can reasonably become impatient with the humanities, as compared with the natural and applied sciences. This is not because of a false prestige of those sciences, or a naive view that they consist entirely of everyday truths. It is rather that everyone knows that there are a lot of everyday truths around in the areas of those sciences, as that some telescopes work and some do not, that some bridges fall down and others do not, and the presence and relevance of those everyday truths give these sciences a claim to seriousness that the humanities can easily lose. The impression of frivolity is enhanced when the humanities adopt a rhetoric of political urgency which represents only the café politics of émigrés from the world of real power, the Secret Agents of literature departments. This suffers the disadvantage of being rightly despised both by those who take liberal politics seriously and by those who do not.

Truthfulness implies a respect for the truth. This relates to both of the virtues that, I shall claim in the following chapters, are the two basic virtues of truth, which I shall call Accuracy and Sincerity: you do the best you can to acquire true beliefs, and what you say reveals what you believe. The authority of academics must be rooted in their truthfulness in both these respects: they take care, and they do not lie. There are more refined virtues in the same direction. It is a good idea, for instance, that academics should resist the comforts of a knowing evasiveness. Much doubt has been cast on Carlos Castaneda's claims about shamanism. The writer of a book about Castaneda and the social sciences says, "It does not matter to me in the least whether any or all of the 'events' reported by Castaneda ever 'took place.'"[11] The declaration may be all right, but the scare quotes are not.

The virtues of truth are not conventional fetishes of academic theorizing. They can be concretely addressed to everyday truths and revealed in the way that one handles everyday truths. Moreover, there is a coherent account of how people's training, which is what helps to convey this authority, is related to what they do. Of course, authority is also displayed in the handling of theory and interpretation, but in the humanities and the sciences alike, one can have confidence in that only if one can respect the writer's dealings with everyday truths. There is a moving and rather bitter example of this in the history of the reputations of Sartre and Camus. For years, bienpensants of the intellectual Left followed Sartre in his brutal marginalization of Camus, his contempt for what was depicted as Camus's fatuous humanism, subjective moralism, and incompetence in philosophy. Camus may have been a less professional philosopher than Sartre, but it is far from clear that he was a worse one. What is certainly true is that he was a more honest man, and his authority as an intellectual lay in that fact, as opposed to the deceitful constructions with which Sartre managed to mislead himself and his followers.

What must be emphasized, however, is that the basic cultivation of truthfulness in relation to everyday truths is only the beginning, not the whole story. There is no way of sticking to everyday truths and no more. Positivism—in the sense, roughly speaking, of thinking that not much more is needed than to establish the concrete facts and set them down—cannot be seen as a minimalist or default position. Any story is a story, and positivism (which is involved in many contemporary forms of conservatism in the humanities) implies the double falsehood that no interpretation is needed, and that it is not needed because the story which the positivist writer tells, such as it is, is obvious. The story he or she tells is usually a bad one, and its being obvious only means that it is familiar. As Roland Barthes said, those who do not re-read condemn themselves to reading the same story everywhere: "they recognize what they already think and know."[12] To try to fall back on positivism and to avoid contestable interpretation, which may indeed run the risk of being ideologically corrupted: that is itself an offence against truthfulness. As Gabriel Josipovici has well said, "Trust will only come by unmasking suspicion, not by closing our eyes to it."[13] While truthfulness has to be grounded in, and revealed in, one's dealings with everyday truths, it must go beyond truth as displayed in everyday truths. That itself is a truth, and academic authority will not survive if it does not acknowledge it.

3. *Nietzsche*

The problems that concern this book were discovered, effectively, by Nietzsche. It is not a book, obviously enough, in any of Nietzsche's styles (for anyone other than Nietzsche to try to write

such a book would be a very bad idea). Nor is it a book about
Nietzsche, but it uses a method for which I have borrowed a name
from him, *genealogy*, and I intend the association to be taken seriously. The deniers, as I have called them, often claim the inheritance
of Nietzsche, and some of their more dramatically extreme positions
have taken the form of an interpretation of him that yields a "new
Nietzsche."[14] Just because little of this book directly discusses him,
something should be said here about Nietzsche's problem and his
own relation to it, if we are to avoid some of the rubble left from
recent cultural wars.

One of Nietzsche's most striking qualities is the obstinacy with
which he held to an ideal of truthfulness that would not allow us to
falsify or forget the horrors of the world, the fact that their existence
has been necessary to everything that we value, or the further fact
summarized in the slogan "God is dead"—that the traditional metaphysical conceptions which have helped us to make sense of the
world, and in particular to bear its horrors, have terminally broken
down. He often calls on honesty and intellectual conscience, and he
prizes those who have to have an argument against the sceptic inside
themselves—"the great self-dissatisfied people." In *The Anti-Christ*,
he wrote:

> Truth has had to be fought for every step of the way, almost every-
> thing else dear to our hearts, on which our love and our trust in life
> depend, has had to be sacrificed to it. Greatness of soul is needed for
> it, the service of truth is the hardest service.—For what does it mean
> to be *honest* in intellectual things? That one is stern towards one's
> heart, that one despises "fine feelings", that one makes every Yes and
> No a question of conscience! [15]

(Those deniers who take Nietzsche's message to be that we should
give up on the value of truth altogether need to consider that this
was written at the very end of his active life.) The value of truthfulness embraces the need to find out the truth, to hold on to it, and
to tell it—in particular, to oneself. But Nietzsche's own dedication
to this value, he saw, immediately raised the question of what it is.
We have taken it for granted, he thinks, and we have seriously mis-

understood it: as he says in *Beyond Good and Evil*, "Perhaps nobody yet has been truthful enough about what 'truthfulness' is."

One of his most illuminating statements of this question occurs in *The Gay Science*:

> This unconditional will to truth—what is it? Is it the will not to let oneself be deceived? Is it the will *not to deceive*? For the will to truth could be interpreted in this second way, too—if "I do not want to deceive *myself*" is included as a special case under the generalization "I do not want to deceive". But why not deceive? But why not allow oneself to be deceived?[16]

The reasons for not wanting to be deceived, he goes on to say, are prudential; seen in that light, wanting to get things right in our intellectual studies and in practical life will be a matter of utility. But those considerations cannot possibly sustain an *unconditional* value for truth: much of the time it is more useful to believe falsehoods. Our belief in the unconditional will to truth

> must have originated *in spite of* the fact that the disutility and dangerousness of "the will to truth" or "truth at any price" is proved to it constantly. "At any price": we understand this well enough once we have offered and slaughtered one faith after another on this altar!
>
> Consequently, "will to truth" does *not* mean "I do not want to let myself be deceived" but—there is no alternative—"I will not deceive, not even myself"; *and with that we stand on moral ground.*
>
> . . . you will have gathered what I am getting at, namely, that it is still a *metaphysical faith* upon which our faith in science rests—that even we knowers of today, we godless anti-metaphysicians, still take *our* fire, too, from the flame lit by the thousand-year-old faith, the Christian faith which was also Plato's faith, that God is truth; that truth is divine.

The title of the section is "In What Way We, Too, Are Still Pious." The idea is developed further in Book 3 of *On the Genealogy of Morality*, where the "ascetic ideal" which has received an unflattering genealogical explanation is discovered to lie at the root of the will to truth, which powered the need to discover that very explanation. But that does not overthrow the will to truth: "I have every respect for the ascetic ideal *in so far as it is honest!*"[17]

The "unconditional will to truth" does not mean that we want to believe any and every truth. It does mean that we want to understand who we are, to correct error, to avoid deceiving ourselves, to get beyond comfortable falsehood. The value of truthfulness, so understood, cannot lie just in its consequences. Various beliefs may be necessary for our life, but that does not show them to be true: "life is not an argument."[18] Already in *Human, All Too Human* he had noted, "*Fundamental Insight*: There is no pre-established harmony between the furthering of truth and the well-being of humanity." When he stresses the historical, indeed the continuing, importance of various false conceptions that have regulated people's thoughts and provided intellectual security, he *contrasts* them with the truth and wonders what will emerge from a battle between them and a growing awareness of the truth: "To what extent can truth stand to be incorporated?"[19]

While he holds on to the values of truthfulness, he is very clear that the truth may be not just unhelpful but destructive. In particular the truths of Nietzsche's own philosophy, which discredit the metaphysical world, may join the forces of a destructive nihilism if they come to be accepted. In the Nachlass there is a revealing note, which mentions the way in which the idea of truthfulness has turned against the morality that fostered it, and which ends with the remark: "This antagonism—*not* to esteem what we know, and not to be *allowed* any longer to esteem the lies we should like to tell ourselves—results in a process of dissolution."[20] In what ways are we "not allowed" to esteem these lies? To some degree, Nietzsche thought that this was already in his time a historical or social necessity: that, at least among thoughtful people, these beliefs simply could not stand up much longer or have much life to them. It is a good question whether this was right, particularly when we recall the secularized, political, forms that are taken, as Nietzsche supposed, by the same illusions. What is certainly true is that Nietzsche took it to be an *ethical* necessity, for himself and anyone he was disposed to respect, not to esteem these illusions. It needed courage: "How much truth does a mind endure, how much does it *dare*? More and more that became for me the measure of value. Error (faith in the ideal) is not blindness. Error is *cowardice*."[21]

There continue to be complex debates about what Nietzsche understood truth to be. Quite certainly, he did not think, in pragmatist spirit, that beliefs are true if they serve our interests or welfare: we have just seen some of his repeated denials of this idea. The more recently fashionable view is that he was the first of the deniers, thinking that there is no such thing as truth, or that truth is what anyone thinks it is, or that it is a boring category that we can do without. This is also wrong, and more deeply so. Nietzsche did not think that the ideal of truthfulness went into retirement when its metaphysical origins were discovered, and he did not suppose, either, that truthfulness could be detached from a concern for the truth. Truthfulness as an ideal retains its power, and so far from his seeing truth as dispensable or malleable, his main question is how it can be made bearable. Repeatedly Nietzsche—the "old philologist," as he called himself—reminds us that, quite apart from any question about philosophical interpretations, including his own, there are facts to be respected. He praises the ancient world for having invented "the incomparable art of reading well, the prerequisite for all systematic knowledge," and with that "the *sense for facts*, the last-developed and most valuable of all the senses."[22] At the beginning of *On the Genealogy of Morality*, he tells us that "the English psychologists" should not be dismissed as old, cold, boring frogs; rather, they are brave animals, "who have been taught to sacrifice desirability to truth, every truth, even a plain, bitter, ugly, foul, unchristian, immoral truth . . . Because there are such truths—"

In his earliest writings about truth and error, Nietzsche sometimes spoke as though we could compare the entire structure of our thought to the "real" nature of things and find our thought defective. The deniers' interpretations tend to rely heavily on writings in this style, in particular on a very early essay, *Truth and Lies in a Nonmoral Sense*, in which he wrote:

> What then is truth? A movable host of metaphors, metonymies, and anthropomorphisms: in short, a sum of human relations which have been poetically and rhetorically intensified, transferred and embel-

lished, and which, after long usage, seem to people to be fixed, canonical and binding. Truths are illusions we have forgotten are illusions; they are metaphors that have become worn out and have been drained of sensuous force, coins which have lost their embossing and are now considered as metal and no longer as coins.[23]

On the account that he sketched in this essay, it is as though the business of using any concepts at all falsified a reality which in itself is—what? Formless, perhaps, or chaotic, or utterly unstructured. Later, he rightly rejected this picture,[24] with its implication that we can somehow look round the edge of all our concepts at the world to which we are applying them and grasp its nature as entirely unaffected by any descriptions (including, we would be forced to admit, the descriptions "formless," "chaotic," and so on). In *Truth and Lies* he suggests that nothing is really "identical" or "the same," that all identity is a fiction.[25] To some degree, this idea shares in the suspect metaphysical conception. To take an example: the concept "snake" allows us to classify various individual things as "the same animal," and to recognize one individual thing as "the same snake." It is trivially true that "snake" is a human concept, a cultural product. But it is a much murkier proposition that its use somehow *falsifies* reality—that "in itself" the world does not contain snakes, or indeed anything else you might mention.

I agree with those who think that Nietzsche overcame the confused formulations of *Truth and Lies*, and that he came to see that there was no standpoint from which our representations as a whole could be measured against the world as (in this sense) it really is. As a remark in the Nachlass puts it: "The antithesis of the apparent world and the true world is reduced to the antithesis 'world' and 'nothing'."[26] This idea of the world "in itself," in this sense, was precisely a relic of the kind of metaphysics that Nietzsche wanted to overcome. We must say "in this sense," because there are other contrasts between the world "in itself" (or "as it really is") and "the world as it appears to us," which, as opposed to this picture, leave it with some properties that it really has: on some philosophical theories, the world really possesses certain properties ascribed to it by natural science, but its appearance as coloured, for instance, is merely relative to us or other perceivers.[27] Such theories may equally be incoherent, but if so, it is not for the reasons at issue here.

Although Nietzsche was keenly alive to what concerns the deniers, he was an opponent of them. The indifference to truthfulness which they encourage would be for him merely an aspect of nihilism. When he discovered that the values of truth and truthfulness, such as the resistance to self-deception and to comforting mythologies, were not self-justifying and not given simply with the concept of truth—unless the concept of truth is itself inflated into providing some metaphysical teleology of human existence, of the kind that he rejected in Platonism—he did not settle for a demure civic conversation in the style of Richard Rorty's ironist, or saunter off with the smug nod that registers a deconstructive job neatly done. He was aware that his own criticisms and exposures owed both their motivation and their effect to the spirit of truthfulness. His aim was to see how far the values of truth could be revalued, how they might be understood in a perspective quite different from the Platonic and Christian metaphysics which had provided their principal source in the West up to now.

In this book I try to contribute to this project, and I use a method which I call "genealogy." It is a descendant of one of Nietzsche's own methods, but only one kind of descendant among others. Nietzsche himself was fully aware that the critique which he directed against old illusions might call in question some of what he said himself. He tried to make sure, by various stylistic inventions, that his writing should not be taken for standard philosophy or standard scholarship, or—and here he was sometimes less successful—for aphorism in a traditional manner. But, however significant his inventions, in the end he not only defends the idea of there being truths but also gives every sign of thinking that he has uttered some. The name "genealogy" can be appropriated to styles of writing which also descend from Nietzsche, but which, in contrast to him, try to avoid that commitment. To a greater extent than his texts, they are obsessionally concerned with their own status, and they hope, in particular, systematically to efface the marks of a writer asserting something to a reader. Alasdair MacIntyre has used the word to apply to such a project and has also brilliantly expressed its difficulties, spelling out the awkwardness that inescapably catches up with the writer, however quick on the turn he may be, who holds up before the reader's lens a sign saying that something is true or plausible or worth considering, and then tries to vacate the spot before the shutter clicks.[28]

My genealogical project does not need these escape and evasion tactics. Some of the story I shall tell, in ways to be explained in the next chapter, will explicitly be fiction; but this carries a claim that the fiction is helpful. Some of it claims to be history, accurate (I hope) in its facts and plausible in its interpretations. Quite a lot of it is philosophy (philosophy, that is to say, before it turns into history), which carries with it whatever claims are appropriate to philosophy, of being reasonable, convincing, or illuminating. I do not have the problem that some deniers have, of pecking into dust the only tree that will support them, because my genealogical story aims to give a decent pedigree to truth and truthfulness. Some of it aims to be, quite simply, true. As a whole, it hopes to make sense of our most basic commitments to truth and truthfulness. Whether, if it were to succeed in doing that, it could as a whole properly be called "true" is doubtful, but unimportant. It is certainly less important than that the story as a whole should be truthful.

2

❖ ❖ ❖ ❖ ❖

GENEALOGY

1. *Real and Fictional*

The subject of this book is truthfulness: various virtues and practices, and ideas that go with them, that express the concern to tell the truth—in the sense both of telling the truth to other people and, in the first place, telling the true from the false. My aim is to explain the basis of truthfulness as a value, and to suggest ways in which we can think about the forms that it has taken, and elaborations that it has received, in different historical circumstances. The kind of explanation I shall appeal to is a *genealogy*; and one of my concerns, alongside the particular case of truthfulness, is to look at the method itself.

A genealogy is a narrative that tries to explain a cultural phenomenon by describing a way in which it came about, or could have come about, or might be imagined to have come about. Some of the narrative will consist of real history, which to some extent must aim to be, as Foucault put it, "gray, meticulous, and patiently documentary."[1] This has a particular importance in relation to our ethical life, the ethical life of modernity. Our ethical ideas are a complex deposit of many different traditions and social forces, and they have themselves been shaped by self-conscious representations of that history. However, the impact of these historical processes is to some extent concealed by the ways in which their product thinks of itself. The most general reason for this is that a truthful historical account is likely to reveal a radical contingency in our current ethical conceptions. Not only might they have been different from what they are, but also the historical changes that brought them about are not obviously related to them in a way that vindicates them against possible rivals. This sense of contingency can seem to be in tension with something that our ethical ideas themselves demand, a recognition of their authority. The tension here is made worse by a feature of modern ethical systems, that they try to combine authority with transparency, and in aiming to be transparent—an aim that is part of their special concern with truthfulness—they encourage reflection on themselves in a style that reveals their contingency. All this means that there may well be something disobliging or disrespectful or critical about genealogical accounts. I shall come back to this idea.

However, genealogy is not simply a matter of what I have called real history. There is also a role for a fictional narrative, an imagined developmental story, which helps to explain a concept or value or institution by showing ways in which it could have come about in a simplified environment containing certain kinds of human interests or capacities, which, relative to the story, are taken as given. This simplified, imaginary, environment, which I shall sketch in the next chapter, I shall call "the State of Nature," a name which of course invokes the traditional use of such stories in political philosophy to explain the origins of the state. In contrast with some stories in that tradition, I shall suppose that the State of Nature does contain a society, a group of human beings who co-operate but are not kin. State of Nature stories have not been confined to explaining the state. One such story figures in Hume's account of the artificial virtue of justice. A recent example is E. J. Craig's illuminating account of the concept of knowledge.[2] In that account, a State of Nature is postulated in which human beings have certain basic needs, including of course a need for co-operation, and it is shown how, granted the powers of observation, recognition, and so on, that human beings have, they would develop a concept with (just about) the properties of the familiar concept of knowledge.

It is a good question, how a fictional narrative can explain anything, and I shall try to answer it in section 4 of this chapter. I hope that, given this answer, we shall be able to say that the fictional genealogy, the State of Nature story, offers an account of the primitive basis of truthfulness—specifically, of what I shall identify as two "virtues of truth." The sense in which it will offer the "primitive basis" of these values is something that the story itself, and the reasons for telling the story, will define. The State of Nature story will, later in the book, lead into some real history. However, before I come to the questions of how such fictional narratives work, and of how the real and the fictional elements are related to one other, I must explain what intellectual needs this whole genealogical enterprise is supposed to satisfy, and how it differs from some other inquiries that might be hoped to satisfy those needs.

2. Naturalism

Genealogy is intended to serve the aims of naturalism (and was understood to do so by Nietzsche, who first applied the term "genealogy" in this sense). Naturalism is a general outlook which, in relation to human beings, is traditionally, if very vaguely, expressed in the idea that they are "part of nature"—in particular, that they are so in respects, such as their ethical life, in which this is not obviously true. There is a well-known difficulty in stabilizing the idea of "nature" so that naturalism is not either trivially true or implausible to such an extent as to be uninteresting. It would be trivially true if "nature" contained whatever there is. Trying to find something that is not trivial, we may say that what naturalism recognizes are just those things recognized by the natural sciences. But then is biology a natural science? If biology is, is ethology? If ethology, what about the ethology of human beings, which includes culture? At this point, it may be that the screw is tightened, and naturalism is required to represent everything—plants, the behaviour of animals, human cultures—in terms of the universally applicable natural science, physics. So naturalism gets tied to the project of physicalistic reductionism. Physicalistic reductionism is an entirely implausible undertaking in itself; and it surely cannot be that the interests of a naturalistic approach to ethics, for instance, must be essentially tied to it.

We should get away from the preoccupation with reductionism. It cannot be that the concerns of those who have wanted to understand human beings, in their ethical as in other aspects, as part of nature, are essentially bound up with the prospects for the Encyclopedia of Unified Science. In trying to do better than this, we may consider the case of life. Living things are, one might think, part of nature if anything is: the study of them is, or used to be, called "natural history." So how could there possibly have been a question about naturalism in biology? However, this is to neglect a significant piece of history. Until the last century, vitalism was an option. It was agreed that there were living things, but there was great unclarity about what kind of property life was, in particular how it related to properties described by the other sciences. Hence there was a question whether life was part of nature, where that meant the *rest* of nature. That question has now been answered positively, and the characteristics of living things can now be clearly understood in a way that is continuous with biochemistry. Thus we can see in scientific terms how living things could have come to exist.

Questions about naturalism, like questions about individualism in the social sciences,[3] are questions not about reduction but about explanation. Of course I recognize that this leaves almost everything open. But that is as it should be, because the questions that are substantial and interesting *are* open. The questions concern what we are prepared to regard, at each level, as an explanation. Moreover, we have no reason to think that what is to count as an explanation, from bits of nature describable only in terms of physics to human beings and their cultures, is at each level the same kind of thing. The question for naturalism is always: can we explain, by some appropriate and relevant criteria of explanation, the phenomenon in question in terms of the *rest* of nature? (We might call this the "creeping barrage" conception of naturalism.)

When we get to the peculiarities of human beings, a special set of problems emerges. The huge innovation represented by *Homo sapiens* is the significance of non-genetic learning, which, with regard to both its nature and its effects, marks an overwhelming ethological difference between human beings and other animals. Every species has an ethological description, and *Homo sapiens* is no exception; but in this case, uniquely, you cannot tell the ethological story without introducing culture (consider, for instance, what is immediately involved in answering the question "In what sorts of places do they sleep?"). Consequently, the story is likely to differ significantly between groups of human beings, and in ways that typically involve history; in many cases, the human beings who are being described will also be conscious, in varying degrees, of that history. All this follows from the peculiar ethological character of this species.

Individual members of the species must of course typically, standardly, or in the right proportion have the psychological characteristics that enable humans to have this ethology, to live under culture. We can then ask: what are those characteristics? What is the best, most revealing and explanatory, description of them? Granted such a description, how might those characteristics have come into existence? In the case of some of them, the answer may be in terms of transmitted social influences operating on general learning capacities, but others may demand an explanation in terms of special, modular, capacities, and then there will be a question (as there is with the general learning capacities themselves) of how they have genetically evolved.

The case that specially interests us is the capacity shown, in some form or other, by humans in all cultures to live under rules and values and to shape their behaviour in some degree to social expectations, in ways that are not under surveillance and not directly controlled by threats and rewards. Call this, begging many questions, (the minimal version of) living in an ethical system. Living in an ethical system demands a certain psychology. But, importantly, it does not follow that all ethical systems demand the same psychology—moral psychology may be opportunistic (an example would be the supposed difference between shame and guilt societies). Nor need it be the case that one and the same ethical system demands exactly the same psychology of each participant. At this level, variation might be not simply individual but, more interestingly, systematic: this would be the case with our prevailing ethical system, if Carol Gilligan's hypothesis were true, that it involves different psychological formations from men and from women.[4]

Granted that there must be a psychology or psychologies underlying any ethical system, we can ask: what do these psychologies have to be like? What is involved in them? Our question here is: what is it for an answer to those questions to meet the demands of naturalism?

We can get to this question by recalling the shape of the naturalist's question in other examples. A naturalist will claim that what is involved in the case of human beings living in ethical systems can be coherently related to the rest of nature. But what exactly is, now, the rest of nature? In the case of vitalism, it meant nature up to living things; in the case of consciousness (which I have not so far mentioned), it will mean all of that, together with living things up to conscious living things. So what does "the rest of nature" mean in the present case? Does it mean: everything, including conscious living things, up to human beings? If this is what is meant, the focus of the naturalistic question will be: is the human capacity to live in ethical systems closely related to characteristics of other, non-human, species? Can it, and its emergence, be explained in basically the same terms as we use in understanding other species?

The naturalistic question about ethics has often been put in this way. Some of those who have discussed it in these terms have answered it in the negative. In particular, there have been those who have been very keen on characterizing human ethical capacities by contrast to other animals ("the brutes," as they were sometimes called in such traditions). Others have understood the naturalistic question in this same way but have given a positive answer to it. These are typically people who are impressed by what used to be called "sociobiology,"[5] and see the capacity needed for living under ethical systems as (for instance) "altruism" in some sense in which a character called by that name can be selected for in other species. But "altruism" cannot be brought across from other species to human beings without our taking into account the differences between the two, which form a major part of the problem.

The crudity of both these approaches, the negative and the positive, suggests that their shared form of the naturalistic question—the way in which they interpret "the rest of nature"—is misguided. Before getting to the psychologies that are distinctively presupposed by ethical systems, we need first to allow for the fact that culture affects almost all of human psychology. We cannot consider the most basic instinctual drives of human beings, those that in some sense they manifestly share with other species, without allowing for the influence of the cultural on them and on their expression. This in itself is simply an application, admittedly a far-reaching one, of an ethological platitude, that the way in which a given instinct or drive displays itself in a given species depends on that species' way of life. It is hardly surprising that the reproductive behaviour of the red deer differs spectacularly from that of the hedgehog or the stickleback, since their ways of life are notably different. If we are going to think in naturalistic terms, or the contrary, about the psychology of human beings as it is most immediately related to their living in ethical systems, we should think in the first place about the relations of that psychology to other aspects of *human* psychology.

There is of course a kind of false abstraction involved in this. I have already said that human beings live under culture, something that follows from the central significance of their capacity for non-genetic learning. I have also said that living under culture involves, roughly speaking, living in an ethical system. If so, we cannot ultimately separate the business of living under culture, together with all the effects that this has on other aspects of human psychology, from whatever it is that enables humans to live in an ethical system. Ultimately, it is true, we cannot. Perhaps, however, we can fruitfully postpone considering all these things together. The relation of at least some basic instinctual drives in human beings, even as they are necessarily modified by language and by culture, to functionally similar drives in other species may be rather more transparent than the psychologies that support ethical systems are. Given these ideas, the naturalist question about ethics will emerge as the question of how closely the motivations and practices of the ethical are related to other aspects of human psychology. With regard to this particular aspect of the very peculiar ethology of this species, this is the special form taken by the recurrent naturalist question which we have identified as arising elsewhere, for instance in the case of life: how does the phenomenon in question intelligibly relate to the *rest* of nature, and how, in particular, might it have come about? As one might put it, we are asking about human ethical life in relation to the rest of human nature. If we can make sense of this undertaking, of explaining the ethical in terms of an account of human beings which is to the greatest possible extent prior to ideas of the ethical, then there is a project of ethical naturalism which is intelligible, non-vacuous, and not committed to a general physicalistic reductionism that is (to put it mildly) dubious and anyway ought to be a separate issue.

3. *The State of Nature Is Not the Pleistocene*

Questions of the relations between culture and psychology, and between both of these and biology, have given rise to a good deal of tiresome and unnecessary controversy between evolutionary theorists and social scientists. Some writers in evolutionary theory have supposed that assumptions made by cultural anthropologists, in particular—the idea has been applied also to other social scientists—are inconsistent with the findings of evolutionary psychology or biology, when it has merely been the case that the anthropologists have, rightly or wrongly, regarded those findings as irrelevant to their interests. Anthropologists have referred, reasonably enough, to "the human capacity to acquire cultural norms," a capacity that enables any human being to acquire the culture of whatever the society may be in which he or she is brought up; the capacity, consequently, is neutral in itself between very different cultural contents. Since the interest of anthropologists is primarily in describing and explaining the differences between cultural systems, some of them have supposed that they will not get much help from a psychology that equally underlies all cultural systems. On the strength of this, some writers about evolution have taken the anthropologists to have a *particular theory* about the nature of the underlying psychological capacity, that it can be no more than a content-free all-purpose learning system, the "blank slate" of traditional empiricism. This theory is certainly incompatible with current psychological understanding and with evolutionary ideas (why should a tabula rasa, of all things, suddenly emerge at this stage of primate evolution?).[6]

Maybe some anthropologists have believed this theory, but their interests in no way imply that they must. You can accept that the psychological mechanisms underlying cultural learning are highly modular or content-directed—that human beings have been formed by natural selection so as to acquire some specific kinds of dispositions and aversions and skills—and still think that understanding this psychology, in particular understanding its evolution, may not contribute much to explaining the differences between cultural systems, since it underlies the capacity to grow up in any of them. However, it would not be reasonable to think this as a matter of principle, still less to suppose that it was somehow a necessity. In explaining cultural differences, we are likely to invoke human psychology, and in trying to show how different environments or circumstances elicit different behaviours from that psychology, we may well call on specific features of it. However that may be, it is certainly a mistake to suppose, as some evolutionary psychologists have supposed, that because culture and its acquisition imply a special psychology, every explanation of the cultural must refer to that psychology.

It is an even bigger mistake to suppose that every explanation of the cultural must be an explanation in terms of the evolution of that psychology—that every cultural development can be shown to contribute to the inclusive fitness of the human beings who live in that culture. Human psychology has evolved by natural selection, and we may be able to explain how that has come about: that is to say, how the development of certain psychological structures and capabilities contributed to the inclusive fitness of the creatures who first displayed them. That psychology is expressed in various cultural practices in various conditions. But there is absolutely no reason to think that the explanation of cultural differences or specific cultural formations will in general appeal *again* to increasing inclusive fitness. The generic human need to make and listen to music, for instance, might be explained at the level of evolutionary psychology, but the emergence of the classical symphony certainly cannot. In fact, the insistence on finding explanations of cultural difference in terms of biological evolution exactly misses the point of the great evolutionary innovation represented by *Homo sapiens*, the massive development of non-genetic learning.

There is another and quite different evolutionary approach, which is to explain cultural variation in terms of *cultural* evolution. This is the idea that cultural change and persistence should be explained, not in terms of biological evolution, but as a process that is analogous to it. Cultural phenomena are to be described in terms of replicating units, analogous to genes, which are subject to selective pressures of various kinds that serve to preserve or extinguish them. The units are such things as "tunes, ideas, catch-phrases, clothes fashions, ways of making pots," as Richard Dawkins has put it; it was Dawkins who introduced the word "meme" for such a unit of culture.[7] It may be that this analogy can be helpful in some connections. I shall not try to discuss its merits at any length, but there are at least two reasons, as it seems to me, to doubt how powerful it can be. One lies in the identification of the supposed cultural units. The history of ideas learned a long time ago to be very suspicious of supposed ideational elements travelling from one head to another. Dawkins gives as one example "the idea of God," but the notion that there is an item that goes under this name and is everywhere the same is a dramatic misunderstanding of the history even of monotheism, let alone of the anthropology of religion more generally.

Another problem concerns the forces of selection. It is accepted that the forces of selection in cultural evolution need not be the same as those that operate in biological evolution: that is to say, the explanation of a meme's survival (continued replication) need not lie in its making a better contribution than its alternatives to *the inclusive fitness of the people* whose culture includes that meme. There are many reasons besides that why a cultural element may flourish or die out; indeed, that is why this evolutionary model is different from the purely biological one. After a very careful discussion of relations between cultural and biological evolution, W. H. Durham concluded that "the single most important force of cultural transformation derives from the secondary-value-driven decisions of culture carriers."[8] In other words, changes in a cultural practice have most often to be explained in terms of other values or beliefs possessed by the people who live in the culture. As a general formula, of course, this does not offer much of an explanation, and it is not intended to, any more than in natural selection the fact that a character is selected for is itself the explanation; we need an explanation of why that itself should have happened. Similarly, you will not have an explanation if you say simply that a certain style of car, for instance, spread—that is to say, was bought by more motorists—because in virtue of their tastes and interests motorists found it an attractive style of car. There has to be some explanation of that fact itself.[9] But that leaves us with the complexities with which the social sciences have always had to live, of what, in a given case, the explanation of such a fact might be. If we can answer those questions, it is far from clear how much work, eventually, the evolutionary model itself will be doing.

If we turn back to the psychology that underlies cultural practices, evolutionary theorists will appeal in explaining it to the circumstances in which they suppose natural selection operated in favour of its various relevant features. These circumstances are standardly identified in the literature as the environment of our Pleistocene hunter-gatherer ancestors. It is important to the argument of this book that this is *not* what I mean when I offer the abstract representation of certain human activities and capacities which I call the State of Nature. My story is not intended as a speculation in evolutionary biology or as a contribution to prehistory. One obvious difference is that my story is explicitly offered as a fiction. To leave it simply at that, however, would be a little charitable, since, whatever the intention, the supposed environment of our Pleistocene ancestors, as it is invoked by evolutionary psychologists, is also a fiction. For many of the distinctive psychological elements in question, we have little idea even of which hominid species developed them, still less in what environment. These models of natural selection, as they stand, are in good part just-so stories. However, the evolutionary theorists' aim is to improve them in these respects, and their stories can be revised in the light of more evidence, in particular from the fossil record. With the State of Nature, on the other hand, while someone may propose a more illuminating version of it, no more can be *found out* about it. Moreover, while the evolutionists' speculations about the Pleistocene may be short of facts, they are required to be consistent with such facts as there are, and also not to violate any known natural laws. Stories about the State of Nature do not have to meet those conditions. They do not even have to be possible. So we come to the question, how can they tell us anything?

4. *How Can Fictions Help?*

Robert Nozick took up this question in connection with the archetypal use of State of Nature stories, to explain the origin of the state.
He starts with the idea, familiar in the philosophy of science, of a
"potential explanation," which is, roughly speaking, an explanation
that "would be the correct explanation if everything in it were true
and operated." A *law-defective* potential explanation is a potential
explanation with a false law-like statement, while a *fact-defective* potential explanation has a false antecedent condition.[10] Some explanations that are fact-defective but not law-defective are useful because
they show that a process is *possible*. This is why just-so stories can be
helpful in evolutionary biology: they can show that it is consistent
with evolutionary theory that a certain character could emerge
under natural selection, even if we do not know how it did so, and
indeed know that it was not exactly like this.[11]

   Nozick himself concentrates on "invisible hand" explanations,
which explain "what looks to be the product of someone's intentional design, as not being brought about by anyone's intentions."
However, I shall not follow him in this. Invisible hand explanations
form an important class, and it may well be that they have, as Nozick
puts it, "a certain lovely quality,"[12] but they are not, for my purpose,
the most significant case. There are interesting and helpful potential
explanations of human behaviour where what has to be explained,
the product of the imagined process, does not even look as though
it had been brought about intentionally. An example is Craig's discussion of the concept of knowledge, which I have already mentioned. His State of Nature gives an explanation, but what it explains, the concept of knowledge, does not look as though it had
been designed. On the contrary: before the story, one may well
never have asked what the function of the concept is, and that is part
of the point. Craig's story answers, in its fictional terms, the question
"Why should we have a concept such as the concept of knowledge?"
and, by answering it, suggests the question itself. What the question
introduces is the notion of function, and that step itself does some
of the work. If one sees the concept of knowledge as having a func-

tion—in particular, a function in relation to very basic needs—this in itself helps one to see why it has the features it has, and can discourage one from less fruitful approaches. A step from function to apparent intention would be a further step, which could not come into this case.

Craig's example, like my own State of Nature story, is an example of what I shall call an "imaginary genealogy"—"imaginary," because, as I said at the beginning of this chapter, there are also historically true genealogies. Imaginary genealogies typically suggest that a phenomenon can usefully be treated as functional which is not obviously so. Moreover, they resemble a larger class of explanations (including those given by natural selection theory) in explaining the functional in terms of the non-functional or, perhaps, in terms of the more primitively functional. The power of imaginary genealogies lies in introducing the idea of function where you would not necessarily expect it, and explaining in more primitive terms what the function is.

Imaginary genealogies are at least fact-defective. But when does fact-defectiveness turn into something more radical? With potential explanations in the natural sciences, one might perhaps hope (if optimistically) to cash out a distinction between the merely fact-defective and something more radical, the law-defective, in terms of the laws of nature, but this is rarely much help with the human examples. This is illustrated by Nozick's own discussion of the State of Nature in political theory. He says, "We learn much by seeing how the state could have arisen, even if it didn't arise that way."[13] But is there a sense in which it *could* have arisen in the way described by his State of Nature story? Nozick derives the political from the non-political, by showing how the state (or a bit less) might arise from a State of Nature in which people have (roughly speaking) only economic motivations and moral ideas of individual right. But everything we know of human evolution, development, and history tells us that there could not have been a pre-political condition with just those properties. Moreover, Nozick certainly regards that point as irrelevant to his project. So he does not mean that the state could have arisen in that way, if this implies that the imagined State of Nature could have existed: the antecedent condition is not just false but impossible. The most he can mean is that if that condition had existed, the state could have emerged from it. But we then face the question again, of what that tells us; all the more so, since a world in which such a condition could have existed might well be a world in which the processes by which one condition could emerge from another would themselves be different from those that operate in our world.

We can get some help with the question of what is involved in imaginary genealogies if we look at another famous example, Hume's derivation of the "artificial virtue" of justice. The state of affairs from which the story starts is one in which people are self-interested and have a capacity for limited sympathy, but have no motives of justice and, correspondingly, no concept of property. Given this condition, and given some further (quite strong) conditions of common knowledge, the story tells how people converge on adopting institutions of property and develop the dispositions of justice. The state of affairs from which this process starts, and hence the process itself, Hume recognizes to have been impossible.[14]

The distinctive idea of Hume's account is that when it becomes common knowledge that everyone would benefit from certain practices, those practices arise, and they involve a new kind of reason for action, one that essentially refers to other people's having similar reasons for action. In a very restricted sense, what has emerged is a collective reason for action: this is still a reason for individual action, though it is possessed collectively, and essentially so.[15] Reasons of the new type, those involved in the virtue of justice, are derived in the story from the primitive type, reasons of individual interest and limited sympathy, even though it may never be the case, and is almost certainly impossible, that there should have been a society in which the supposedly more primitive kind of reason existed without (some version of) the reasons of justice.

If this is so, what use is the story, and how could it explain anything? I suggest that it offers three elements. First, it shares with Craig's account of knowledge the feature that a functional account is given of something that not everyone would expect to have a functional account; and the account is given in terms of motivations that people must be granted to have anyway. Second, the account is functional because the relation between the derived, more complex, reason and the simpler, "more primitive," reasons or motivations is rational, in the sense that in the imagined circumstances people with the simpler motivations would welcome, and, if they could do so, aim for, a state of affairs in which the more complex reasons would operate. This rational relation might even be represented, very fancifully, by the story's describing the outcome as the conclusion of a deliberation. But it would weaken the genealogy to represent it in that way, just because of genealogy's third feature: like evolutionary explanations, it derives the functional from what is not functional or is functional only at a lower level. A story which offered a collective deliberation as the route to the outcome would presuppose what the story is supposed to explain: the people in the "earlier" situation would have already to appreciate the content of concepts such as justice and property, and their connections with reasons for action, but it is an important aim of the story to illuminate what is involved in these things.[16] An imaginary genealogy with these features is explanatory because it represents as functional a concept, reason, motivation, or other aspect of human thought and behaviour, where that item was perhaps not previously seen as functional; the explanation of the function is unmysterious, because in particular it does not appeal to intentions or deliberations or (in this respect) already purposive thought; and the motivations that are invoked in the explanation are ones that are agreed to exist anyway.

Why not just give a functional account without the story? Do the diachronic fictions of genealogy add anything except colour? They do. In relation to institutions, practices, expectations, and values that actually exist, of justice, promise-keeping, truthfulness, and so on, functional accounts are simply false. As Robert Brandom has said about language in general:

> Linguistic practice is not *for* something . . . [it is not] a means to secure some other end specifiable in advance of engaging in linguistic practice—not adaptation to the environment, survival, reproduction, nor co-operation—though it may serve to promote those ends. Even if . . . those functions explain why we came to have language, once we did have it, our transformation into discursive creatures swept all such

considerations aside. For discursive practice is a mighty engine for
the envisaging and engendering of *new* ends.[17]

To take the example that is the subject of this book, it is just not true
that the dispositions of truthfulness that we have, or that anyone
else has had, can be adequately explained in functional terms. As we
shall see in chapter 4, their value always and necessarily goes beyond
their function. Nevertheless, at a more abstract level, function plays
a role in explaining them. These dispositions have taken different
forms in different historical circumstances, and in grouping them
and explaining them as examples of the same kind of disposition, we
are relying on a functional interpretation, that every society needs
there to be dispositions of this general kind and also needs them not
to have a purely functional value. This interpretation, which requires an abstraction from actual historical variation, is then expressed in the fiction of the State of Nature, which is represented
through many other abstractions as well. We could not appeal to
some actual, very early, hominid society instead, because any actual
society would always already (as some thinkers are fond of saying)
present the features from which the abstraction has to be made.

The fiction is uniquely useful because—so far from confusing
genuine history and fiction—it enables us to keep count of what is
history and what is abstraction, and it helps us to avoid two errors.
One is that of going straight to our actual society with the apparatus
of functional explanation; this would distort our understanding of
our own cultural situation, debar us from seeing what is peculiar to
it as opposed to others, and lead us to a stupid reductionism. The
other error is to construct pictures of very early societies on the
basis of functional ideas and suppose that this was actual hominid
prehistory. Genealogy keeps historical fact and functionalist abstraction in their places.

5. *Shameful Origins*

A genealogical explanation such as Hume's is sometimes said to be
"reductive." As I have emphasized, in any strict sense this is false.

The genealogy gives no way of translating language that mentions
the resultant item into terms that mention only the original items,
nor does it claim that "justice" or "property" or "knowledge" introduces nothing over and above the original items—on the contrary, it
shows what new thing is introduced, and why it is new. Genealogical
explanation makes such things intelligible without getting involved
in reduction.

However, there is a looser sense in which genealogical explanations may be said to be reductive, to the extent that they explain the
"higher" in terms of the "lower"—knowledge in terms of beliefs and
everyday needs, the moral in terms of the non-moral. I said that
justice might be something that not everyone would expect to receive a functional account. It might be said, further, that the motivations of justice have a tendency to resist a functional account, on the
grounds that it will represent as instrumental and "lower" what is
properly seen as intrinsic and "higher." (This idea is very prominent
in Plato's *Republic*.)[18] Of course, "higher vs. lower" does not map
onto "intrinsic vs. instrumental" as simply as this suggests; moreover, the Humean account is not simply instrumental. But, however
one deals with these complexities, it looks as though only those who
already have an ethically ambitious view of justice will be dissatisfied
for these reasons with Hume's account of it. If one looks at what
might called the common interest in justice, as opposed to a Platonic
idealization of that interest, an account in the Humean style need
not represent justice in terms that fall too far short of what people
expect of it. One might, that is to say, accept Hume's account (understand justice in terms of that genealogical story) and still give
justice, its motivations and reasons for action, much the same respect as one did before one encountered the explanation—or perhaps more respect, if one had suspected that justice had to be a Platonically other-worldly idea if it was anything. In such a case, one
may say that the genealogical explanation is *vindicatory*.[19] Nozick's
derivation of the minimal state aims to be vindicatory, by his own
standards of right, and has the particular aim of showing that by
those standards there is no vindicatory genealogy of any more ambitious state.

Not all genealogies are vindicatory. The famous example from which the name itself is taken, Nietzsche's genealogy of morality,[20] is certainly a lot less benign. There are at least three features of Nietzsche's account that contribute to its unsettling or destructive effect, and which, for the same reason, distinguish it from Hume's example. What is being explained is the whole of morality, where that is identified through notions of obligation, blame, and guilt,[21] and Nietzsche rightly claims that morality in this sense demands to be understood as self-sufficient, and to resist explanation in terms of anything else at all. The resistance to a functional style of explanation, here, is very deep. Second, the explanation is in terms of forces that are not merely simpler or more primitive or non-moral or "lower," but are among the supposed enemies of morality—hatred and resentment and baffled self-assertion. Third, because of this, the process invoked in the explanation does not merely avoid being understood as intentionalist or deliberative; it must be unconscious, since no-one could arrive at that result while acknowledging this route to it. For the same reason, people who are identified with the result, the outlook of morality, must be resistant to this explanation of it, and if they come to accept the explanation, their outlook will have to change.

The element in Nietzsche's account that needs to be unconscious—the formation and operation of ressentiment—raises a problem about his conception of genealogy. It sounds like a psychological process, one that happens in an individual. But genealogy, in Nietzsche's own use of it as much as in Hume's, explains a social phenomenon. Nietzsche is trying to explain a new kind of collective reason, the shared consciousness of morality, and there is a problem about the role played in this explanation by what is seemingly a type of individual psychological reaction. Moreover, Nietzsche's genealogy is by no means meant to be entirely fictional. It has something to do with history, though it is far from clear what history: there are some vaguely situated masters and slaves; then an historical change, which has something to do with Jews or Christians; there is a process which culminates perhaps in the Reformation, perhaps in Kant. It has been going on for two thousand years.[22]

It may be that Nietzsche himself was relying on a type of historical explanation in psychological terms that owes more to Hegel's idealism than he would have wanted to acknowledge. If we are to see his explanation as having force, we shall have to integrate the references to individual psychology with the account of an actual social and historical process, and how exactly this should be done remains a question. A central point must be that in this case, unlike Hume's, there is a real genealogy that provides a location for the imaginary one. Morality, in Nietzsche's sense, is not a universal human phenomenon but a particular historical formation. The account resembles Hume's in making psychological and social sense of the system by reference to motivations that people have anyway, but Nietzsche's functional account is applied to a system of reasons—in this case, literally a *new* system—which very powerfully resists being understood in such terms; this why the psychology that he invokes in explaining it necessarily involves unconscious processes. The fact that Nietzsche's account has somehow to be placed in real history in one way presents a difficulty, but it also gives it an advantage over purely imaginary genealogies. Because we can refer to real history, we have some concrete idea of what it is for human beings—the ancient Greeks, for instance—to do without the particular outlook that the genealogy hopes to explain, and so a sharper sense of what may be added or lost by the development of that outlook. This itself may help us to find a place for the psychological elements in the historical account.

6. *The Genealogy of Truthfulness*

In setting out my own State of Nature story, I shall invoke some very basic human needs and limitations, notably the need for cooperation, and I shall consider ways in which they are related to discovering and telling the truth. The aim is to derive within the story *values* connected with these activities. A central question will be how the values derived can be regarded as intrinsic, as opposed to instrumental (and also what this distinction itself, in these connections, should be taken to mean). As I have explained in this chapter, I am not concerned with speculations about the evolution of the hominids (though if there is anything relevant to be known from such studies, I unsurprisingly hope that what I say will be consistent with it). The State of Nature story is a fiction, an imaginary genealogy, which proceeds by way of abstract argument from some very general and, I take it, indisputable assumptions about human powers and limitations. In virtue of that, and in line with other examples we have considered, I take it to be an example of philosophy.

While the account claims to show some conclusions that can be reached by these abstract arguments, it will also help us to see what cannot be achieved in this way. We can give an account of truthfulness and its value, I believe, in the particular philosophical mode of a fictional genealogy, but we shall see that such an account is essentially incomplete, and that after a certain point, or, rather, various different points, we must turn to real genealogy—to cultural contingencies and to history. We could put this by saying that philosophy goes only so far, that it gives only some kinds of explanations and not others. However, if we consider different ways in which the abstract account is incomplete and needs real history, and if we go back to the concerns that prompted this inquiry in the first place, I think it will be better to say that philosophy itself must involve more than abstract argument, and that, in confronting this kind of question, it must engage itself in history. In this as in other respects, philosophy cannot be too pure if it really wants to do what it sets out to do. We can leave the question of what we should call "philosophy."[23] What is certainly true is that if we want to understand our own attitudes to truthfulness—which is the original aim of the inquiry, the anxiety from which we started—the imaginary genealogy will take us only part of the way, and in order to go further, we shall need history. This is for three different reasons, each of which provides a theme for this book. One is that the imaginary genealogy itself reveals a gap in the motivations to truthfulness, a gap that can be filled by one or more of various values or attitudes, and what values or attitudes perform this role at a given time in a given society is a matter of fact. In this sense, culture and history *fill in* the abstract, fictional, account. This kind of development will be the concern of chapters 5 and 6.

Second, cultural developments *extend* what is offered in the imaginary genealogy. In certain connections, the State of Nature story delivers only a restricted or, as I shall put it, local conception. The story might be designed to deliver this much and no more simply because the local conception was an interesting abstract possibility, but in the case that concerns me there is another reason, that the local conception has existed as a matter of historical fact. The example is a certain conception of telling the truth about the past, and in chapter 7 I shall try to explain what this local conception was like, and also how at a given historical juncture it was replaced by another conception, which is the one that we now have. The local conception is bound to seem unsatisfactory from our later point of view, and that itself raises philosophical questions, in particular whether we have to see the development of the later conception as a growth in rationality: but certainly it is a development, one that is dimly anticipated, at best, in the State of Nature story.

Third, cultural changes have their own momentum and can involve elaborations of the idea of truthfulness that are more and more distant from its primitive base. The historical process to this extent is *autonomous*. The elaborations themselves need philosophical analysis and understanding, but in relation to the original account they are entirely contingent and, one might say, gratuitous. Yet they have occurred, and in doing so they have contributed to our conceptions of truthfulness, and so, once again, to the hopes and anxieties that we are trying to understand. A particular example of such a development, the rise of notions of personal autonomy in the eighteenth century and their relations to sincerity, will concern us in chapter 8.

All this is for later. We can now turn to the State of Nature story.

3

❖　❖　❖　❖　❖

THE STATE OF NATURE:

A ROUGH GUIDE

1. *The Division of Labour*

In the State of Nature there is a small society of human beings,
sharing a common language, with no elaborate technology and no
form of writing.

In supposing that these people are a linguistic community, I shall
assume that they speak a language which we (you, I, other human
beings) could come to understand. We need not make this assumption too strong. In particular, we need not assume that if we came
to understand their language, we could translate everything they
said into an equivalent in our own language. We would be able to
do this, if only roughly, for much of what they said, but we may
suppose that their language contains terms for which we have no
way of forming equivalents to sentences in which they occur. Where
this is so, however, what we would be able to do, if we encountered
them, is to enter imaginatively into the practice of using the term,
identifying with their use of it, and when we reflected on this, we
would get the hang of what they were saying.

The account of the fictional people in the State of Nature story
will be stripped down to certain functional ideas implicit in their use
of language for basic human purposes. Of course, any actual society
would also have many more cultural practices, more determinate
and, no doubt, locally peculiar. The model does not say what they
are, but this is expressly an abstraction. It is not simply that they

would not be human if there were not more to them than is presented in this story; beyond a certain point, they could not do what they do in the story unless there were more to their life than the story itself reveals. That this should be so was already implicit when I said in the previous chapter that the State of Nature was designed to bring out, in an abstract form, functional elements in the explanation of truthfulness; that every society not only needs there to be dispositions of this kind but needs them to have a value that is not purely functional; and that the State of Nature is supposed to be a society. This implies that the State of Nature story is essentially cumulative. Its first abstractions, offered in this chapter, are *too* abstract, and more will have to be added to them. This chapter offers only the basics, even of the State of Nature, and more of their implications will come out in the following chapters, until we eventually arrive at real history.

It is uncontroversial that a basic function of language is communication, where this includes, notably, telling other competent language-users things that they do not know. To embody this, we should include right at the beginning the idea of what may be called a *purely positional advantage*. This is the idea that a speaker can tell someone else about a situation because he is or was in it, while his hearer is not or was not. There are of course different kinds of purely positional advantage: I may be unable to observe what you can observe because you are there now and I am not; you can tell me what happened here a while ago because you were here then and I was not; and so on. All these differences of point of view or position, implicit in the idea of a purely positional advantage, presuppose, of course, another difference, that between one person and other. However, I do not want to treat the difference between "I" and "you" or "he" as *itself* an example of a positional advantage—as though not being you, or not being inside your mind, constituted my difficulty in knowing what you are thinking or feeling; this would point us firmly in the wrong direction.[1]

To express the differences between observers with respect to space and time in terms of "I" and "you" is anyway a little misleading, to the extent that it implies an egoistic point of view. In fact, each person in a collective group needs information which he or she is not in the best position to acquire: they are all, at various times and with respect to different pieces of information, at an advantage or disadvantage (purely positional, or otherwise) in relation to each other. What they need, in fact, is to pool information, and this implies, very significantly, that there will be a division of epistemic labour. In the State of Nature, this does not imply that there are specialists in some particular kinds of knowledge; at this stage of the story, it means only that on a given occasion one person does one thing and another does another.

The idea of a positional advantage is implicit in the idea of what one can come to know by observation. If someone has this idea, for instance of a person's coming to know something by looking and seeing, then he has the idea of things that this person, so placed, could not come to know by looking and seeing, and of other people who are placed in such a way that at the moment they could not come to know this thing in this way. These ideas contribute to an understanding of the epistemic division of labour, though naturally the people involved need not have formulated such ideas in any general way, any more than they need to have formulated the idea of a division of epistemic labour itself.

We have said that the participants in all this are people, human beings. They are not just recording devices; rather, they have beliefs, which they can express in the things they say.[2] Moreover, they can reflect on the beliefs they have, and on such questions as whether to express a belief on a particular occasion, or how much effort it is worth spending to get the answer to a particular question. What exactly is involved in these various capacities is something that will concern us later on. Later on, too, we shall have to consider more precisely what part belief plays in communication, and also some less obvious ways in which other people play a part in a person's having beliefs.[3] These will be particularly important when we move beyond beliefs that straightforwardly embody pieces of information. But for now, at our entry to the State of Nature, we concentrate on the basic phenomenon of people's beliefs' contributing to there being a shared pool of information: various observers are in different situations, and they then transport to the pool beliefs (in the favourable case, true beliefs or, again, knowledge) which each of them has acquired from being in that situation.

With this, we have the idea that one person may, on a given occasion or more generally, do better in this than another; and that people may be discouraged or encouraged, sanctioned, shamed, or rewarded with respect to this. One significant way in which these processes will work is through encouraging individual dispositions to do these things well. Since we are considering people, who have beliefs and desires and intentions, and who may or may not express their beliefs, it is already natural to think of these dispositions as falling into two different kinds. One kind of disposition applies to their acquiring a correct belief in the first place, and their transporting that belief in a reliable form to the pool. The other desirable dispositions—desirable, that is to say, from the social point of view of those using the pooled information—are necessary because reflective creatures will have the opportunity within this structure for deceit and concealment; they will also have the motives for them, as when a hunter has found a prey which he would rather keep for himself and his immediate family. (This is the force of Voltaire's famous remark to the effect that men have language in order to conceal their thoughts.) This second group of dispositions centrally contains the motivation, if one is purporting to tell someone something and the circumstances are right, to say what one actually believes.

The distinction between these two kinds of disposition is not only natural but also, I think, basic to questions about truthfulness, and I shall register this by treating each of the two groups, a lot of the time, as one generic disposition. I shall label the two kinds of disposition respectively as Accuracy and Sincerity. These are terms of art, and I shall use the capital letters to mark that fact. (In both cases, and particularly in the case of Accuracy, treating the set of relevant characteristics as one disposition involves some large over-simplifications: we shall be concerned with a more complex and realistic picture later on.) I shall call Accuracy and Sincerity the two basic *virtues of truth.*[4] The choice of the term "virtue" is meant to make a point about the way in which the distinction is to be understood. In everyday usage, it may be natural to think of Sincerity and its relatives as virtues, as being morally commendable, while the dispositions of Accuracy, care in acquiring correct information and so on, are more like skills or capacities than virtues. It is hard to say whether this is everyday usage: "virtue" is now to a considerable extent itself a philosophical term of art, and it is hard to detach it from one or another set of philosophical prejudices. In any case, to distinguish between the two in this way is unhelpful. It may easily suggest that that Sincerity is largely a matter of the will, while Accuracy is not. This is wrong on both counts. Sincerity basically involves a certain kind of spontaneity, a disposition to come out with what one believes, which may be encouraged or discouraged, cultivated or depressed, but is not itself expressed in deliberation and choice. Equally, Accuracy does involve the will, in the uncontentious and metaphysically unambitious sense of intention, choice, attempts, and concentration of effort. Indeed, as we shall see at many points, each of the basic virtues of truth involves certain kinds of resistance to what moralists might call temptation—to fantasy and the wish.

2. Plain Truths

In taking up at the beginning of the story the use of language to communicate, in the limited sense of one person's telling another something that the second person does not know, I have passed over something presupposed by this—that the language has to be learned. Children learn language in many ways and in many different kinds of situation, but one essential way is that they hear sentences being used in situations in which those sentences are plainly true.

This is such a salient part of the process that it has been privileged in many empiricist theories of language in the form of the idea of an "ostensive definition." This was the idea that there can, indeed must, be a primitive deixis of the semantic relation itself—that by being shown the (kind of) thing to which a linguistic item T applies, you are shown that T applies to it. It is a familiar criticism of ostensive definitions in their classical form that T was a subsentential item, typically a common noun: when the parent said "dog," pointing to a dog, the child was supposed to pick up from that action the syntactic role of "dog" along with its semantics. But the idea of an ostensive definition is no better if the linguistic item is a sentence. Take a sentence T of which it is intuitively plausible that a learner grasps its meaning by hearing it uttered in situations in which it is true.[5] Exaggerating a little, we may say

> (a) there is a type of situation S such that the utterance of T in S is necessary for grasping the meaning of T.

We can agree that (a) obtains because assertions of T in S are plainly or obviously true. The distinctively empiricist turn comes in not with (a) itself, which is unobjectionable, but with a certain explanation of it, namely,

> (b) T has a particular semantic relation to S: plainly observable features of S are what make T true in S.

That is to say, S plainly presents to a competent and suitably placed observer all the truth-conditions of T; as one might put it, T is true not only *in* S but *of* S.

This is the empiricist idea. But it must be wrong: given that a truth-condition of T is a condition such that if it is not satisfied, T is not true, many sentences that are examples of (a) fail to be examples of (b). To take a significant kind of case, let T be "Mummy has just gone out of the room." The truth-conditions of this are not plain to someone who can observe just the here and now, namely, a situation consisting of a room without Mummy, though it is a situation of that kind (and not, say, of a room from which Mummy is right now departing) in which the sentence is true. Children do learn the meaning of such sentences, and do so in situations in which they are true; they have or acquire the capacity of short-term memory, which is what enables them to recognize the truth of such sentences in such situations. They could not learn them—that is, acquire an explicit concept of the past—just by being taught to make inferences from a class of present-tense observational sentences.[6] But now the empiricist idea that (b) elucidates or explains (a) collapses. If S is identified solely in terms of what a competent observer can observe here and now, (b) is false. If, on the other hand, S is taken to include the fact that Mummy was here recently, and the competent observer is taken to have been here at that time and to have an appropriate memory span, (b) is true, but it adds nothing to (a): there is no particular or special *semantic* relation in such a case, but only the familiar relation that T is true just in case that T, together with some information about the uptake of this particular kind of sentence.

However, it remains true and basically important that there are many kinds of sentence for which (a) is correct. How do plainly true statements which help the learner come to be made? Sometimes, competent language-users make such statements to the learner, or in the learner's presence, solely by way of instruction. (In the next chapter, we shall see a little more of how this works: in particular, the speakers may be giving the learner words for something that he already, in some form, believes.) Often, however, they make some plainly true statement which may indeed help a learner who happens to be present, but they do so without that intention: they assert things to other competent speakers which the hearers might just as well assert, and perhaps do assert, themselves. There are all sorts of reasons that people have for stating the absolutely obvious. The obvious truth may be important, as when two people have both been looking out for the same thing ("Here he is!"). Again, an exchange may be merely companionable, as when two people comfortingly rehearse that they do see the same things, share the same familiar scene. It is true, of course, that a primary use of language is to tell people things they do not know—it is the point from which we started—but it is a mistake, one predictably made by instructors, to forget the immense importance that human beings find in exchanging assertions which offer no news to any of them. The point is not confined to comments on what is immediately obvious; human beings notoriously love being told stories they already know.

There is another significant way in which plain truths can come before the learner: they may be implied or presupposed by other speech-acts made by competent language-users. These may be other assertions, not themselves plainly true ("This chair was given to me by my grandmother"), or they may be speech-acts of other kinds ("Is this your purse?" "Get that cat out of here!"). These possibilities involve the idea not only of what a speaker says but of why he says it. If a speaker actually asserted the plain truths implied by these questions and orders, that there is a chair here, or a purse, or a cat, there might well be a question of why, speaking to another competent observer, he should do so. There is an excellent exchange in Sheridan's *The Critic*, which takes place at the rehearsal of a play:

> DANGLE: Mr Puff, as he *knows* all this, why does Sir Walter go on telling him?
> PUFF: But the audience are not supposed to know anything of the matter, are they?
> SNEER: True, but I think you manage ill: for there certainly appears no reason why Sir Walter should be so communicative.
> PUFF: 'Fore Gad now, that is one of the most ungrateful observations I ever heard—for the less inducement he has to tell all this, the more I think, you ought to be obliged to him; for I am sure you'd know nothing of the matter without it.
> DANGLE: That's very true, upon my word.[7]

The idea of the point of saying a certain thing, in particular of asserting a certain thing in given circumstances, was present at the very beginning of our story, with the activity of imparting information. This does not mean that we should confuse truth-conditions or content with the conditions of appropriate assertion.[8] On the contrary: the examples illustrate ways in which the point or pointlessness of making a given assertion to a given person in a given situation can help someone in picking up the content of that assertion. For some purposes, such as the theory of deductive inference, the content of assertions can be treated in abstraction from their appropriateness, but basically there is no understanding of the one without the other. Equally, in ascribing content to assertions, hearers must make assumptions about the cognitive capacities of speakers; we have already met two examples, of what someone can perceive from a given point, and of what people can be expected to remember. All of these things the child who does not yet know any language has to pick up together, while the interpreter of a strange language who knows another language will necessarily bring to his interpretation, in ways made familiar by Davidson,[9] assumptions about the similarity of the other people's psychology to his own.

A significant feature of the situation in which the learner can come to understand a sentence through its being uttered when it is plainly true is that there is no need to rely on the speaker's Accuracy or Sincerity, because there is no question of his having a positional advantage. The assumptions governing the situation are that the speaker, whether speaking for the learner or simply stating the obvious to someone else, is asserting something that the hearer can observe as easily as the speaker can. Since this is so, there is no room within this structure for the idea of a deceitful intention: such an intention, granted the rest, would simply be unintelligible. Of course, a speaker could deceitfully pretend that a situation was of this kind, but learners will proceed pre-reflectively on the basis that this is not so. They will usually be right, and if language is to be learned, it will have to be the case that they are usually right.

Of course none of this can be available to the learner, or at least the early learner, in the form of explicitly formulated belief: it must be pre-reflective. This means that language-learning must in the first instance be conducted in circumstances of pre-reflective openness or, as we might also say, primitive trust. In a more developed social and political perspective, it is no accident that it begins in the family.

From what has been said about the empiricist idea, it will be clear that a sentence's being plainly true does not imply that in some absolute sense it is *indubitable*. Moreover, what is plainly true is itself not absolute; the plainness of a truth can be relative to a technology, or to a technology and a set of skills in using it. It may be plainly true that a circle is drawn on this surface, though you need a magnifying glass to see it. It may be plainly true that a speaker is saying a certain thing, though we are hearing it on the radio. Two astronomers may agree that it is plainly true that this photograph from the telescope shows a double star. If we refuse to count such cases as plain truths because they involve complex assumptions which in an exceptional case might turn out to be false, we shall be committed once more to the hopeless empiricist or Cartesian path: the plain truth that there is a cat in front of us also involves complex assumptions, which (as friends of the argument from illusion always remind us) could in an exceptional case turn out to be false. In a genealogical perspective we can straightforwardly draw a line between plain truths that are relative to a technology and those that are not, and, so far as these considerations are concerned, we can think in terms of absolutely plain truths, for in the State of Nature there is no observational technology, unless perhaps one counts such things as climbing a tree in order to see farther.

We have to consider another relativity. What can be plain truths for the inhabitants of another and simpler society will depend on their language, and in particular on the classificatory terms that occur in it. This will not come out when we are thinking simply about these people; we shall consider merely their recognition of plain truths which are expressed in sentences of their language, and this takes for granted the vocabulary of that language, the ways in which it carves things up. However, as soon as we put ourselves into (or alongside) the picture, as people who speak a different language, a question does arise. Certainly for us, who live in a more complex society and have artefacts and institutions unknown even in quite recent times, let alone in a simple society, there are many plain truths ("The telephone is over there") that are not available to them. But equally, they may have plain truths not available to us, not just because they can observe things that we have not learned to observe (though that will no doubt be so), but because they classify some of the items in the world around them on principles unfamiliar to us. This may well mean that we cannot produce in our own language an equivalent of some things that they say; the best that will be available to us in those cases may be a paraphrase of what they say, which is helped by an explanation of why they say it, one that reveals the point of their classifying things in this way. We find, that is to say, an explicit interpretation of what they are doing in speaking in this way, and this, certainly, will not express a plain truth to us, though the sentence of theirs which we were trying to understand can be used to express what is a plain truth to them. Having gone through this process of understanding, however, we may pick up their use and come to speak as they do, and then we shall be able to recognize the same plain truths. There will be an element of pretence or role-playing in this, to the extent that our identification with their world is only partial. We see how it goes for them in this part of their language use, but we do not (really) belong to their world, unless we merge entirely into their life, forget our original presuppositions and attitudes, and (in a phrase with significant imperialist overtones) "go native."

Even when our identification with their world is only partial and episodic, and our own perspective, the one that we really live with, does not contain some classification system of theirs, we need not deny that statements they make—or which we make, when we speak as they do—are true: indeed, in certain cases, plainly true. Yet there may well be other types of statement they make and which they treat, sometimes, as plainly true, which we shall regard as false. They may, for instance, see it as plainly true that some god has passed that way, or that some other kind of "supernatural" force (as we would put it) is at work.[10] Here, everything turns on the interpretation which we put on what they say. If we are to say that some of their statements are false, not just in the occasional sense in which every-one makes some false statements, but systematically false, then we have to give an interpretation which leaves room for the possibility that this whole dimension of their speech is ill-founded, and which explains at the same time how it is that they can make sense of their environment in these terms.

It is important that, in any actual case, we shall not be able to do this by merely taking their language together with a "principle of charity" which asks us to interpret what they say in such a way that, in our language, as much of it as possible comes out true. When we try to make sense of these people, we must at the same time make sense of their relations to us, and so of ourselves in relation to them.[11] This process is likely to have a significant historical dimen-sion. For instance, one reason we might have for saying that some of their statements refer to "gods" or similar agents, and that all those statements are false, is that they seem to imply a certain kind of explanation of happenings (happenings which we ourselves recog-nize), a kind of explanation which we reject. Why should we think that they imply such an explanation? One reason might be that when, with our arrival, these people become familiar with our expla-nations of those happenings, and with the technology that our expla-nations make possible, their statements of that kind go out of business, or at least go underground; moreover—and this is an important addition—we have reason to interpret that change as an intellectual process of learning, not merely as the social triumph of one style or organization over another. Those interpretations are no doubt contestable. But so are their alternatives, and we cannot escape accepting some interpretation or other of such changes if we are to make sense of these people and of what they say at all.

An idle relativism often breaks out at this point, to the general effect that what they say is true "for them" while what we say is true "for us." If this can be made coherent at all, it represents one kind of interpretation, one which, in particular, understands their and our statements in such a way that they do not imply mutually conflicting explanations. This style of interpretation may suit some cases, but if it does, this has to be shown to be so in the light of what more generally we understand about the relations between ourselves and the others. This style of relativism often complacently presents itself as a witness to human equality, a refusal to impose our conceptions on others, but in fact, if it does anything at all, it simply imposes one of our conceptions rather than another. It gives up before the real work of understanding human similarities and differences even begins.

All these are questions for our relations to actual societies. But how do they relate to the fiction of the State of Nature? In relation to that, we are not social anthropologists; no-one can visit it as an interpreter, and it is no place in which to go native. We create it, and in doing so we already determine the interpretation of what its inhabitants say and do. But it is just for this reason that it is important to remember, in telling a State of Nature story, the problems of interpreting a real society. They remind us of how much we are taking for granted in telling the story in one way rather than another, and of what is presupposed by our putting in some elements and leaving out others. For instance, it is very natural to suppose, and in telling the story I do suppose, that many of the plain truths recognized in the State of Nature are not only plain as opposed to obscure but plain (so to speak) as opposed to coloured: that a lot of these truths will concern everyday features of the environment which we ourselves readily pick out—people, animals, trees, fruits, bodies of water, the sun and the moon, and such things. I do not, on the other hand, put into the basic account references to gods or supernatural agencies.

This procedure involves an assumption. It is not, of course, an assumption about the State of Nature, since the State of Nature is whatever we say it is, but it is an assumption about the relevance of a State of Nature constructed in these terms to our understanding anything else. The assumption is that the identification of such everyday objects (not that all of them will appear in every environment) plays such a basic role in human thought that our interpretations of other actual societies, and hence our understanding of human beings in general, can take it for granted. It might indeed be true that every human society, at least in the past, has had some beliefs about gods or other supernatural agencies, but the assumption is that those can safely be left out of the abstraction which is the State of Nature, because the genealogical account will come to them later; for instance (it is only one possibility), because they will be best understood as attempts to explain everyday happenings which we ourselves recognize. These are substantive assumptions. They are part of the general naturalistic outlook to which, as I said in the previous chapter, the genealogical project is committed.

3. *Space, Time, and Indeterminacy*

There is a further question about the State of Nature and the use of language that we should ascribe to the people in it, one that raises a sensitive point about our relations to the story. The story concerns a small society of human beings. This immediately implies to us the idea of their existing at some place rather than another on the earth, and at some time rather than another. The story does not say where or when, and since the story determines what questions can be answered, there is no answer to the question of where or when; but this does not mean that the story is one about a society which, remarkably, exists at no time or place, any more than the fact that there is no answer to the question "How many children had Lady Macbeth?" means that she is represented in the play as a woman with no deter-

minate number of children. In ascribing concepts and beliefs to the
people in the story, we need not insist that they have quite the same
idea as we have of the space and time in which any given human
beings exist. We need not assume that they understand themselves
as living at one place rather than another on the surface of the earth,
for they need not have an appropriate idea of the surface of the earth.
Again, they need not have any very determinate idea of their living
at one time rather than another. We can say that their conceptions
of these things are *local*. I do not mean just that their conceptions
differ from ours, but that in some sense which needs to be made clear
the content of their conceptions is local, restricted to a perspective
that is determined by the space and time in which they actually live.

In giving them even the few capacities and practices that we have
already considered, which involve (as I put it) the notion of a purely
positional advantage, we have supposed that they have some notions
of space and time. They can think of some things as being farther
away than others, not just from each of them or from a group of
them, but from the place where they all live. They can think of
events as past, and of some of them as longer ago than others. We
can reasonably imagine, however, that their thoughts are carried by
such concepts only so far. Their ideas of what is beyond a certain
distance are vague or non-existent, and although they tell tales of
what happened before their grandfathers' time, these tales do not
have much of what we would call temporal structure. We can lay
down that this is how it is in the State of Nature, and there is a
reason for us to do so, that we know that this is how it is or has
been with actual societies. Human beings can live with very local
conceptions of where they are and of what has happened.

The important question is what we should say about this state of
affairs and the people who are in it. One thing we say is that they
lack knowledge: that there are things distant from them and earlier
in time about which they do not know. (Once again, it is worth
considering what happens when an actual isolated society meets for
the first time people who come from somewhere else.) We may very
readily—too readily—go on to say that to the extent that they are
rational and reflective, they must themselves recognize that if their
ideas of what is distant in space or time are vague, this must be just

because they do not know. After all, they operate locally with such ideas as *what is farther away* and *the farthest that anyone has travelled*; so, we may insist, what except lack of thought could stand in the way of their forming the idea of *a place which is farther away than the farthest that anyone has travelled*, and recognizing that if their idea of what is at such a place is vague, then that is simply because none of them has been there?

In the case of space, this line of thought is very compelling. It is hard not to understand their outlook in this way, because the notions of distance which they must have are so closely related to the ideas that however far someone has actually gone, he might conceivably have gone a little farther, and that having gone there, he could conceivably come back again. With space, the idea of a purely positional disadvantage, which is implicit already in our people's ideas, does seem naturally to lead in thought to the idea that however far away a place may be, it is at some determinate distance from where they are. But is it equally so with regard to time? They must have the notions of *before* and *after* and *earlier than* and, it is reasonable to suppose, *yesterday*. Then they have the notion of *yesterday's yesterday* or *the day before yesterday*. This surely introduces the idea of *so many days before yesterday*. Since they not only have memory of events but can use the notion of memory in understanding and assessing testimony about the past, they have the idea of *a day that he can remember*. Putting all this together, they must be able to reach the idea of *days earlier than anyone of us can remember*. But that should give them *days earlier than any day remembered by anyone whom anyone of us can remember*—and so on. Then, we may finally insist, they really have, at least implicitly, the same idea that we have, that if anything really happened in the past, then it happened within some definite period in the past, a period that is so many days or years or other temporal interval earlier than now. (I shall call this the "objective" conception of the past.) Then, if they have only vague ideas of what happened at that earlier time, this must be because they do not know, and if they are rational and reflective, they will realize that that is their difficulty: that they are situated at a certain point of time at which it is natural, given their sources of knowledge, that they know some things and do not know others.

Some of these arguments we can accept. It is reasonable to insist, I think, that just in virtue of the local conceptions which they necessarily have, our people must have within their reach all the ideas that I have mentioned up to and including *days earlier than anyone of us can remember*, or something like that, but we should not insist that just in virtue of their local conceptions they must have really, if implicitly, the same "objective" conception of the past as we have.[12] It is very tempting to put our own conceptions of past time into the State of Nature, and of course we are free to do so—it is our story. But the point of the story is to illuminate our own actual understanding of truth and truthfulness, by offering an abstract basis to which real historical developments can be added. In deciding, therefore, what conceptions of past time to put into it, we need to consider what real historical developments there have been. We need to see whether, in our understanding of past time, we may be different from other people who have actually existed. If we assume that the State of Nature story, the simplest and most basic account of human activities, must contain our conceptions, we shall be drawn to some descriptions rather than others of people who seem not to have shared those conceptions (and perhaps of actual people who do not share them now). We are likely to say that they would arrive at our objective conception of the past if they were rational and reflective enough. But these phrases offer not much more than a compliment to ourselves. We need to ask what might actually be involved in forming the objective conception, and we cannot consider that question if we assume that the conception must be there from the beginning and that only stupidity or lack of reflection stops people from operating with it. So we shall put no more into the State of Nature than what is readily implied by the capacities and interests that we have already assumed. This will include a locally restricted or perspectival conception of the past.

There are various reasons why we might ascribe to people in a State of Nature story ideas less determinate than our own. What those ideas might be, and the ways in which they may be, from our point of view, indeterminate, will depend on our reasons for telling that story. In the present case, I have a particular reason for picking out ideas of past time. When we come to consider (in chapter 7) the origin of the objective conception of the past, it will turn out to be intimately linked to ideas of telling the truth about the past, ideas appropriate to the development of written history. But history is (in ways that chapter 10 will examine) quite central to our political and cultural grasp of our world. This feature of the State of Nature, then, is connected to our confronting finally the concerns from which I set out, the hopes of truthfulness in the humanities.

It is important that the local and the objective conceptions are equally conceptions of *the past*. The objective conception, just as much as the local, involves tenses: it thinks in terms of so many years' having passed since a given event, of its having happened so many years before now. The difference is that the objective conception insists that it is a truth-condition of a statement about a real past event that it occurred some determinate temporal interval before now, while the local conception does not insist on this. How it can avoid insisting on it will become clearer when, in chapter 7, we shall take a lesson from real history and see how it was, so far as Western thought is concerned, that the objective conception of the past emerged at a particular historical moment. The emergence of the objective conception will turn out to go with a certain conception of telling the truth about the past, one that is extended beyond the minimum given in the State of Nature. In this respect, too, the real historical story will itself be part of the genealogy of the virtues of truth.

4. *Value: The Story So Far*

I have called Accuracy and Sincerity "virtues of truth." The State of Nature story, as far as we have come in it, has suggested reasons why those virtues, and the fact that people possess those virtues, have a value. They are useful, indeed essential, to such objectives as the pooling of information, and those objectives are important to almost every human purpose.

In taking us so far, the story has led us some way toward the idea that truthfulness has a value. However, there is more than one way in which what the story has given us so far is limited. First, it is not

clear whether the virtues of truth, as so far understood, represent
values that can be recognized from an impersonal or general point
of view. There is a lack of fit between the value of these qualities to
the community and their value to the people who possess them. This
is less significant in the case of Accuracy, but it radically affects the
value of Sincerity. The community has an interest in having correct
information about the environment, its risks and opportunities, and
so does each individual. So each individual (roughly speaking) has
an interest in possessing the quality of Accuracy, and (even more
roughly) it is equally in the interest of the individual that others
should have it. However, this does not extend to particular pieces of
information. We already met in the previous chapter the age-old
observation that while a given person needs correct information, it
may well be a good idea for him to keep it to himself.[13] It is this that
has an effect on the value of Sincerity. The value that attaches to
any given person's having this disposition seems, so far as we have
gone, largely a value for other people. It may obviously be useful
for an individual to have the benefits of other people's correct information, and not useful to him that they should have the benefit of
his. So this is a classic example of the "free-rider" situation, much
studied by game theory, in which each participant wants there to be
a practice in which most of the others take part, without, if he can
get away with it, taking part in it himself. So there is a problem, that
without some help, the collective value of Sincerity (and in *that*
sense, its value to each person) does not translate itself into a reason
that each person has for possessing that quality himself. We shall
consider that problem, and how from a genealogical perspective it
is overcome, in chapter 5.

In that chapter, too, we shall consider another limitation of what
we have so far, that the values of Accuracy and Sincerity alike are
instrumental: they are entirely explained in terms of other goods, and
in particular the value of getting what one wants, avoiding danger,
mastering the environment, and so on. We shall see there that the
two limitations are connected: particularly with regard to Sincerity,
the fact that it is exposed to free-riders and its value is in that way
unstable comes about, in good part, because its value, as it has so far
been identified, is purely instrumental. These are in the first place

questions about the construction of the State of Nature itself, of how we can conceive of the imaginary community and its activities: the question at this level is, What would be needed for it to work? These problems are immediately connected with the point, mentioned earlier, that the State of Nature is itself supposed to be a society, and that no society can get by (I shall argue) with a purely instrumental conception of the values of truth.

However, the question whether truthfulness should have a more than instrumental value is not a matter simply of what we put into the State of Nature, the place from which the discussion starts. It applies also to our current situation. Some people, and in particular some among the "deniers," as I called them in chapter 1, will cheerfully leave the values of truthfulness as instrumental and accept that there is no intrinsic value to these qualities at all. They will be happy to do without it. But there is a serious question whether they can do without it. They want everyone to agree that the virtues of truth have a purely instrumental value. But what makes them think that if everyone agreed with this, the virtues of truth would still have the same instrumental value—indeed, that they would exist at all? The reason why useful consequences have flowed from people's insistence that their beliefs should be true is surely, a lot of the time, that their insistence did not look just to those consequences but rather toward the truth: that it was bloody-minded rather than benefit-minded.

At the very least, the cheery souls should address the question, and it is surprising how rarely they do so. The work of Richard Rorty[14] provides striking examples of what in this respect might be described as running on empty. Those who appear in Rorty's texts as "we pragmatists" encourage us to get beyond fussing about something called "the truth," and address ourselves just to technical and social benefits, solidarity, democracy, the discouragement of cruelty, and other laudable ends. It seems not to occur to them that even if the ideals of discovering and telling the truth were in themselves illusions, if the idea of "the truth" were itself empty, those illusions might well play a vital part in our identifying and pursuing those objectives. The pragmatists' claim to have overcome traditional obsessions with the differences between appearance and reality, truth and illusion, and so on, is offered in a setting that not only relies on such ideas itself—we shall see in chapter 6 how this is so[15]—but reflects the most elementary Enlightenment optimism associated with them. These pragmatists think that we can do without these illusions, and get on as well or better without them, but they believe this only because they really assume that the truth (their truth) will set us free. If they had attended more to Nietzsche, they would have a better sense of how far they need to go in order to get away from that assumption.

In fact, most people do think, in some way or other, that these qualities have a more than instrumental value (the pragmatists do, out of school). They think that, other things being equal, it is better to be honest rather than not—as one might say that Sincerity, at least in good surroundings, is a good thing in its own right. Similarly, up to a point, with Accuracy. "Truth has had to be fought for every step of the way, almost everything else dear to our hearts . . . has had to be sacrificed to it"—a vivid statement, but it says something that most people can still recognize.[16] Something like that outlook is part of what has counted as (really) believing in the value of truthfulness. There is nothing yet in the State of Nature story that gives us such an outlook or even, it seems, prefigures it, but as we develop the story further and also move beyond it into real history, we can hope to get some insight into what that value is, and why we need to recognize it.

The limitations I have mentioned relate to what the story has said so far about the value of the virtues of truth, Accuracy and Sincerity. The objection that they have, and need to have, a value that is more than instrumental is to the effect that not enough has been said about the value *of these qualities*. However, some may complain that there is another and more radical limitation, that it is simply these qualities that, so far, are supposed to bear the value. People have spoken of the value of *truth*: is this what they had in mind? Are we right to consider only certain human attitudes toward the truth, people's dispositions to discover it and express it? My answer is yes—it is right only to consider human attitudes. Indeed, it is part of the naturalistic outlook of this inquiry that it should be seen as an exercise in human self-understanding. It may be that there have been metaphysical outlooks which have associated truth and goodness in ways that represented these things as altogether prior to a human interest in them. It is in fact harder to find such an outlook than one may suppose. Plato's account of the Form of the Good in the *Republic* indeed looks like the paradigm of a metaphysical account which represents the objects of our knowledge and their value as in themselves entirely independent of our thoughts or attitudes. But we must consider the fact that on Plato's account "we" in our intellectual aspects are supposed to be of the same character as those objects, and that our deepest aspiration is to be at one with them. If this transcends human life, then that is because, for Plato, "we" are only contingently and temporarily human. That view is in any case not my concern, nor is any other that sets truth and goodness even further above us. I can only suppose, with Nietzsche, that such views, precisely in their obliteration of human interests, must be an expression of human interests.

The inquiry is, then, into human concerns with the truth. A basic form of that concern lies in the virtues of truth. But it does not follow that in thinking about human attitudes toward the truth we should consider only the virtues of truth. My inquiry will consider other matters as well, such as belief, assertion and communication, and the changes that I have already mentioned in conceptions of past time. One thing I shall not consider, however, is the history *of the concept of truth*, because I do not believe that there is any such history. The concept of truth itself—that is to say, the quite basic role that truth plays in relation to language, meaning, and belief—is not culturally various, but always and everywhere the same. We could not understand cultural variation itself without taking that role for granted. There are indeed scholarly books that describe themselves as histories of the concept of truth, but they typically describe conceptions, varying over time, of belief-formation, or of knowledge, or of the metaphysical structure of the world. Often, they are histories of philosophical theories of the truth. Some of those philosophical theories are themselves exercises in metaphysics or the theory of knowledge; others stick as closely as possible to the task of elucidating the essential role that truth plays in relation to such things as assertion and belief. The present point is that philosophical theories of truth, whether more or less ambitious, quite certainly have a history, whereas the concept of truth itself does not.[17]

I shall not try to give any history of theories of truth, nor shall I pursue very far the disputed question of how much such theories (if they stick firmly to their subject) can have to say. But in giving the State of Nature story to this point, and in introducing the virtues of truth, I have already taken for granted belief and assertion. I need to look more closely at them and at the ways in which they are essentially involved with truth, and this will be the subject of the next chapter.

4

❖ ❖ ❖ ❖ ❖

TRUTH, ASSERTION, AND BELIEF

1. *Truth Itself*

What about truth itself? If we are going to say that beliefs and assertions in some sense aim to be true, or, as the State of Nature story has assumed, that it is a good idea (at least from some of the participants' point of view) that they should be true, should we not say something about what it is for them to be true?

We should say something, but not very much. In particular, we should resist any demand for a *definition* of truth, principally because truth belongs to a ramifying set of connected notions, such as meaning, reference, belief, and so on, and we are better employed in exploring the relations between these notions than in trying to treat one or some of them as the basis of the others. It is also true that if any of these notions has a claim to be more basic and perspicuous than the others, it is likely to be truth itself. As Davidson has put it:

> [W]e cannot hope to underpin [the concept of truth] with something more transparent or easier to grasp. Truth is, as G.E. Moore, Bertrand Russell and Gottlob Frege maintained, and Alfred Tarski proved, an indefinable concept. This does not mean we can say nothing revealing about it: we can, by relating it to other concepts like belief, desire, cause and action. Nor does the indefinability of truth imply that the concept is mysterious, ambiguous, or untrustworthy.[1]

In discussing the truth of beliefs and assertions, I shall also speak, in various connections, of the truth of sentences (which are used to express beliefs and make assertions) and of propositions (which are

their content). Most modern discussions of truth accept a requirement which Tarski put at the centre of his theory,[2] that any adequate
account must in some sense explain the correctness of sentences
(often called "T-sentences") of the type

(T1) "Snow is white" is true if and only if snow is white.

The point that an account of truth should explain the correctness
of T-sentences is widely agreed, but there is less agreement about
what this means. Some have supposed that we should read them in
the light of the idea that in any instance of them the left-hand side
introduces a piece of language (in the case of (T1), the English sentence "Snow is white"), and the right-hand side introduces a fact,
so that T-sentences represent a relation of *correspondence* between
language and the world.[3] The basic objection to this account of truth
is that there is no systematic way of identifying the fact which supposedly makes a given sentence true, and there is no useful content
to the idea that a given fact makes a given sentence true.[4] This is
clear when we consider the point that if T-sentences gave us the idea
of a "corresponding fact," they would have to do so quite trivially. So

(T2) "Lucy is in the kitchen or Lucy is in the garden" is true if and
only if Lucy is in the kitchen or Lucy is in the garden

would give us a disjunctive fact to make the disjunctive sentence
true. But it is clear that if the correspondence theory is to have any
interest or intuitive appeal, it will have to say that if the sentence
"Lucy is in the kitchen or Lucy is in the garden" is true on a given
occasion, then what makes it true will be a fact expressed by one of
the disjuncts rather than the other: the fact—let us suppose—that
Lucy is in the garden. That same fact, moreover, will make true the
sentence "Someone is in the garden"—or, if there is more than one
person in the garden, should we say that *each* of the facts, that Lucy
is in the garden, that Mary is in the garden, and so on, makes that
sentence true? Equally, any one of those facts will falsify the sentence "No-one is in the garden"; but what would make that sentence
true, if it were true, will presumably have to be just the fact that
there was no-one in the garden. And so on. There is no account of

facts that at once is general enough for the purpose and does more than trivially reiterate the content of the sentences for which it is supposed to be illuminating the truth-conditions. That is to say, there can be no interesting correspondence theory.

Others have supposed, in strong contrast to the correspondence theorists, that the significance of T-sentences for the understanding of truth lies in their showing us that there is very little to the idea of truth at all. They take T-sentences simply to express the relation between two *sentences*, one of which (the left-hand side) refers to the sentence which occurs on the right-hand side. This can be taken as suggesting that "true" is merely a device of disquotation, or that it is used for signifying agreement with an assertion or with some class of assertions which we cannot or do not want to express ("What Jones said was true"). Some put their view by saying that truth is not a property; others accept that it may be taken to be a property, but only trivially so. Such theories have been called "minimalist."[5] We need not consider their details; what matters here are certain supposed consequences that have been drawn from such theories for the value of truth. It has been argued that since truth does not, on these accounts, come to much, so the value of truth cannot come to much. In particular, the value of truth "in itself" comes to nothing, so what is sometimes called "the value of truth" must be (the argument goes) the value of something else, and the so-called value of truth must be entirely instrumental.[6] This conclusion does not follow at all. All that minimalist theory requires is that occurrences of "true" can be eliminated and replaced by references to sentences or propositions. Suppose for the sake of argument that this programme could be carried out. Then we could represent the claim

(V1) There are matters concerning which we reasonably set a high value on the truth, quite apart from any instrumentalist interest

as

(V2) For some P, we are reasonably very interested in the question whether P, and want to believe that P if P and to believe that not-P if not-P, quite apart from any other benefit following from that inquiry or that belief.

Critics of such formulations convincingly object that the letter "P" has to play a fatally incoherent role in them.[7] If that problem is insoluble, minimalism fails anyway, but if it can survive such problems and sentences such as (V2) can be made coherent, (V2) will be an adequate representation of (V1). Nothing ties minimalism to an instrumentalist view of the value of truth.

The kind of attitude expressed in (V1) does of course presuppose that the matters in question are interesting. Even if we are motivated by pure curiosity, we are not curious about everything. Moreover, the issue whether a given question is interesting must be relative, in a broad sense, to our concerns, but this does not imply that our interest in that question must be instrumental, or really directed to something else. An interest in music, and in some music rather than other music, is obviously relative to one's background, temperament, experience, and so on, but it would simply be a reductionist conjuring trick to draw from this the conclusion that an interest in music is really an interest in something other than music.[8]

2. *Assertions and Truth*

A sentence uttered makes a world appear
Where all things happen as it says they do;
We doubt the speaker, not the words we hear;
Words have no words for words that are not true.

—W. H. Auden[9]

I said in the previous chapter that, quite apart from the question whether Accuracy and Sincerity might have a more than instrumental value, an account of the instrumental value itself must rest on notions of belief and assertion which are somehow essentially involved with truth. We must now consider how they are involved with it, and how they are related to each other.

Philosophers often say that assertions "aim at" truth, or that speakers, in making assertions, aim at truth. In the same spirit it is said that the "norm of assertion" is truth. We may equally say that assertions are supposed to be true, or—to exploit a helpful ambigu-

ity—that they are expected to be true.[10] There must be something
in these formulations. They hint at something basic about language,
a feature of it that we have already assumed in the State of Nature
story, that it must involve speakers coming out with a sentence in
circumstances in which they claim or are taken to claim (or something like that) that it is true. At the same time, the connection between assertion and truth tells something about the point of distin-
guishing sentences into the true and the false; it is not just one
classification among others, because, where the true and the false
are an issue at all, the aim of speaking must in some sense be to
come out with, to assert, the true rather than the false.[11]

But what exactly is the connection between assertion and truth?
If it is constitutive of assertions that they are subject to norms, in
particular norms of truth, what are these norms, and in what ways
are assertions subject to them?[12] We can start with an obvious contrast. Beliefs also can be said to aim at the truth, to be supposed to
be true, to be subject to norms of truth. It is an objection to a belief
that it is false. In fact, in the case of a belief, it is a *fatal* objection,
in the sense that if the person who has the belief accepts the objection, he thereby ceases to have the belief, or at least it retreats to
the subconscious: if a person recognizes that the content of his belief is false, in virtue of this alone he abandons his belief in it. But
there is no comparable way in which falsehood is a fatal objection
to an assertion.

"Assertion," like "belief," has an act/object ambiguity: it may refer
to what someone asserts (the content of his assertion), or to his asserting that content. In the act sense, there may be many other objections to an assertion, that it is rude or tactless or reveals a secret,
and so on. Falsehood is certainly an objection to an assertion; intuitively it seems to be a more basic objection than these others, and
clearly it must be so if the line of thought we are exploring is correct.
It might be thought that there is a simple explanation of why it is
more basic: falsehood is a property of the content and not of the
act, and therefore the objection of falsehood is an objection to the
content, not to the act. But this would be a straightforward mistake.
What A asserts, the content of his assertion, may equally be what B
supposes or C denies; it is just a content, what Frege called "a

thought." If it is false, it is false in all these connections or presenta-
tions, but its falsehood is an objection only in A's case, not in B's or
(least of all) in C's. Though the objection to A's assertion is
grounded in a fact about its content, the objection is to his asserting
it. Equally, we cannot say that the other styles of objection to someone's assertion are objections only to his act of assertion and are not
grounded in its content—it is the content, after all, that makes it in
the circumstances offensive, tactless, or whatever.

Is falsehood the basic objection to an assertion because it is the
only universal objection, the one that every assertion must accept or
rebut just because it is an assertion? Or, slightly differently, is it the
only absolute objection, the others being variously relative to audience, circumstances, and so on? What is tactless or rude if said to
one listener is not if said to another, but what is false is false whoever
is listening.[13] But now everything turns on what counts as "an objection." No-one can hold that if A's assertion is recognized to be false,
it follows that he ought not to have made it. He may have made it
in good faith, on convincing evidence, and so on. Indeed, there was
no such implication in the case of belief: if what one believed turns
out to be false, it does not follow that one ought not to have believed
it. What does follow is that if one recognizes the falsehood, one does
not carry on having the belief—that is what it was for the objection
to be fatal. So will the objection of falsehood be fatal to an assertion
in this sense, that if a person recognizes that an assertion of his is
false, he cannot go on making it? No, since it is a sad truth that he
can. Perhaps he ought not to, but that merely reminds us of what we
knew already, that falsehood is one kind of objection to assertions,
and does nothing to show that it is fatal. The most that could be
claimed is that he cannot go on making the assertion to the same
audience, or rather—and this is a substantial qualification—to an audience about which he knows that they have also recognized the
falsehood. At least in that case, it may be said, what he would be
doing would no longer be assertion. But if that is the point, we shall
have lost the idea that the objection of falsehood is absolute.

There is no way in which, parallel to belief, falsehood is a fatal
objection to assertions. Indeed, we still need to find out the precise
sense in which it is an objection at all.

Michael Dummett has written:

The roots of truth and falsity lie in the distinction between a speaker's being, objectively, *right* or *wrong* in what he says when he makes an assertion. Just because the notion of assertion *is* so fundamental, it is hard to give an account of it that does not take other notions relating to language, or at least psychological notions such as intention and belief, as already understood: but it is plain that, for anything classifiable as an assertion, an understanding of the force of the utterance depends upon having some conception of what it is for the speaker to be right or wrong in saying what he does ... Suppose that an assertoric utterance is such that it is possible, within a finite time, effectively to discover whether or not the speaker was right in what he said: and suppose that he was not right, so that he is compelled to withdraw his statement. What possible content could there be to the supposition that, nevertheless, the conventions governing that utterance were such that ... he was not actually *wrong*? How could he have gone further astray than by saying something in saying which he was conclusively shown not to have been right, than by being forced to take back what he said?[14]

What concerns me are the circumstances that Dummett takes for granted in this passage as those in which an assertion is assessed.[15] It is notable that he equates the question whether the speaker was "right in what he said" with the question whether he was "right in saying" it; he is concerned with the former. He has in mind a situation in which, as he puts it in the last quoted sentence, the speaker is "conclusively shown not to have been right"; while that phrase covers several possibilities, I take it to mean that the speaker is at least confronted with clear proof that what he said was wrong. Then, it is claimed, he is "forced to take back what he said." *Forced*? How, by whom, to do what?

In this talk of force and compulsion, there seems to be a blend of several different necessities. First, if a speaker is confronted with information which clearly proves that what he said was false, and he admits the truth of the information, and will not accept that what he said was false, and has nothing at all to say on how that can be so, this can cast doubt on what he meant, because it may be unclear by now what he would count as making his statement true or false. But this point applies just as well to what a speaker has conjectured or suggested and so forth. It is a point about the connections between meaning, truth, and content, and has nothing specially to do with assertion. It reminds us, however, that if we are looking for norms that connect truth and assertion, we are not going to find them simply by putting together the ideas of truth and of the utterance of a sentence. David Lewis has said that the convention by subscribing to which a speaker uses a given language $\mathfrak{L}$ is that of being truthful in $\mathfrak{L}$, where this means "to try never to utter sentences of $\mathfrak{L}$ that are not true in $\mathfrak{L}$."[16] There is more to Lewis's notion of a convention of truthfulness than this implies, but certainly this formulation cannot be right. We appropriately utter—that is, come out with—false sentences in all sorts of contexts.

We get nearer to the idea of assertion if we take up some other necessities implicit in Dummett's description. We have already noticed the point that if the speaker admits that he was wrong, and goes on saying the same thing to people who have themselves shown him that he was wrong, then it may readily become unintelligible what he is up to. If, by contrast, the speaker is sincere, responsible, and so on, and he has been convinced that he was wrong, then he will not assert the same thing to anyone, including people who do not know that it is false, and he may, in some circumstances, experience this reluctance as a necessity—that he *cannot* tell this person (at any rate) what he believes to be untrue. (He has, in one of its forms, the virtue of Sincerity.) Again, if he does assert what he believes to be untrue and is discovered in doing so, he will, quite often though not always, be the object of criticism; in an extreme case he will be shamed, if he is capable of being shamed, and this can give a further, social, sense to the ideas of force and compulsion.

We can understand the idea of an assertion in a way that makes sense of these various reactions only if we introduce, as Dummett indeed suggests, psychological notions such as belief and intention. Taking the first phenomenon, that we cannot typically make sense of someone who seems to be asserting something that he does not believe to people who, as he well knows, know that he does not believe it, an explanation of it might be this: that an assertion is an utterance intended to bring it about that the hearer believe its content, and this is not an intention which, in these circumstances, the speaker can intelligibly have. This places assertion firmly in the context of one person's *telling* something to another. We might try to capture this idea by saying that the basic idea of A's asserting P to B lies in this, that A utters some sentence to B with the intention of bringing it about that B believe that P. This does not yet quite give what is wanted for such an account, because it does not say enough about the sentence that A utters. To use an example of John Searle's,[17] an American captured in World War II might want to induce in his Italian guards the belief that he was German, by uttering the only German sentence he knew, "Kennst du das Land, wo die Zitronen blühn?" but this does not make it true that in saying this he has asserted that he is German. To deal with this, we can add a further condition, that the sentence which A utters *means that P.* (Of course, if we were trying to explain meaning, this would be unhelpful. But we are not trying to explain meaning, only to give an account of what assertion is.)

We can find a place for Sincerity in this proposal: a sincere assertion will be one made by someone who himself believes that P. This at any rate gives us a class of assertions which are sincere, though it must be said that it does not, in itself, do anything to explain why Sincerity seems to be so basically connected with the idea of an assertion. Further considerations beyond this account of assertion itself would be needed to explain why assertions are expected to be sincere, or, indeed, why, as I put it at the beginning, they should be expected to be true.

It would not be impossible, though it might not be very appealing, to bolt such considerations onto this account. But we should not go further in that direction, because there is an objection to this type of account altogether. It is simply not true that someone who makes an assertion has to think that he is informing his hearer. What Searle has called "a preparatory condition" for the assertion of P, that it should not be obvious to the speaker and the hearer that the hearer knows that P,[18] is not a condition on assertion, though it is no doubt a condition on some other speech-acts, such as informing someone of something. As we noticed in the previous chapter, people constantly come out with truths which they know are as plain to their hearers as to themselves, and if P is such a plain truth, the speaker will still have asserted that P. This is not just a matter of a marginal counter-example. As we also saw earlier, the fact that speakers assert the entirely obvious is very important, in particular for the processes by which language is learned. If a competent speaker utters a plain truth expressed by the sentence "S" for the benefit of a child learning the language, it is rarely helpful to say that what he is doing is informing the child of that truth. In some cases, one might say that the speaker cannot do that, since the child is not yet in a position to grasp it; the aim of the speaker's utterance is to help him to grasp it, and so put him in a position where he can be informed of such things. In many other cases, and more interestingly, we can say that the child already believes in some form or other the truth expressed by "S," and, just because it is pre-reflectively plain to the child that the same truth is plain to the speaker, the speaker's utterance can give the child words to express this belief. The speaker says, for instance, "The cat just jumped off the wall," and in doing so gives the child words for a belief which in some form the child already has in virtue of the fact that he saw the cat jump off the wall.

Statements which are plainly true perform other functions as well. They remind us that we share the same world and find the same things salient, and help us to discover where we do and do not agree—consider, in our own life, conversations that take place when we visit some entertainment or exhibition or landmark, and comparable talk takes place in any society. Of course, as the State of Nature story has made clear from the beginning, the transmission and sharing of information is a basic function of language, but, very importantly, it does not follow that this function must figure in the account of assertion itself. All that the account must do is help us to understand how assertion plays its part in that process.

Let us drop the reference to affecting the hearer's beliefs. Then the basic idea of an assertion might seem to lie just in a speaker's expressing a belief by uttering an appropriate sentence. Rather more strictly, we might say that A asserts that P in uttering a sentence which means that P, in doing which he expresses his belief that P.

But this cannot be the only kind of assertion. A can express his belief that P only if he has that belief, that is to say, if he is sincere. An account of assertion must leave room for insincere assertions, and this suggestion does not yet do so.

What does an insincere assertor do? In a certain sense, he pretends to express his belief, and this means, as with all pretence, that up to a point he does exactly what someone does who is doing the real thing: for instance, he utters the same sentence, in the same manner, as one who was expressing that belief. There is a phrase in Homer which captures the idea quite naturally and, in (rightly) making it seem very simple, suggests some of the complexities it implies. When Odysseus, coming back to his home in disguise, is telling a lot of lies to Penelope, the poem says of him, "[H]e spoke, and said many false things that were like true things,"[19] and this means both that he spoke as one who believed those things, and that they were things which he made it seem reasonable to suppose were correct.

It is tempting to say that someone who insincerely asserts that P *pretends* to express a belief that P. But that formulation would apply just as well to someone who was, for instance, speaking ironically. The point is not merely that irony is distinct from deceit, but that an ironical assertion is not an assertion; if someone says of an embarrassing attempt at wit, "That was very amusing," he has not asserted that it was amusing (since he did not mean what he said), nor that it was not amusing (since he has merely implied it). The formulation would also apply to someone who was merely *pretending to make an assertion*. The problem raised by both these objections is that the idea of pretence does not in itself make precise enough the intended effect on the hearer. I think it is clear that in giving an account of insincere assertion, we do have to put back the idea of a speaker's trying to affect the beliefs of the person he is addressing. I have made the point that sincere assertions do not necessarily have the aim of informing the hearer; but insincere assertions do have the aim of misinforming the hearer. In the primary case, they aim to misinform the hearer about the state of things, the truth of what the speaker asserts. Derivatively, they may aim to misinform the hearer merely about the speaker's beliefs: the speaker may know that the hearer will not believe what he falsely asserts, but he wants her to believe that he himself believes it. We should say, then, that the standard conditions of A's asserting that P are that

> A utters a sentence "S," where "S" means that P, in doing which either he expresses his belief that P, or he intends the person addressed to take it that he believes that P.

This is not meant to be a strict statement of sufficient and necessary conditions: especially in this field, I take it that it is impossible to produce such a thing without circularity. But I do take it to be an adequate account of what assertion centrally is. It explains the connection between assertion and truth and provides a natural place for the expectation of sincerity. It also fits well with a point made by Williamson: "In natural languages, the default use of declarative sentences is to make assertions."[20] I take this to mean that if a speaker comes out with a declarative sentence not as part of a larger sentence (as one might say, by itself) and there are no special circumstances, then he is taken to have asserted what is meant by that sentence. Something on those lines follows from the present account. If we share a language with a speaker who comes out with "S" in such circumstances, we shall take it that he is expressing a belief which we shall describe as a belief that S, or at least that he is doing just what somebody does who is doing that. What better expression could there be of that belief than that sentence, and what belief could be better expressed by its utterance? There are of course other ways of expressing one's beliefs; we can say that someone who asserts that P and is sincere says something that is a *direct expression* of his belief that P.

It may be wondered why the account has to take a disjunctive form. Might we not say more simply that a speaker, whether sincere or insincere, asserts that P if by uttering "S" (where "S" means that P) he intends his hearer to believe that he (the speaker) believes that P?[21] But this reads sincere assertion too much in the light of insincerity and, in doing so, pays too much attention to effects. A speaker can sincerely assert that P, and to some purpose, without supposing that his hearer thinks that he is sincere, and without caring whether he thinks so or not. If we want a unitary formula,

we shall have to say, rather, that a speaker asserts that P if he intends what he says to be taken as an expression of a belief that
P. But formulations of this kind take for granted the notion of
"an expression of belief" and return us to acknowledging the fact
that this idea has to be understood first, and that insincerity is para-
sitic on it.

Quite generally it is true that we have to understand what it is to
do X before we can understand what it is to pretend to do X. But in
the case of belief (and more broadly in cases of expressing some
feeling or attitude) there is a further and very important point, that
in their most primitive form expressions of belief are spontaneous.
This does not mean that the utterance is involuntary, though even
that can be true in some circumstances. While in the most basic case
the utterance is not, as we might put it, involuntary as to *whether*, it
is involuntary as to *what*: in the first instance and in the simplest
cases, we are disposed spontaneously to come out with what we believe.[22] This fact not only helps to link assertion and belief, but also
helps to explain the connection between belief and truth. A disposition to come out with the sentence "S" is an appropriate and standard reaction on my part to a situation in which it expresses a plain
and salient truth—a situation, for instance, in which I can be described as "seeing that S."

The connections between belief and truth explain why, in the case
of sincere assertion, a speaker's intention to inform the hearer about
the truth, and to inform him about the speaker's beliefs, fit naturally
together—they are two sides of the same intention. The speaker
who makes an insincere assertion has neither of these intentions.
Moreover, as we have already seen, the intention to deceive the
hearer about these two things may come apart. In asserting that P,
the deceitful speaker may not intend his hearer to believe *that P* at
all; he may know that the hearer firmly believes the opposite, and
his aim may be, for some reason, only to get her to think that he,
the speaker, believes that P.

Sincerity at the most basic level is simply openness, a lack of inhi-
bition. Insincerity requires me to adjust the content of what I say.
Of course, this does not mean that all adjustment or reflective
thought about what I should say is insincerity, though some Puritans

or Romantics may have thought so. There are other demands on what I say, and, again, I may have reasons not for concealing the truth but for expressing it very carefully.

It follows from the basic spontaneity of assertion that Sincerity does not typically involve a special exercise of Accuracy, namely, Accuracy in discovering what it is that I believe; rather, in the simplest case I am confronted with my belief as what I would spontaneously assert. There are of course other cases in which I do have to discover by inquiry what I believe. Some of the inquiry will be reflective, and some of the reflective inquiry may take the form of, so to speak, trying out various assertions. In other cases I may have to go further than reflection and look to other people for evidence. Some of these complexities will concern us later—in the last section of this chapter, for a start, but more extensively in chapter 8. In that chapter, too, we shall have to consider what Sincerity involves when it is a matter of expressing or describing other states of mind such as desires and intentions. But it is certainly true that not all cases of declaring one's beliefs can require inquiry, and where there is inquiry, it must finally be based on the primitive type of situation in which one is simply disposed to come out with one assertion rather than another.

3. *Assertions and Knowledge*

It has been claimed that the norm attached to assertion is knowledge, in the sense that in asserting that P one represents oneself as knowing that P.[23] The force of the claim might be thought to lie in the idea that one can be criticized for asserting what one does not know ("You should not have said it if you did not know"). This represents the criticism as a criticism of the assertor, but the speaker, after all, may not be in the position himself to apply the norm effectively, because, at the point of asserting that P, he may reasonably think that he knows that P when he does not. In such a case, it is not reasonable to criticize him, in the sense, at least, of *blaming* him for not having remained silent rather than speaking, or for not having said that P only in some qualified or doubtful way.

It may be said, as it can in the case of many other rules, that he has broken the norm, but that in these circumstances he is not to blame for doing so. But then we still need to know how the supposed norm applies, and what the consequences of its obtaining are supposed to be. Here it seems sensible to look for analogies in other types of speech-act to which notions of authority, warrant, and so on, clearly apply. If the idea we are examining is sound, there should be some such analogies to help us to get a hold on it, and all the more so if the idea represents the application to assertion of a more general theory of the authority that is required to perform a given kind of speech-act.[24] The most obvious example to consider is that of commands or orders, cases of A's authoritatively telling B to do something, as compared with A's authoritatively telling B that something is the case.

The formulation of the analogy, however, immediately suggests that there is something wrong with it. Commanding or ordering someone to do a certain thing is a special kind of telling-to, one done with authority, as contrasted with mere ground-level telling-to, done without any special authority, as when an aggressive road-user tells another to get out of the way, or a helpful one tells another to look out. This ground-level telling-to parallels ground-level telling-that—merely telling someone that P, without any special entitlement. But ground-level telling-that is surely *already* assertion.

If there is an analogy, it presumably runs like this. If A tells B to do something, but lacks authority to do so (even if, we may add, A reasonably thinks that he has that authority), what follows is that B has no reason to obey him. This does not necessarily mean that B has no reason to do the thing in question—he may have some other reason to do it. What it means is that B has no reason to do it *which lies just in the fact that A has told him to do so*. Similarly, it may be said, if A tells B that P, but lacks authority to do so (that is to say, he does not know that P), this will not give B a reason to believe that P; B may have some other reason to believe that P, but he will not have a reason which lies just in the fact that A told him that P.

It may be said that a hearer never has a reason for believing that P which lies just in the fact that a given speaker has told him that P. He has to believe also that the speaker (on such matters, and so on) is a reliable informant. This, in itself, does not destroy the analogy: equally, B's reason for doing what A tells him to do does not lie simply in the fact that A has done so, but in this together with a belief that A has the relevant authority. But these considerations do point to a deeper disanalogy, which stems from the significant point that there is no analogy in the field of action to the idea of truth in the field of belief. In the case of commands, it is a *particular* objection to doing what someone tells one to do that he has no authority to give such orders. The act of telling another to do something can be "subject to a distinct norm of authority" in the sense that there are many situations in which, unless the speaker has authority, the hearer has no reason to do what he is told. In the case of assertion, if B, the hearer, doubts whether A is a reliable informant on this matter, then, other things being equal, he has no reason to believe what A has told him. But this means that he doubts that the belief that A has expressed is true; or he may doubt that what A asserted is really his belief. These doubts or objections do not imply any distinct norm, involving the idea of authority, which is attached to the speech-act of assertion. The objections that the supposed expression of belief is insincere, or that the belief expressed may not be true, are appropriate simply in virtue of the nature of assertion as the direct expression of belief. The initial impression stands, that assertion is just ground-level telling-that: it is this just because it is taken as the direct expression of belief.

A related point comes out if we consider the role of assertion in the transmission of knowledge. As I have already said, the account of assertion must make sense of that role, but assertion need not itself be explained in terms of that role. If A tells B that P, and B in turn tells C, then we want it to be a possible outcome of this process that if A knows that P, then C does. It is obvious, and it is central to the State of Nature story, that testimony can convey knowledge. The process implies that C at least, and usually B, should have reason to believe what they are told, and, as we have just seen, this implies a belief or assumption on their part that their informants are reliable. If C, at the end of the chain, is to know that P, a further condition has to hold: on some accounts, that C has to know that this informational chain was reliable, on other (and, as I suppose, more reasonable) accounts, simply that the chain has to be reliable. This implies only the transfer of true belief by reliable, or detectably reliable, informants. Assertions play their role in the transmission of knowledge just because they are taken to be direct expressions of belief and the speakers are taken to be reliable. It is in virtue of this that in situations of trust, where the hearer relies on the speaker, he takes the speaker's assertion to be *giving* him the information in question.

A message can be reliably transmitted from one person to another through a chain of people who pass on a sentence without understanding it themselves. This establishes the principle that knowledge can travel through the utterances of people who do not themselves have the knowledge. But the more common case is that in which each party asserts the same thing to the next party.[25] If the final recipient is reflective and critical, he may consider how reliable this process has been. What he is considering, in these reflections, is whether he should or should not believe what he has heard, and similar reflections are available to any recipient on the way. These reflections are appropriate just in virtue of the fact that assertions are direct expressions of belief, and it is in virtue of the same fact that a chain of assertions can transfer knowledge.

4. *Beliefs and Truth*

Someone who asserts something to another standardly gives the hearer to understand that he can rely on the truth of what has been asserted, in particular that he may base his actions on that assumption. This calls to mind another speech-act to which assertion might be compared, promising.[26] Just as there are legally enforceable promises, there are legally underwritten sworn statements of fact, and even without legal sanctions there are ceremoniously emphasized statements of fact which share some language with promising: "I give you my word that . . . ," indeed "I promise you that . . ." These formulae in themselves are hardly likely to make a doubter more likely to believe the speaker. The force of them lies rather in the realm of informal sanctions—recriminations, loss of reputation, apologies, forms of compensation will be in place, certainly if the speaker was insincere, probably if he was careless, possibly if he was merely wrong. Assertions without the ceremonious formulae, mere assertions, often carry some of the same consequences. This has no doubt encouraged the idea that assertions by their very nature involve a norm of knowledge. What is true, rather, is that assertions perform one of their most basic functions, to convey information to a hearer who is going to rely on it, in circumstances of trust, and someone who is conscientiously acting in circumstances of trust will not only say what he believes, but will take trouble to do the best he can to make sure that what he believes is true. This, as I have already said, makes no demands on the account of an assertion beyond its being taken to be a direct expression of belief, but it does imply a lot about the roles of both Accuracy and Sincerity in certain standard kinds of communicative situation.

These considerations will concern us in the next chapter, when we take up the basic matter of trust. However, it is relevant here to point out one very basic *disanalogy* between assertion and promising, because it reminds us, again, of the connections between belief and truth. Promising, even in its less formally contractual forms, does have one particularly important function, that it is supposed to protect the promisee against the possibility that the agent fails to deliver simply because he has changed his mind. Intentions may always vary with the change of desire, and desires do very readily change. Indeed, an agent can change his intentions capriciously, at will. Promises are meant to provide a protective hedge against such changes. But beliefs, just because they do aim at the truth or are subject to a norm of truth, cannot intelligibly be changed at will.[27] So if I have genuinely expressed my belief, there is no question of my *simply* changing my mind. I may change my mind because I have, as I suppose, come to know more, and then I may have a reason to warn someone who is relying on what I first said. But I cannot simply change my mind as a matter of choice, fancy, or inclination, and it follows that those who rely on what I assert do not need the kind of protection which, in the field of intention and action, it is a prime purpose of promising to provide.

The facts that beliefs cannot be adopted or changed at will, and that their expression is also, in the basic case, involuntary (as to *what*, as I put it earlier, if rarely as to *whether*), are extremely important to the relations between belief and truth. This is connected, too, with the point made earlier, that the objection of falsehood to a belief is fatal. All three points go together. We may take the simplest case, plain perceptual truths: if a person who speaks a language which allows him to form the sentence "S" is confronted with a situation in which "S" is plainly true,[28] he will enter a state in which he is disposed to say "S" if, for instance, he is asked about that situation. This is a disposition which he will need to inhibit if he wants to mislead people, and it is not one that he can change at will. Moreover, if the content of what he is disposed to assert in this way conflicts with some other disposition of the assertive kind that he has, or if it conflicts with the content of assertions made by other competent people whose utterances are hard to explain unless they are expressing their beliefs, he will, for instance, look again, or take other steps as a result of which the disposition will change to one that has a content in harmony with those other dispositions, his own or others'. All of this has an explanation which is basically very simple, however much philosophical and psychological elaboration it may need: that the situations in which people find themselves act on the perceptual and linguistic capacities of those people to cause these dispositions. This is known pre-reflectively to every mature and capable speaker, and it is common knowledge—that is to say, it is known to everyone that it is known to everyone.[29] All this together makes it clear why the points about belief are not simply points about the word "belief" or its equivalents. If I am confronted with some objection to the content of my belief, for instance, it is not that I am left with the same disposition with the same content, but I no longer *call* it a belief: in the simplest case, at least, the disposition itself changes.

In the simplest case, but the simplest is far from being the only case. I have described assertion in terms of the direct expression of belief, but this is not meant to imply a one-way relation, by which belief is not at all to be understood in terms of assertion.[30] Sincere assertions are indeed expressions of belief, but what beliefs I have can often be a matter of what I am disposed or prepared to assert. One very obvious reason for this is that in language-users, the conceptual content of their beliefs is to a significant extent the conceptual content of their language, of what they are able to assert.[31] But there is another reason, which is more interesting. It is far from being true that every thought swimming around in one's mind is already the content of a belief as opposed to some other mental state such as a guess, a fancy, or (very importantly) a wish. We may have a picture of discrete beliefs lodged in a person's mind, waiting to be expressed. In the simplest cases, as I have said, this is a crude picture of something real: we do have very determinate dispositions to assert certain things. But in many other cases, it is not merely that we do not know what we believe (though this is of course often true), but that a given content has not come to be a belief at all. What makes it into a belief may be that we are asked about the matter or about the belief and then have to decide whether we are prepared to assert it or not. How can that be, if assertions are expressions of belief? The answer is that assertions (as we have seen) often give others a reason to rely on what we say, either as a statement of how things are, or as an expression of how they seem to us. So, on such an occasion, when I accept the demands of being under oath, or I am concerned to be helpful, or I want my friend to understand how I see things, I have to consider what I am prepared, sincerely and responsibly, to assert. I ask myself what I believe, and that is, in such a context, the same question. The question should not be understood, however, as simply one of what I already believe; in trying to answer it, I do not simply review my dispositions but consider my reasons for taking a given content to be true, and this is a question of what *I am to* believe. The formula that assertions are expressions of belief works in both directions: what, after all or in the end, I believe, is often a matter of what, all things said and in contexts I care about, I am prepared to assert. In such ways, the virtues of Accuracy and Sincerity, and our relations with each other, help to construct the beliefs that each of us has. (We shall see more of this in chapter 8.)

There are other ways in which we have to go beyond the simplest case. The contents floating in my mind may not merely fall short of being, all things considered, beliefs; they may be, as I just suggested, the contents of wishes. Just in virtue of this they may have some tendency to turn into beliefs, or at least to do so if there are no defences against it. The phenomenon of wishful thinking is very basic and not a great mystery: the steps from its being pleasant to think of P, to its being pleasant to think that P, to thinking that P, cover no great psychological distance. The interesting question concerns the disciplines and structures that are needed to stand against this process. That will be a significant part of the story about Sincerity and Accuracy.

It is basic, I have claimed, that beliefs are not subject to the will. This fits in with the point that when beliefs are the products of wishful thinking, or in other ways become hostage to desires and wishes, they do so only as the result of hidden and indirect processes, against which the disciplines of the virtues of truth are directed. But while this is so, and it is indeed a conceptual truth that beliefs cannot be changed at will, it is not a conceptual truth, or true at all, that we cannot consciously adopt a strategy to cultivate some beliefs or lose others. It was such a strategy that Pascal famously recommended in the light of his argument about the Wager.[32] Such an undertaking is possible only for some kinds of beliefs: one requirement, for instance, is that I must be able to forget that this is how I acquired the belief, or, if I remember that I acquired it in this way, I need an explanation of how that is supposed to be connected with the belief's being true. In Pascal's own example, if the *libertin* arrives at a belief in God by such a route (choosing to be conditioned into it because he fears even a small risk that there may be a Hell), he will also come to believe that it was the wisdom and benevolence of God that set him on this route. Besides the constraints on such projects, however, there is a deep distrust, contempt, and indeed fear of them, a strong reluctance to acquire beliefs by methods that have nothing to do with their truth. Why this should be so is again something that our reading of the virtues of truth should help us to understand.

5

❖　❖　❖　❖　❖

SINCERITY: LYING AND OTHER
STYLES OF DECEIT

1. *Value: An Internal Connection?*

The previous chapter showed that truth has an internal connection
with beliefs and assertions. In a sense, truth figures in that connection as a value. Genuinely asking a question, wondering how things
stand, I aim at a true answer. Assertions can be assessed for truth,
and they would not be assertions if they could not. The assessment
of beliefs and assertions as true is a favourable one. These facts involve valuations in terms of truth. In one direction, all this takes us
quite a long way in the direction of truth as a value. The situations
in which these things have their place and work well necessarily
form an important part of experience in any human society, and to
that extent we can see that truth must be regarded as a value.

In another direction, however, all this takes us nowhere at all. If
we define the belief-assertion-communication system in the narrowest functional terms, the story so far tells us something of how that
system works; it shows a role of truth as (in a sense) a value in that
system; and it reminds us that a lot of the time the system does
indeed work. That means, moreover, that a lot of the time people
simply tell the truth and have no need of a virtue of Sincerity in
order to do so: in appropriate circumstances, they come out with
their beliefs. But as soon as a *question* comes up, whether an individual or group should on a given occasion continue to work the system
(defined in those same narrow terms)—whether, for instance, they

should tell a lie—the sense we have recovered so far in which truth is a value gets us nowhere. Indeed, these people could not tell a lie unless there were assertions, and utterances would not be assertions if they were not expected to be true, and they would not be expected to be true if they did not, a lot of the time, express true beliefs. All this may be correct, and these people may know that it is correct, but it does not answer their question. They know that they can tell a lie, as every day millions of people do, and the heavens will not fall; if the heavens were going to fall, they would have fallen already.

It is very important that the internal role of truth in the belief-assertion-communication system gets us *no further at all* in delivering the values of truthfulness, once the questions arise to which truthfulness helps to provide the answer—questions that inevitably arise granted that the participants in the system are people, reflective agents, to whom such questions can occur. It may be said that, whatever the implications may be for individuals and their reasons, failures in truth-telling are at least failures *of the system*, as it has so far been described in the State of Nature story. Even this is true only if "the system" is identified (as we identified it at the beginning) in the narrowest and most basic terms, as a system for pooling information among the participants. In that perspective, a lie, or indeed less than adequate disclosure, is a failure, like a failure in any communication system. But no social system, even the State of Nature, is just *that* system, and the people who live in the society have interests in other things besides being maximally efficient communicators. They may have relations with people who are outside the society. Within the society, some other members will be rivals and some may be enemies. Their relations to people who are neither of these things involve many aims besides that of imparting information, and may conflict with that aim. Even within the closest possible group, the scene of primitive trust, call it the family, many things are not shared, and many things need to be shared besides information.

Despite the fact that there are norms which lay it down that assertions are supposed to be true, many assertions are not true, often because they are not sincere. Granted this, it is a good question, how the assertion system replicates itself. Moral philosophers have been fond of the fantasy that the rules against lying and promise-breaking are sustained by the consideration that any particular lie or breaking of a promise tends to damage the institutions of assertion and promising.[1] It may perhaps be true, at the limit, that promises and assertions could become worthless if the respective institutions were overwhelmed with defaulting behaviour. But, quite apart from the question of how this consideration is supposed to affect any given agent, it is quite unclear where the point of breakdown is supposed to be reached, and without some idea of that, and of the kinds of causality involved, this idea does not do much to help us understand how these linguistic practices survive the level of abuse which year in and year out they regularly receive.

The answer lies partly in the fact that the cases in which the norms are broken can be to some extent segregated from the others, and that there is more than one way in which this comes about. This in turn depends on a very basic and significant fact, that the norms in question are not sustained by just one kind of reason or motive. The norms are, trivially, "social," but this does not tell us much about the motives that sustain them. It is tempting to think that because assertion is essential to language, and norms of truth are essential to assertion, those norms sustain themselves in the behaviour of language-users just as other linguistic norms sustain themselves: that since all these norms are involved in there being the kind of collective behaviour that constitutes the existence of a language, the mere existence of the language sustains the norms.[2] For many linguistic norms, such as the local lexical and syntactic rules, the language indeed carries its speakers along, and there is rarely a question of what reason they have for observing them: their reasons for doing so are simply their reasons for speaking that language. (This does not rule it out, of course, that on occasion they can have interesting and creative reasons for breaking these rules.) With the norms of assertion, something similar is true to the extent that a lot of the time, as I put it, people simply tell the truth. However, there are also various substantive and everyday reasons for deciding to observe the norms or to break them, and once the question has arisen, there is no way in which it is going to be answered by the mere fact that any speaker is, by definition, involved in the practices of a language. There is indeed a tradition that tries to conjure substantial norms of truthfulness—in particular, a certain interpretation of Sincerity—out of the mere fact that we are all committed to the linguistic practice of making assertions; but, I shall argue in section 5 of this chapter, this is based on an illusion. Before we come to that, however, we must consider the significance of the fact that there are many different motives for telling the truth, and that among those motives an important part is played by a virtue of Sincerity. In order to do this, we must consider the notion of trust.

In this chapter, we shall be principally concerned with one of the virtues of truth, Sincerity. However, it is worth noting here that, just as the norms that relate assertion and truth do not by themselves deliver the virtue of Sincerity, so the internal connections between truth and belief do not deliver the virtue of Accuracy. Once a question has arisen, as I put it before, the internal connections are not going to provide the answer. Of course the questions are not going to be the same, or even exactly parallel, in the two cases. We may recall the differences that we noticed in the previous chapter between belief and assertion and their respective relations to truth. In the territory of Sincerity, it needs only a moment of reflection, the thought of inhibiting or shaping an assertion, to leave room for the questions "Shall I tell the truth?" "How much of the truth shall I tell?" But, in the territory of Accuracy, there is no such question as "Shall I believe the truth?" Beliefs necessarily aim at the truth, and this is not a merely verbal point. There is indeed the question "Shall I have a belief about this?" and this, in the more recognizable form "Shall I bother to find out about it?" is an innocent and necessary part of the system, an aspect of the epistemic division of labour. It introduces the idea (which we shall look at more closely in the next chapter) of what may be called an *investigative investment*, the idea that information, acquiring a true belief about a given question, can have a cost, in time, energy, opportunities lost, perhaps dangers run. So there are questions such as "How much trouble is it worth to find out about this?" Moreover, they can be questions directed to what one already believes or is disposed to believe: "Do I really believe it? Should I?" It is questions of these kinds that signal the need for the virtue of Accuracy. This is the virtue that encourages people to spend more effort than they might have done in trying to find the truth, and not just to accept any belief-shaped thing that comes into their head. The questions that signal the need for Accuracy do so all the more because they often do not get asked. Part of the point of Accuracy is that it encourages people to ask them. In contrast, encouraging people to ask the question "Shall I tell the truth?" does not, at first glance, look like one of the aims of Sincerity; but, as we shall see, it is more of an aim than it seems to moralists who suppose that the triumph of Sincerity would consist in its never occurring to anyone to tell a lie.

2. *Trust*

A necessary condition of co-operative activity is trust, where this involves the willingness of one party to rely on another to act in certain ways. This implies that the first party has some expectations about the second party's motives, but (in its most basic sense) it does not imply that those motives have to be of some specific kind. A may trust B to do something because A knows that B expects punishment if he fails to do it. In this case B's motives for co-operating are crudely and immediately egoistic. They may be less crudely and immediately egoistic: B may have an interest in long-term co-operative activities with A and may believe that if he defaults on this occasion, A will not trust him again. This is the motivation that Adam Smith famously found reassuring in his baker.[3] It implies, of course, that A and B will meet again, and that A will be able to recognize him. Again, A may have reason to believe that B is a trustworthy person, in the sense that in situations of trust he is generally disposed to do what he is expected to do just because he is expected to do it.[4] In this section, we shall be concerned with trust and trustworthiness in general; in the next section, we shall come to the connections between trust and truth.

There are some general forms of trust on which all social interaction depends, in particular the expectation that other people's behaviour will not be unpromptedly aggressive. These kinds of trust may be sustained in rather desperate circumstances[5] merely by beliefs about the other party's immediate or medium-term self-interest, but in better times and places one can count on most people's having entrenched dispositions against attacking their fellow citizens. While these dispositions provide the basis of trust, it would be misleading to say that they were in themselves dispositions of *trustworthiness*. One is not likely to be reassured by someone who says, "I promise not to murder you." There may be mafioso circles in which such a promise makes sense, but in general, if you cannot rely on someone not to kill you, you can even less rely on him to keep his word. Trustworthiness as a *particular* type of disposition comes in against a more settled background, in which patterns of co-operation are established, and people are standardly trusted to do their part in a venture in which, for instance, they make their contribution after the other parties have made theirs.

Relationships that involve trust give rise to game-theoretical problems about securing assurance. We do not have to make the lowest-level assumptions in favour of egoism, that each party really prefers an outcome in which he defaults and the other person delivers. Let us assume that each party prefers a situation in which they both co-operate, rather than a situation in which he wins at the expense of the other.[6] It is still true that each party ranks lowest a situation in which the other defaults and he himself delivers: so each of them needs assurance. This implies that the situations in which one can rely on the other party need to be segregated from those in which there is good reason to suspect that one cannot. In some cases, the self-interest of each party, immediate or medium-term, so obviously favours co-operation that they need look no further. But more generally the appropriate expectations can be secured only through its being common knowledge that the parties do prefer the co-operative outcome and have an internalized disposition to act in ways appropriate to bringing it about.

Here we have to recall once again the point that has been central to the State of Nature story throughout, that the parties are not devices which have dispositions merely in the sense that reliable predictions can be made about their behaviour. They are human beings, who are understood by one another to have desires, temptations, a sense of what is most important to them, and so on. This implies that there are further questions to be asked about the way in which the dispositions of trustworthiness are secured. One important way of securing them is that the parties come to think that trustworthy behaviour, such as keeping one's word, has an *intrinsic value*, that it is a good thing (many other things being equal) to act as a trustworthy person acts, just because that is the kind of action it is. Moreover, since it has to be common knowledge that the parties think in this way, the idea of this intrinsic value has to be shared, and it has to be understood as part of the culture that it is shared.

This immediately raises a very important question: how intrinsic is intrinsic? There is a danger that if trustworthiness (or anything else) is regarded as having an intrinsic value, it will be supposed that there is nothing else to be said about its valuableness—it is good because it is good, and that is all there is to be said about it. If, on the contrary, one gives an account of how its value might relate to other, perhaps more primitive, values and needs, such as securing co-operative activity which is in everyone's interests, one seems to be giving a reductive and instrumentalist account of the value— which shows (it will be said) that it is not really an intrinsic value at all. But this opposition must surely be unreasonable. It offers us only the choice between an inexplicable and self-subsistent intrinsic good, the value of which is self-explanatory, and, alternatively, a good which has to be understood merely in instrumental terms.[7] What we want, rather, is some insight into these values, some account of their relations to other things which we know that we need and value, but an insight which does not reduce them to the merely instrumental. What we want, once again, is explanation without reduction, and as I have suggested earlier, one aim of the genealogical method is precisely to help one to get it.

It may be said that no line of argument which sets out from a game-theoretical formulation of the problems of trust could possibly show that trustworthiness had an intrinsic value: the most the argument could show is that it is useful for people to treat it as though it had an intrinsic value. It may even be said that it is a question of their *pretending* that it had an intrinsic value. It is true that if the basic resources of understanding are too limited, this charge will be just. If an agent has no more than the thought that it is instrumentally useful for him to think that a certain value is not merely instrumentally useful, the structure will indeed come to no more than a pretence, and for that reason it will be unstable under reflection. This is what happens to indirect Utilitarianism, the kind of theory that recommends, on strictly Utilitarian principles, rules or dispositions which will lead us to choose certain actions that, in themselves, would not be chosen by a Utilitarian. The trouble with this is that an agent who needs to reflect on a situation in which he is disposed to do such an action has no thought to fall back on except that it is Utilitarianly valuable that he should have this disposition, and this leaves no content to the disposition: he has no thoughts with which to counter the consideration that some alternative action in this situation is the one that has the best Utilitarian consequences.[8]

The problem is not peculiar to indirect Utilitarianism. The same structural difficulty is inherent in David Gauthier's contractualist argument,[9] according to which entirely self-interested agents are supposed to reflect on the fact that in the Prisoners' Dilemma players who try to maximize their immediate advantage will each get no more than their third preference, and to see, merely in virtue of this reflection, that they have a rational basis for becoming "constrained maximizers," that is to say, for acquiring some of the dispositions of justice. As Gauthier's critics have insisted, it is very hard to see how a self-interested agent who is armed with this reflection and no more, and who knows that the other parties are in the same situation, will not simply be returned to the Prisoners' Dilemma: each party will fear that the other party will not act as a constrained maximizer, and so reasonably does not act in that way himself. The trouble with indirect Utilitarianism, and with Gauthier's construction, is that the lack of fit between the spirit being justified and the spirit of the justification is so radical that, if the construction is exposed to reflection at all, it is bound to unravel.

So what is required for trustworthiness to have an intrinsic value is that those who possess it should not be related to it merely in the empty way that is illustrated by indirect Utilitarianism and by Gauthier's argument. Those who treat it as having an intrinsic value must themselves be able to make sense of it as having an intrinsic value. This means that its value must make sense to them from the inside, so to speak: it must be possible for them to relate trustworthiness to other things that they value, and to their ethical emotions. I suggest that it is in fact a sufficient condition for something (for instance, trustworthiness) to have an intrinsic value that, first, it is necessary (or nearly necessary) for basic human purposes and needs that human beings should treat it as an intrinsic good; and, second, they can coherently treat it as an intrinsic good. This means that it is stable under reflection, as the examples just mentioned were not. What is essential for this to be so is that the agent has some materials in terms of which he can understand this value in relation to other values that he holds, and this implies, in turn, that the intrinsic good (in this case trustworthiness), or rather the agent's relation to it, has an inner structure in terms of which it can be related to other goods. If these conditions do hold, then I claim that we have not simply adopted an illusion or a pretence of there being an intrinsic good. In fact, if these conditions hold, that would be a very odd thing to say, implying as it does that there is something further which would count as its *really* being an intrinsic good, of which these conditions offer only a surrogate or mock-up. If the conditions are satisfied, then we shall have *constructed* an intrinsic good. Another way of putting it is that in a genealogy the value can be represented as arising from more primitive needs and desires, and that when we reflect on that story, we can find the value intelligible without at the same time losing our hold on it.[10]

Of course, the construction has to be more than the idea of a construction. For us to get clear about trustworthiness as an intrinsic good, we need to answer two kinds of question. First, we have to decide what disposition or set of dispositions trustworthiness is; as we might also say, what it needs to be. For instance, one thing it needs to be is the disposition of an agent to be reliable, not in the sense that you can rely on him to help you (that is a different disposition, helpfulness), but in the sense that he will help you if he has told you that he will help you or, perhaps, if he has led you to believe that he will. (That last distinction will turn out to be important in the case of Sincerity.) Second, we have to see what those other values may be that surround trustworthiness, values that provide the structure in terms of which it can be reflectively understood. The two questions are related, since the psychological and ethical backing that the dispositions of trustworthiness receive itself affects, to some extent, their content. We have a general idea of what kind of content is involved, and without it we would not know that we were talking about trustworthiness rather than some other disposition, but the exact demands and expectations involved will vary with the framework of values and sentiments in terms of which trustworthiness makes sense.

That framework has been different in differing cultural circumstances. Everywhere, trustworthiness and its more particular applications such as that which concerns us, Sincerity, have a broadly similar content—we know what we are talking about—and everywhere, it has to be related, psychologically, socially, and ethically, to some wider range of values. What those values are, however, varies from time to time and culture to culture, and the various versions cannot be discovered by general reflection. At this point the fictional history of genealogy, which aims to bring out the necessary, structural features, is replaced by the real history of specific cultural determinations. General reflection can show that something has to support the disposition of Sincerity, and that an agent should be able to make inner sense of the structure in which Sincerity is embedded. But what particular range of values in a given cultural situation will perform this role is a matter of real history, and this history has been quite various and dense.[11] In our own time we find it particularly natural to think that deceiving people (or at least some people, in some circumstances) is an example of using or manipulating them, and that that is what is wrong with it. But there have been other ways of looking at it: Sincerity has a history, and it is the deposit of this history that we encounter in thinking about the virtues of truth in our own life. This is why at a certain point philosophy needs to make way for history, or, as I prefer to say, to involve itself in it.

3. Trustworthiness in Speech

Truth, and specifically the virtues of truth, are connected with trust. The connections are to be seen in the English language. The word "truth" and its ancestors in Early and Middle English originally meant fidelity, loyalty, or reliability.[12] (Rather similarly, in modern English the primary sense of "honesty" can be summarized as "not lying, not stealing, keeping promises.")[13] Truthfulness is a form of trustworthiness, that which relates in a particular way to speech. "Truthfulness," in fact, like the German *Wahrhaftigkeit*, can refer to both Sincerity and Accuracy, and this is entirely natural. If we are to rely on what others tell us, they had better be not just sincere but correct; moreover (in the other direction, so to speak) if we take care to be right, we need to be honest with ourselves.[14] Of course, other forms of trustworthiness also involve speech, because they require fitting action to words: if he says, "I will do it," and he is trustworthy, he does it, and he makes what he said true. This very general relation between speech and trust is not the main point in this chapter. We are concerned with the trustworthiness in speech that constitutes Sincerity. The question is, what dispositions does a speaker need to have if he is to be trusted to say what he believes about some matter which it is not up to him to bring about?

As with other forms of trust, the reasons for trusting what someone else tells one can be various. It is vital that on many occasions there are obvious reasons of self- or group-interest for speakers to tell the truth as they see it. This can be true in situations of primitive openness, and there are many other occasions on which the parties are using language instrumentally to their needs—it may be, their shared needs—where it is mutually obvious that their interests are served by their telling the truth. In such ways, constant injections of reasons for action which are obviously self-interested help to warm the tubes of the normative circulatory system.

This can extend to relations between strangers where there is no obvious reason for one to deceive the other, but this is more problematic territory. In some places, people may lack good will toward strangers, may indeed be simply bloody-minded, and nothing about the nature of language as involving norms of truth is going to tell one whether they are or not. A further complication is that one cannot necessarily assume that good will leads people to tell the truth. It is said that in some regions, if a stranger asks for directions, he is given not the correct answer but a more encouraging one. If this is not a myth, and the practice can continue to exist, it can only be for one of two reasons: either enough strangers can be expected not to understand the practice, or the answers are supposed to be heard not as assertions aiming at the truth but rather as happy pictures of an alternative world, much as someone might sing the traveller a snatch of a song to cheer him on his way.

Between the cases in which there are shared interests, and those in which dependence on others is recognizably hazardous, we need something else. We need to rely on assertions' being sincere not only where this is guaranteed by obvious self-interest, immediate or medium-term, but in a range of interactions wider than these. We need people to have dispositions of Sincerity, and this implies that people treat Sincerity as having an intrinsic value.[15] As we saw in relation to trustworthiness generally, this raises two questions. What does Sincerity need to be? And what structure of other virtues and values will surround it, in such a way that the reflective agent can make sense of it as an intrinsic value? We saw also that the two questions are related: the surrounding of other values itself affects what Sincerity needs to be.

The answers to both the questions have varied in different historical circumstances. I cannot give a history of those historical variations: I wish I could.[16] What I shall try to do in this chapter is to trace some features of the structure that give rise to the variations; mention a few of the historical divergences; and make some suggestions about an interpretation of Sincerity that makes sense to us now. In doing this, I shall move from the most general demands on the structure of Sincerity to some values that are most familiar to us, ideas in terms of which *we* see it as having an intrinsic value or being a good thing in itself. Just because we—that is to say, I myself and, I shall assume, the reader—do have this view of Sincerity, we see it as having a value that goes beyond anything ascribed to it in the basic State of Nature story, where it first emerges as, roughly, the solution to a co-ordination problem. At the same time, we understand that it has been given rather different interpretations in the past. Some of these we may want to criticize, as I shall criticize what I call "the fetishism of assertion": we are not bound to a relativistic vow of silence about the past, though comments about it are not obligatory, either. All these elements, the basic construction of Sin-

cerity, our own interpretation of it, the history of other interpretations, and our view of those interpretations, can be brought together
in a genealogical story.

4. *Dispositions of Sincerity*

What, then, does Sincerity need to be?—where that means, first,
what does *anyone* need Sincerity to be? From the earliest stages of
the State of Nature story, we have the idea that Sincerity consists in
a disposition to make sure that one's assertion expresses what one
actually believes. The assertion system, narrowly and functionally
conceived, aims to communicate beliefs, so a speaker will not only
have expressed his belief, but, if he is trusted, he will have led his
hearer to have some beliefs. What is the relation between the speaker's beliefs and the beliefs with which the hearer ends up? If we
identify the belief which is expressed in the assertion (granted that
the speaker is sincere) with the content of the assertion, as we did
in chapter 4, then the beliefs which the hearer acquires will certainly
include that belief. But the speaker has beliefs which are not expressed in his assertion, and also, very significantly, the hearer will
come to believe more than the speaker said.

The speaker says, "Mary was in Paris when she telephoned, or
she was in Rome," and the hearer reasonably gathers from this
that the speaker does not know which is true. But that was not part
of what the speaker asserted: what he said will be true just if one of
the disjuncts is true, whether he knows which it is or not. What a
hearer may reasonably gather in such ways from what a speaker says
may lead to many other kinds of conclusion. "Someone has been
opening your mail," she helpfully says, and you, trusting her, take it
that it was not the speaker herself. If you discover that it was the
speaker, you will have to agree (if through clenched teeth) that what
she said was true. So, you must also agree, she did not tell you a lie.
I take a lie to be an assertion, the content of which the speaker
believes to be false, which is made with the intention to deceive the
hearer with regard to that content.[17] I also believe that this is what
most people understand by the word "lie"; despite a very promiscu-

ous use of it by some theoretical writers, it seems to me that in everyday use this is clearly its definition. Of course, it is another question how clearly a given utterance fits the definition. It may be very uncertain, or actually indeterminate, whether the speaker is really making an assertion; whether he or she believes it is false; whether the intention is to deceive the hearer. This is notably so with children, who are in the course of learning what all these things are, and have to be taught what it is to lie, as they are, in part, by being taught when not to do it.

It can be vague in these ways whether someone is telling a lie, but the woman who talked about the mail was definitely not telling a lie, though she may well have deceived you, misled you, intentionally led you to believe something untrue. So far as her assertion's content was concerned, it was all right: it expressed a true belief of hers. Admittedly, it failed to express another belief of hers (indeed, a piece of knowledge) which was very closely related to what she did assert. That much is true of every assertion, but in this case, the fact that she said so much and no more was exploited by her in order to mislead you. Although she did not lie, you may well not want to trust her again. So if Sincerity is trustworthiness in speech, it seems that it must be more than what we first took it to be, the disposition to make sure that any assertion one makes expresses a genuine belief. Trustworthiness is more than the avoidance of lying, and if we want Sincerity to be the virtue of trustworthiness in speech, there must be more to be said about it. We have to ask what beliefs, and how much of one's beliefs, one may be expected to express in a given situation.

In these connections, it looks as though the distinction between lying and some other forms of misleading or deceptive speech fits rather neatly with a distinction in the philosophy of language, between the content of an assertion and what Paul Grice called "conversational implicatures"[18]—the implications of a speaker's choosing to perform a speech-act with one content rather than another. Implicatures are not entailments; if an entailment, a logical consequence, of what she asserted is false, then so is what she asserted, but, as we have seen, this is not the case with such things as her suggestion, in saying "someone," that it was not herself, which is an example of an implicature. We have strong intuitions about what someone can be said to have actually asserted, and these are not confined to the term of art (as it more or less is) "assert." If you were asked about the supposedly helpful person and the mail, "But did she actually *say* that she had not opened it herself?" you would be bound to deny it. What she said (in the sense of her *saying that* . . .), or what she stated, is in our ordinary understanding identified with its truth-conditions, whereas implicatures lie outside the truth-conditions.

This natural conception of an assertion's content helps to pick out ways in which we may be uncertain what a speaker has asserted. The sentence he used may be lexically ambiguous: "She was homeless and helpless, and he took her in." Or structurally ambiguous, as in "I left the chocolates in the box in the garage." Or there may be an ambiguity of reference: "Paul told Bruce to go into the shop, and as soon as he got through the door, he shot the shopkeeper." In such cases, if we do not know what sense or reference the speaker intended, we do not know what belief he expressed when he used the sentence, and we do not know what assertion he made. In the case of the implicature, we could equally be unsure "what she meant," as we naturally put it: we could have been unclear whether the woman who said, "Someone . . . ," meant us to understand that she was excluding herself. In that case, however, we can identify exactly what belief it is that her assertion expresses: we know one of her beliefs, at least, and the problem concerns others she may have.[19] All these possibilities for uncertainty and misunderstanding can be deceitfully exploited, and we shall see more of this in the next section.

Even if the sentence which the speaker used was not ambiguous, we should not assume that we can get directly from its words to what he asserted. I suggested in the previous chapter[20] that an ironical assertion is not an assertion, because the real content, what the speaker wants one to believe, is only implied. But there are other cases in which a sentence is indeed used to make an assertion, though its content cannot simply be recovered from its words. It may be meant, for instance, metaphorically. The old member of an Oxford college who wrote to the alumni magazine and said, "Since my retirement, I have literally buried myself in my garden," said something false only because he used the word "literally"; without it, he would have made a true assertion, one expressed by the use of a metaphor.[21] It may be unclear whether we are presented with a metaphor, an unusual or special meaning of an expression, or a mere implication. Another story, also true, concerns a philosopher who was asked by his wife to watch the soup cooking on the stove and who, when she came back, was staring intently at it as it boiled over. He clearly had not done what she wanted. He said that he had done what she asked, but if we agree that he failed to do that, too, should we say that this was because he wrongly took what she said *literally*? Surely not, at least if that is opposed to *metaphorically*. If this is taking a metaphor literally, what would he have done if she had asked him to keep his eye on it? There is room for a good deal of theory here, but we shall leave it aside.

Not everything that one can infer from a person's making a particular assertion is an implicature. It is not a matter of implicatures if one reaches the conclusion from the tone of his speech that he is not a native English-speaker, or, again, if one gathers from the timing of his interruption that he is tactless, offensive, or does not know that this is the dead man's widow. All sorts of inferences may be reasonably made from what people say and the ways in which they say it. Implicatures more resemble matters of linguistic rule, and it is a striking fact that competent speakers can standardly recognize an implicature if they are presented with a sentence and are invited to think of it as asserted in normal circumstances (though, as we shall see, this assumption is not as simple as it sounds). To take two examples from Grice, someone who says, "I went into a room yesterday and spoke to a woman . . . ," would normally be taken to imply that this woman was not, for instance, his wife, and that the room was not in their house; while if he said, "I broke a thumb yesterday," he would, on the contrary, be taken to mean that it was his thumb (it takes on an unexpected ring if it is heard as a wrestler's boast).

Grice explained these expectations in terms of rules which are understood by speakers as underlying efficient linguistic exchange. One rough formulation that he offered of the most general rule was "Make your conversational contribution such as is required . . . by the accepted purpose or direction of the talk exchange in which you are engaged." One particular purpose, not the only one, is to secure "a maximally effective exchange of information." The basic rule, he suggested, might be labelled "the Co-operative Principle."[22] It is immediately clear that implicatures do not presuppose language as simply a practice involving semantic and syntactic rules, together with the norm that certain kinds of utterances are taken to be true; they look to the use of language under favourable social conditions which enable it to be indeed co-operative. They are *conversational* implicatures, but not everyone who is talking with someone else is engaged, in the required sense, in a conversation. What is required for that to be so are certain understood levels of trust.

The discussion of implicatures helps to bring out a fundamental point, that hearers gather more from a speaker's making a particular assertion than the content of that assertion. As I put it earlier, the speaker expresses one belief, but they acquire many. Speakers have countless beliefs and many different ways of expressing them. They could always have said something else, mentioned a different matter, made their statement more or less determinate. The fact that in a given context the speaker says one thing rather than another gives information to the hearer, and this of course is itself a means of communication. Moreover, it is an essential feature of language. There may be special circumstances in which it is understood that a hearer is to ignore everything about an assertion except its content, but they are very special. In general, in relying on what someone said, one inevitably relies on more than what he *said*.

5. Fetishizing Assertion

Consider cases in which a speaker has the intention to deceive. The familiar distinction between lying and other forms of misleading speech is that between the speaker's making an assertion the content of which he believes to be false, and his asserting something which he takes to be true, but in such a way that he leads the hearer to believe something false, in particular by exploiting the mutually understood operation of implicatures. This distinction is not altogether definite, which is what you would expect, but the indeterminacies are not what are interesting. The interesting question is whether the distinction is morally relevant. If someone deliberately brings it about by what he says that you have a false belief, getting you to rely on something which he knows is untrue, what moral difference, if any, does it make whether he does this by lying or by relying on an implicature?

It is important that this is the issue. When someone bases a moral position on some distinction, and it is said that the distinction is "unreasonable" or "baseless," this can mean two different things. It may mean that the distinction itself is unreal or hopelessly vague or subjective. For instance, if it is a question of an action that will lead to someone's death, moral theorists sometimes invoke a doctrine of "double effect," which seeks to draw a line between different ways in which the death may be causally and intentionally related to the action. Is it a direct consequence or a side effect? Is the action intended as a means to the death, or has it some other aim?[23] This doctrine is often criticized on the ground that it does not offer enough of a distinction: it is too easy to redescribe cases so that they fit one pattern or the other. In contrast to this, a distinction may be clear and robust enough, within the demands of practical affairs, but the objection is that it is not relevant. Someone who knowingly sits by and watches a blind man walk off the cliff, when he could easily have prevented it, certainly did not kill him, but how much difference does that make? He may be, in the circumstances, as much to blame for the blind man's death as if he had pushed him.[24] In the present case, it is this second kind of objection that has to be considered. In ordinary thought, the distinction between a lie and other forms of misleading speech is, by the standards of such things, fairly robust. The question is: in the many cases where it is clear whether a deceitful utterance is a lie or not, how much does the difference matter?

A surprising number and range of powerful moral thinkers have thought that it was quite basic to the morality of truthfulness: in particular, that lies are never really justifiable (though they may be forgivable), while other forms of deceitful speech can be justified.[25] Aquinas wrote:

All lies are by definition wrong, acts out of tune with their matter, since words should by definition signify what we think, and it is perverse and wrong for them to signify what is not in our mind. So since lies as such are out of order, they cannot be used to rescue others whatever the peril; rather the truth must be cleverly masked in some way.[26]

Kant, much later, in a very different social and religious context, and for moral reasons which are also, at least on the surface, very different, held much the same view, famously claiming that if a murderer came to the door seeking an innocent fugitive who was hiding in your house, and asked where he was, you would violate the moral law if you told a lie.[27] (The example itself goes back to Augustine.) Some in the Catholic tradition who favour the distinction are fond of the edifying story of Saint Athanasius:

If we read the lives of the Saints, we see how they managed to avoid lying in crises. St Athanasius was rowing on a river when the persecutors came rowing in the opposite direction: "Where is the traitor Athanasius?" "Not far away", the Saint gaily replied, and rowed past them unsuspected.[28]

As Alasdair MacIntyre has rightly said, one's reaction to this story reveals something fundamental about one's attitudes to lying.

These writers do not think that there is nothing wrong with other forms of misleading or deceitful speech. They do not necessarily think that all lies are equally bad, though Kant at least seems to have thought that in the vital dimension of duty they were all alike, "the greatest violation of a human being's duty to himself regarded merely as a moral being."[29] The point is that an overall moral distinction is drawn by this tradition between lying and other forms of deliberately deceitful speech, by which lying is unqualifiedly wrong (even if in human weakness and peril we are sometimes drawn into it), while other forms of misleading speech are not (though they are always undesirable and sometimes wrong). The tradition distinguished various different ways of avoiding a lie. Besides the obvious resources, innocent but not always available, of refusing to answer, changing the subject, meeting a question with a question, and so on, there was "equivocation," which in the strictest sense lay in using an ambiguous sentence which in one of its meanings expressed a true proposition: the speaker hoped that the hearer would take it in the other meaning, in which what it said was false. It is a good question, in fact, whether this hallowed device even saves the speaker from telling a lie. Suppose that in virtue of an ambiguity of sense or reference the sentence that the speaker utters can mean one thing, which is true, and also mean another thing, which is false. The speaker says, "The man you are looking for has not been here this year," where "here" would mean, on a natural understanding, this house (in which sense what he said is false) but could mean the very spot the speaker is standing on (in which case what he said is true). When I mentioned ambiguity earlier, I said that if the hearer does not know what sense or reference was intended, he does not know what assertion the speaker made. In those terms, we should surely say that if the equivocator asserted anything, he asserted the falsehood, that the fugitive had not been in the house. There is at least a reason for saying this, that he intended the hearer to take what he said as meaning this rather than the other. But if he asserted this, he told a lie. An alternative would be to say that he made no assertion at all but, in effect, pretended to. On that interpretation, he did not tell a lie, but there is an odd consequence. Let us call the proposition which is the unobvious meaning of the sentence, the "second" proposition: this is the one that the equivocator hopes that the hearer will *not* pick up from what he says—in this case, the proposition that the fugitive has not stood on this very spot. The doctrine of equivocation requires the second proposition to be true. But why should it have to be true? If the correct account is that the equivocator avoids a lie because he does not assert anything at all, it will not matter if the second proposition is false as well.

This makes it clear that the doctrine of equivocation must hold that the speaker does assert one proposition rather than the other, and that the one he *really* asserts is the second proposition, the one that is true. There is not much going for that in terms of the relations between speaker and hearer: the equivocator, after all, really intends the hearer to pick up the meaning in which what he says is false. So what might make one say that he *really* asserts the truth?

We can get some insight into this by looking at a more extreme device recommended by some casuists, in particular as a way for Catholic priests, under persecution, to preserve the secrets of the confessional. This was the device of "mental restriction" or "reservation": what the speaker said was, as it stood, false, but he supplied mentally some addition or qualification, given which it was true. So a report about a certain Father Ward in 1606: "First, he swore he was not priest, that is saith he [in a subsequent explanation], not Apollo's priest at Delphi. Second, he was never across the sea, it's true he saith, for he was never across the Indian seas."[30] And so on. Clearly this device could license any lie at all—it comes to much the same as a child's crossing his fingers behind his back. It attracted severe criticism and was condemned along with other excesses by Innocent XI in 1679. The rationale for it, however, is revealing: that God knows what you are asserting even if the hearer does not, because you speak always in the presence of God. He knows what you *really* assert, because he knows your intentions. But what intentions? Deceit, after all, is a relation between you and your earthly hearer, and the question of what you meant must be answered in terms of intentions directed toward that hearer. God may know my intentions in the sense of my good intentions, but the intentions that form my meanings cannot rest with him, independently of the uptake I aim to secure in the world. At most, his understanding of my meaning would make all the difference if I were addressing him: but in addressing him, there is no place for deceit.[31]

Both equivocation and mental restriction were defended, under conditions of persecution, by a Jesuit, Henry Garnet, who published anonymously in 1595 *A Treatise of Equivocation; or, Against Lying and Fraudulent Dissimulation*. A lie, Garnet said,

> consists in this, that a man intends to deny with words the very truth he conceives in his mind. But this is not so in these cases, for he contraryth not the truth which to himself he conceiveth, but rather signifyeth another diverse truth . . . it mattereth not whether those I speak to understand it amiss or no so long as unjustly, rashly or wickedly I am asked by them.

The considerations about what the speaker "conceives to himself" and what he "signifies" do not make much of a case that the victim of persecution who answers in this style is not lying. But it is clear where the weight of the argument really rests. The last qualification, about the questioners, not only lays down the conditions under which mental reservation could rightfully be used, but, Garnet makes clear, provides the most significant content to the reservations: "I do not know [in such a way that I can state publicly]"; "the priest is not there [in such a way that it can be declared to you]." This consideration in itself, that there is every reason not to tell these people the truth, is eminently sensible, and the idea that some people "have no right to the truth" is one that I shall come back to in section 6. But someone today who is sympathetic to that idea is likely to take its force to be that in extreme cases, at least, and certainly in the circumstances faced by the persecuted Church, you can tell a lie to wrongful questioners. That is the conclusion that this consideration leads us to, not to a desperately shifty attempt to re-arrange the boundaries of what counts as a lie.

The underlying purpose of these casuistical manœuvres, and more generally of the doctrine which distinguished morally between lying and other forms of deceitful speech, is clear enough. It was to deliver a prohibition on lying that could be exceptionless. If there are to be no exceptions to the rule against lying, and yet the world sometimes requires, for the greater good, that people should be given false beliefs, then this must be done by means other than lying. But why should one expect the rule to be exceptionless? Many other prohibitions, including some very important ones, are certainly not. In any case, the tradition did not see this purpose, of making the rule exceptionless, as self-justifying, or as justified merely in terms of consequences (as people sometimes say that if rules are not exceptionless, there is a slippery slope of exceptions, and you end up with no rule at all). Rather, there was supposed to be an independent basis for the distinction between lying and other forms of deceit, from which it would helpfully follow that the rule against lying could be exceptionless. The justification lay in the idea that the definition or essence of assertion involved truthfulness: an assertion, just as such, is "meant to be true." The very nature of this communicative device, which is essential to the relations between human beings as rational creatures, was itself supposed to determine how it should be used. This is the thought that is expressed in the passage that I quoted from Aquinas, and the same idea, for all their differences, is at work in Kant. He puts it in terms (mountingly hysterical terms, one may think) of the speaker's relations to himself as a rational being:

> But communication of one's thoughts to someone through words that yet (intentionally) contain the contrary of what the speaker thinks on the subject is an end that is directly opposed to the natural purposiveness of the speaker's capacity to communicate his thoughts, and is thus a renunciation of his personality, and such a speaker is a mere deceptive appearance of a human being, not a human being himself.

And further:

> The human being as a moral being (*homo noumenon*) cannot use himself as a natural being (*homo phenomenon*) as a mere means (a speaking machine), as if his natural being were not bound to the inner end (of communicating thoughts).[32]

I accept the account of assertion on which the idea is based; I have agreed that there is a sense in which assertions are "meant to be true." But nothing follows from that about the use that may appropriately be made of assertions. This is what I meant when I said in section 1 of this chapter that the "value of truth" recovered from the account of assertions *gets us no further at all* in delivering the values of truthfulness, once the questions have arisen to which truthfulness is supposed to give the answers. If there is a temptation to think that it does get us further, it is likely to come from some relic of a teleological assumption, as old as Plato or older, that essences—for instance, the nature of assertion as essential to our life as rational beings—can show us how to behave when we have a choice about how to behave. But this idea is dead (even if the news that it is has not yet reached everyone), and its death should be among the assumptions of any adequately naturalistic account. If essences can be said to rule out anything at all, they can do so only by making that thing impossible, and if they leave a course of action possible, such

as lying, it is too late for them to try to stop it by signals directed
through morality.

It is not surprising that the teleological assumption should have
operated in the thought of Aquinas or, indeed, Kant, and it is not
that in itself which makes their insistence on this doctrine seem, as
it seemed to Benjamin Constant, so unreasonable. What is more
peculiar is that the teleology of assertion should have been thought
to have just this consequence. The "definition" of an assertion may
indeed refer just to its being an expression of belief, but as soon as
one considers the role of assertions in informative communication,
which is the context in which these problems arise and also, one
would suppose, one in which their function in the life of rational
creatures should be considered, it is obvious that the ways in which
assertions work essentially involve the matter of what assertion a
speaker chooses to make. If lying is inherently an abuse of assertion,
then so is deliberately exploiting the way in which one's hearer can
be expected to understand one's choice of assertion. The doctrine
makes the assertion into a fetish by lifting it out of the context in
which it plays its part and projecting onto it in isolation all the force
of the demand for truthfulness.

Kant himself informally explains the idea of a lie with a Latin tag
which means "to have one thing shut up in the heart and another
ready on the tongue,"[33] a formula which naturally covers more than
a lie. More substantially, he says that a lie makes one an object of
contempt in the eyes of others and, "what is still worse," contemptible in one's own eyes. He tells us that another disposition that similarly offends against one's duties to oneself is servility. These ideas
of honour are admirable (and all the better when not presented in
the unhelpful vocabulary of duties to oneself). We shall come back
to them. But if deceit is justified at all, as in defending the innocent
fugitive, something is wrong if one thinks that it is more honourable
to find some weasel words than to tell a lie.

The tradition—Kant for one—has spoken sometimes in terms of
distributing responsibility. I have a responsibility to speak the truth,
no more and no less, but it is *up to the hearer* whether to accept the
implicatures of what I say, so if I mislead him, I leave him free to
form his conclusions, as I do not if I lie. There is something in the

idea that to deceive people can be to attack their freedom, and we
shall encounter it in the next section. But that is a point about deceit,
and it does nothing for the distinction between lying and other
forms of deceit. If the circumstances are those of "normal trust"—
we shall come back to the question of what they might be—the
hearer will take for granted as much what I imply as what I assert;
if he has reasons to be suspicious, he is as free to apply his suspicions
to what I assert as to what I imply. Again, this is not a matter to
which one can apply that well-known moral resource, a distinction
between doing and merely allowing something to happen. It is not
that when I lie, I bring it about that the hearer has a false belief, but
that when I mislead, I simply allow him to have a false belief. There
is such a thing as the latter, as when I allow someone to continue in
a false belief which I could correct. But in the cases we are considering, I deliberately bring it about that he has a false belief, whether
I do so by intentionally making a false assertion or by intentionally
choosing a misleading one.

The cases we are considering are those in which the person to be
deceived is a murderer or a persecutor or otherwise in the wrong,
and there, as it seems to me, it makes no difference whether deceit
takes the form of lying or of something else. But this does not mean
that lying is in all respects on the same level as other forms of verbal
deceit. Many share a feeling that in some circumstances, and among
people who in general have reason to trust one another, there is
something particularly odious or insulting about the "lie direct,"
that it is a special kind of affront. In the next section, I shall try
to find a place for this thought. Moreover, there are some special
institutional circumstances in which the tradition's distinction between lying and misleading people does make sense. If we consider
what they are, this may shed some light on the ethical state of mind
that gave rise to the traditional doctrine and its mistaken attempt to
rule out lying altogether.

In the British Parliament, there is a convention that ministers may
not lie when answering questions or making statements, but they
can certainly omit, select, give answers that reveal less than the
whole relevant truth, and generally give a misleading impression.
(There is indeed an offence of "misleading the House" which falls

short of straight lying, but the general idea is on the lines of the traditional distinction.) When a minister lied in the House in 1963 about his affair with a woman called Christine Keeler, a limerick went round:

> What on earth have you done, said Christine,
> You have wrecked the whole party machine;
>   To lie in the nude,
>   That is just rude,
> But to lie in the House is obscene.[34]

It is clear what the point of this convention is. No-one can expect a government to make full disclosure about everything, and often it is unclear anyway what full disclosure would be. It is equally undesirable that they should be able to get away with anything they like in order to deceive the public. The rule makes it harder to get away with deceit, since answers will be suspiciously inspected and questions pressed, and ministers who are debarred from lying can be forced to a position in which they either produce the truth (if they know it) or are left seriously embarrassed and with nothing to say.

These are quite special circumstances: the situation is at once adversarial and rule-governed. The rule works, a good deal of the time, because it has a point and there are strong sanctions against breaking it. There are other situations with a similar structure, such as courts of law, and areas of commercial activity that lie between the gentlemanly on the one hand and the utterly unscrupulous on the other. But, apart from such cases, not much of life has just this structure of expectations. Most of it is either better or worse. It is better when we can more or less rely on what people imply as well as on what they assert; it is worse when we cannot even rely on what they assert. Perhaps the tradition rested on a picture of the world in which it was all, ultimately or at the limit, adversarial but rule-governed. Much of life, in this picture, is adversarial and there is little to rely on, but it is still wholly rule-governed, and as the ministers who do not lie under pressure emerge with their credit intact, so, if we hold on to the rule, we can emerge from life altogether with an adequate answer to give. This implies a dimension beyond this life. Rather as the idea of what one "really asserts" implied a God who was lis-

tening, this picture of things surely implies a Judgement. Kant's
supposedly secularized version of such ideas was, as Nietzsche and
other critics noticed, running on borrowed time. But even for those
who believed in a literal Judgement, there is still a question. Where
could their great confidence have come from that these would be
the rules of the court? Athanasius used his little trick to save himself
and so took his own chances, but others who have followed his example in not lying to avert evil might well have wondered from some
indications in the Scriptures themselves, such as the parable of
the talents, whether they were not taking a rather narrow view of
their responsibilities.

6. *Deserving the Truth*

The tradition I have just considered offered a rule, one that was
supposed to be exceptionless in the case of lying, though it left much
room for judgement about misleading people. Apart from the merits
of that rule, however, and the question whether any rule could be
exceptionless, there is a deeper issue, whether what we want is a *rule*
at all. We started out, after all, looking for a disposition, one fit to
be the disposition of Sincerity. Perhaps this is a matter not of following a rule but of having a set of values that shape one's attitudes to
the people to whom one may be speaking.

In discussing Grice's implicatures, I have referred to the circumstances of "normal trust." These are the circumstances that he and
other theorists have in mind when they discuss what is presupposed
by co-operative communication. But what are those circumstances?
More precisely, from what field are they being picked out? Do we
principally have in mind a kind of society, one that is relatively
well functioning in these respects, as opposed to one that is on the
verge of pervasive Hobbesian conflict and mistrust? Or do we mean
some relations within our familiar society, those that we have to
some people (most people?) as contrasted with people whom, for
instance, we have special reason to distrust? Do we mean certain
situations or domains, as it is often said that no sensible person expects to hear the truth when buying a used car from a dealer? Or,

again, do we have in mind certain aspects of our relations to other people, determined, for instance, by particular social roles, as when the Opposition member of Parliament who is a friend of a minister will expect him to be cagey when answering in the House, and perhaps in private conversation about some government business, but would be upset if he were that evasive on personal matters? We mean all of these things, and this implies that in referring to "normal trust" we are not really looking for one particular kind of circumstances. We noticed that Grice's implicatures are like features of the language: competent speakers can identify them when they are asked to consider a sentence as uttered in normal circumstances. In thinking about those circumstances, they are in fact imagining that they are engaged in some kind of co-operative and trustful conversation. But, as I said earlier, not every linguistic exchange is in that sense a "conversation."

It may be said that the idea that a linguistic exchange is a "conversation" is the *default* assumption.[35] But it is far from clear what this means. It might mean that if we know absolutely nothing about someone except that we share a language with him, then we should start by trusting him. This is not a theoretical assumption but a piece of bad advice. It may mean, differently, that a large proportion of linguistic exchanges in a well-ordered society are "conversations," rather than any of the other things they may be, such as contributions to a relation which is rule-governed but antagonistic. This may be true, but it does not support any interesting presumption, as opposed to a rather better piece of advice, to make sure what sort of exchange you are engaged in. It may mean, again, that if we can reasonably assume (it does not have to be a matter of calculation or conscious reflection) that our relations to this speaker are of the trustful kind, so that we are indeed in a conversation, then we have reason to sustain that relation of trust and to speak in a way that is appropriate to it. That is correct, and it represents a commitment which is a central expression of the ethical disposition of Sincerity. In trying to understand Sincerity, however, we cannot simply assume those relations. We need to consider the various kinds of communicative expectations that obtain between people who have different kinds of relations to one another—either in general, or in special situations defined by their roles (as when the two friendly politicians confront one another across the House). When we have considered some of these possibilities, we shall perhaps be able to see what general notions may help us to describe the variations.

I have mentioned the special cases in which the relations between speakers are adversarial but rule-governed, and I said that most relations are (from the communicative point of view) better or worse than this. We can consider some that are better, and first, those that are shaped by some degree of friendly acquaintance. I said in the previous chapter that it is a mistake to assimilate assertions as such to promises, but there is a significant point about promises and intentions which has an analogy in the area of saying and implying. Philosophers and moralists have exaggerated the difference between promises and mere statements of intention. In legal contexts there is an important distinction between what I have undertaken, the terms of the contract, and what I have not; the idea is that this should be made as clear as possible in advance. But if I say to a friend or a colleague or a well-disposed neighbour that I am going to do a certain thing, and I know that he or she will rely on this in some significant respect, and he or she knows that I know this, there is room for recriminations and a retreat from these relations if I do not do the thing and also do not try, if possible, to avert the effects on this person. It may be said that this shows that promises can be made without the formalities of promising. But this would be to overlook the main point, that considerations of this kind may come up only *after* the utterance: you discover that the other person is counting on some (reasonably understood) implication of what you said, and you feel that you must do something about it. Equally, promises in informal contexts are less than contracts: neither the agent nor the recipient need fall back on every word of what was originally understood. Flexibilities and understandings of these kinds help to define an entire territory of friendship, trustful acquaintance, and much else. Human relations would be drastically and unrecognizably impoverished if there were only two maxims that applied to such things, "Keep your promises" and *Caveat auditor.*[36]

Some of these points apply to speech more generally. How far people may reasonably rely on the implicatures and presuppositions of assertions, and more generally on what they imply, as much as on their content, and how far a speaker has any reason to concern himself if they do rely on them, is a matter of the particular relations between these people and the speaker. The degree to which people can rely on such things, as also on the meaning of silence, is, platitudinously, one mark of how close relations are between people (though it is equally a platitude that it is only one mark, and not a certain one: some couples live off each other's deceits). As with intentions, also, it will often make a difference what the hearer *turns out* to be relying on, as this comes to light only after the utterance. One expression of friendship may be, in certain circumstances, to make it clear what exactly has been said and what has been understood, but another, more frequent and more relaxed, is not to fuss or fall back on it. This is the world in which trust and reliance are the main idea.

We might go on to say that in this world deceit is not called for, or is not expected, or is ruled out, but that would be a mistake. As social psychologists and novelists remind us, people in friendly and trustful circumstances widely lie to others or mislead them or give them false impressions, in order not to wound them or to expose themselves, and in general to sustain systems of mutual esteem. How far this exchange of mis-statement, exaggeration, simulated agreement, conventional falsehood, and so on, adds up to *deceit*—how far, that is to say, anyone believes what is said or expects it to be believed—differs in different places, and to a large and helpful extent the question has no determinate answer. In some very sophisticated societies, such as the eighteenth-century Parisian salons that Rousseau so detested, no-one expects anyone to believe any of it, but then these are no longer circumstances of friendly trust; here, as *Les liaisons dangereuses* unnervingly demonstrates, trustfulness falls back into being a fatal idiosyncrasy.

Leaving aside the level (whatever it may be) of social falsehood that is needed to sustain the world of friendly trust itself, that world will contain in addition distinct violations of the normal expectations. The violations may be justified, as when it is a matter of protecting someone else's secret, and in those cases, if it comes to deceit, there is not much reason to think that Athanasian evasions are better than lies, and they may be worse. This may apply, too, to another kind of violation that is sometimes justified, often called "paternalistic" deceit. Nothing but pointless pain will follow if we tell the truth to the old lady about her daughter's illness or her son's disgrace, and—she is a sharp listener—there may be no effective alternative to a lie. But if you could get away with misleading her through implicatures, would that necessarily be better? Here, I suspect, people differ in their reactions. Some will think that a lie in such a case is a special kind of affront; others feel that if they were in the old lady's situation and they found out about the lie, they might perhaps be indignant, but their indignation would focus naturally on the paternalism itself and on the kind person's wish to hide the reality from them at all, rather than on the methods that he used.

We cannot be friends or friendly acquaintances with everybody, and no sane person would want to be. But there are other relations which, with regard to communication at least, are better than those which are antagonistic but rule-governed. One is that of manifestly coincident self-interest, which I mentioned earlier in considering trust in general.[37] Another example, emphasized by MacIntyre, is that of a shared enterprise to find out the truth, where each party understands that it would be simply beside the point not to speak frankly, or to mislead the others. Another is that phenomenon so typical of the modern world, the expectations generated by a well-ordered impersonal enterprise, as when I expect not to be deliberately misled by an official or employee whom I have never seen before.

Some relations between people are, on the other hand, notably bad—aggressive, extortionate, structured by threats. In such a case, and that of the murderer at the door is an example, a lie may be a necessary form of defence. Here, it must surely seem to most people now that Constant was right, and that to "have a problem" about lying in such a situation (except perhaps in the sense that you may not be very good at it) is a sign that there is something wrong in your conceptions of what truthfulness requires. We naturally say, as Constant said, that a person with those objectives does not deserve the truth, that he has no right to it, and that it makes no ethical difference at all how I deceive him. To understand this is part of what it is for someone's dispositions of Sincerity to be correctly shaped.

Moreover, if it is right to lie, in this kind of case it is no sign of a good disposition to feel bad about it, and anyone who had a sleepless minute over having told a lie to this murderer has, once more, his Sincerity out of shape. This further point is not true of all cases in which deceit is justified. The lie to the old lady may have been rightly told out of kindness, but we have reason to regret it, to feel bad about it, to think that something has been lost, because our relations to her were in general structured by a sense that we deserved the truth from each other.

The bad feeling in this case will be a kind of guilt: not fully guilt or remorse, since we continue to think that we did the right thing, but an ethical regret, that we had to bring about something, in this case a kind of violation, which we wish we had not had to bring about. There is no reason to feel this, certainly, in the case of the murderer, toward whom there need be no regrets at all. But guilt and its associates are not the only bad feelings that are tied up in the dispositions of Sincerity. There is also shame, the feeling that even if a lie or another piece of deceit was appropriate in the circumstances, and even if, further, it was exactly what the hearer deserved, nevertheless there was something low or contemptible in resorting to it. Adam Smith thought that this reaction was appropriate even to cases like that of the murderer. Discussing the situation of a man from whom a promise is extracted by a highwayman, he agreed that there was no question of one's having to carry it out, and that the highwayman had no right to delivery, but that, all the same, breaking the promise entailed some degree of dishonour to the man who made it.[38]

The application of the idea to this kind of case may seem distinctly odd, but the idea itself is an important one. One traditional and important way in which an internal structure for the value of Sincerity has been culturally available has been through ideas of honour or nobility. So Neoptolemus in Sophocles' *Philoctetes*, a noble boy, believes, and only temporarily is persuaded to forget, that it is shameful to get one's way by a shabby trick. These motivations are connected, of course, with fear and with courage; such a person is in a position to defend himself, and is not so dependent on others that he has to hide what he is and what he wants. The anticipation of shame is at work, but it is precisely not a shame that takes the form of fearing what people in general will think. The fear, rather, is of disgrace in one's own eyes, and in the eyes of people whom one respects and who one hopes will respect oneself.[39] It was this kind of thing that Maynard Keynes had in mind when he splendidly said about an American official that he had his ear so close to the ground that he could not hear what an upright man said.

The motivations of honour and the avoidance of shame have historically played a large part in the dispositions of Sincerity, and they still have a part to play. But, left entirely to themselves, they are an unreliable support to truthfulness, because there is an ambivalence in them, which surfaces in ancient Greek literature, in Nietzsche, and in writers such as Yeats. The honour that despises deceit represents a form of self-sufficiency, a capacity not to have to worry about the accommodations that deceit can secure. But the feeling that one must be open with others can itself be seen as a need, as expressing fear or indignity, and noble self-sufficiency may then take the form of defeating people's expectations, of being unhelpfully misleading or ironical, or deploying masks. The man who is for others, on this line of thought, is no-one in particular. A predominant emphasis on the motivations of a self-sufficient nobility in relation to Sincerity, and equally this style of reversing them, are most naturally rooted in hierarchical or aristocratic societies, or, again, in association with a very highly cultivated aesthetic. (We may recall Oscar Wilde's remark that all bad poetry is the product of genuine feeling.)

In one way, Adam Smith's thought about the dishonour of making a false promise to the highwayman does engage with a feeling we have now: the situation involves a humiliation. But the humiliation comes from being coerced into making the promise, as it would come from having to give up one's money on the spot. It does not come from breaking the promise, and similarly there is no humiliation in lying to the murderer. Adam Smith may have thought that a well-placed gentleman should not be reduced to breaking any promise, even one made to a highwayman. If he did, it may be a hangover from an age before the modern world he did so much to inaugurate. Even under the *ancien régime*, however, the thought would surely have been something of a luxury, and we do not have that luxury, if it ever existed. We have, or think we have, a more significant luxury, of living in a world understood as a community of moral equals; we want to believe that what people deserve or are owed is determined not by considerations of social position but, at the most basic levels of morality, from a position of equality. This does not mean that considerations of honour or shame fall away. The conception of moral equality was expressed with notable power by Kant, and Kant was deeply influenced by the vision of Rousseau, a vision, one has to remember, of a society in which everyone would be a noble because nobody was. The motivations of honour and shame have to be brought into relation with ideas of what we deserve and can expect from one another, when that is no longer a matter of given hierarchies but of the particular relations in which we socially and personally find ourselves. Some of what we expect from each other is a matter of social roles in which we are engaged. Some, very significantly, are a function of how individual people behave.

How are such ideas expressed in a disposition of Sincerity? Not everyone, certainly, equally deserves the truth. People can put us in situations in which deceit is a necessary defence or precaution against their threats or manipulations or other damaging intentions. Again, and differently, they may have driven us into a corner by their importunate demands for information. Even in the State of Nature, not everyone has a right to know everything. Of course, a State of Nature may well take the form of a village, and it can be a tiresome feature of villages, as John Stuart Mill observed, that everything is everyone's business. Indeed, small traditional societies are typically full of lies, because it is so hard to keep anything secret. In our world, in which there is much private life and many particular contracts, it is easier to keep a secret without telling lies, and there is a marked difference between the two. If someone wants to know too much, the first resort, as the casuists said, is a refusal to answer, and a proper pride drawn from the motivations of honour and shame can be a great help in this regard, but under pressure, and particularly if other interests need to be protected, silence may have to turn into evasion, and evasion into deceit.[40] This familiar progression may contribute something to diagnosing the traditional doctrine I have rejected: there is a sharper distinction between lying and other forms of deceit

than there is between the other forms of deceit and ways of withholding information which are not deceitful at all, so it may be easier
to think of the other forms of deceit as simply not telling. The notion of an evasion lives in this dank area, which occupies a lot of
ground between evading the question, at one end, and answering
the question with a evasive statement, at the other.

In these cases, there is no need for regret; it is the questioner who
in one way or another is at fault and no longer deserves to be told
the truth. In other situations where deceit may be necessary, from
kindness as in the case of the old lady, or for some reason such as
protecting another's secret, we may well feel that there is room for
regret, or a sense of loss or of there having been, as I put it, "a
violation." That is a strong word for many cases, but it is in place
for some and in the right area for others. A violation of what? Manifestly, of trust: I lead the hearer to rely on what I say, when she has
good reason to do so, and in abusing this I abuse the relationship
which is based on it.[41] Even if it is for good reasons of concern for
her, I do not give her a chance, in this particular respect, to form
her own reactions to the facts (as I suppose them to be), something
that I would give her if I spoke sincerely, but give her instead a
picture of the world which is a product of my will. Replacing the
world in its impact on her by my will, I put her, to that extent, in
my power and so take away or limit her freedom.

All the more, this is what someone does who for reasons of mere
self-interest[42] lies to a victim who trusts him. It is this case above all,
I think, the case of sheer betrayal, that provides a place for the
thought that there is something peculiarly odious or insulting about
a lie as contrasted with other forms of deceit. The victim is of course
angry above all at the deceit, but he may well feel a peculiar and
extra resentment at its having taken the form of straight lies. If this
is so, it is because assertion purports to be the direct expression of
belief, and so to *give* the hearer the truth. A deceiver in any case
manipulates his hearer's beliefs, but in the lie this substitution of the
will for the world becomes as immediate as it conceivably can be.
Hearing the truth is of course not the same as being presented with
the real, and, correspondingly, lying is different from the deceiver's
arranging a simulated scene which, as in a Jacobean tragedy or a

Mamet movie, makes his victim believe that a certain thing is happening in front of him when it is not. Because of this difference, a trustful hearer knows all along that in relying on what the speaker says, he is dependent on him and in a sense dependent on his will: but in trusting him, he thinks that he has merely gone through a gate held open by that will. In allowing himself to accept the other's belief as his own, and taking it that he has been given the truth through the speaker's assertion, he will feel that he has come as close to the real thing as anyone in his situation could do. When he realizes that he has been betrayed, there is a complete reversal: the speaker's will was entirely out of the picture, but now the picture is nothing but a product of that will. The victim recognizes the barefaced lie as a pure and direct exercise of power over him, with nothing at all to be said for it from his point of view, and this is an archetypal cause of resentment: not just disappointment and rage, but humiliation and the recognition that in the most literal sense he has been made a fool of.

Deceit involves manipulation, specifically of people's beliefs, and it may be part of "using" someone more generally. Kant's phrase about treating other people as ends and not "merely as a means" comes naturally to hand when we try to say what is wrong with it. But if we want to use that phrase, we need to preserve a sharper sense than Kant himself did that it makes a great difference whether I deceive an unoffending hearer in my own interests, as in the case of betrayal; or on behalf of people whose interests I am rightfully defending; or in the hearer's own interests. It is at this last point, particularly, that the famous phrase becomes famously misleading, suggesting as it does that it must always be wrong to "use" other people "merely as a means" to their own happiness.

One of the questions that will arise is whether a given hearer is indeed unoffending, or, rather, he is someone who no longer deserves the truth. Here is it is tempting to think in terms of reciprocity. The reason why the murderer or even the intrusive questioner does not deserve the truth is that he is no longer in a relation to us which is structured by the normal expectations of trustful exchange. Seen in this light, Sincerity will involve in a certain way the sense of justice, and there doubtless are some ideas of justice and injustice involved: it is a very natural thought, for instance, that it may be perfectly *fair* to deceive the importunate questioner, because he has put himself out of line. But it is certainly not in any straightforward way a matter of reciprocity. If it were, the fact that someone was an inveterate liar would be a complete justification for lying to him, but most of us probably do not think that it is. If it matters to us that he is a liar, and we do not see this characteristic of his as just an eccentricity, as it is with some mythomaniacs, we are more likely to react by withdrawing relations and not having dealings with him. Here I think that the motivations of honour and shame play an important part. The intrinsic value that Sincerity bears makes it an unlovely idea to turn into a liar, even in relation to this person. It is unlikely, too, that one will have become a liar merely in relation to this person, not so much because lying becomes a habit, but because news of lies travels and one comes to be seen as a liar. We would be ashamed to be seen in such a light, and rather, if we can, we keep away from such a person.

It has always been a problem for those who ethically explain truth-telling and promise-keeping in terms of abusing people's trust that such accounts seem to let the known liar and promise-breaker off the hook. Since no-one trusts him, no-one is damaged or let down. But surely, the objection goes, he did something wrong? Well, he certainly tried: he presumably did not know that the other party did not trust a word he said. But the important point about this person is rather the kind of person he is: in respect of truthfulness, he is not as we want people to be. Blame, the moral weapon that is carried by the word "wrong," in a case such as his has become obsolete. It is too late to be angry or disappointed, and, if you can, you will ignore him, do such things as warn other people about him, and generally treat him with less respect. That is an expression of the motivations of honour and shame: you, for one, would not want to be seen as such a person, one who does not care enough about the effect of what he says on the component of trust in the relations that he has to other people, and does not mind carelessly or deliberately manipulating them.

Sincerity is a disposition, and it cannot be understood just as the disposition to follow a rule. Of course, there have to be some general

considerations to which Sincerity attends, or the disposition would
have no content. We have just considered some of them. But they
do not add up to a rule, in the traditional sense of a requirement
which is relatively simple and does not leave most of the work to be
done by judgement. If there were a rule, what would it be? If it were
merely a rule against lying, or against deceit more generally, it would
be a rule with many and various exceptions, since there are all sorts
of cases in which the best thing to do is to deceive, and in some of
them it is not a good thing to feel bad about it, either. What is
essential to the disposition is to have a good grasp of what those
cases may be, the ones that would count as exceptions to the rule,
and that grasp will not be given by the mere disposition to follow
the rule. Moreover, if there were a rule, it could not be a rule only
against lying to people who trust you, since that would indeed lead
to the old problem that the more notorious you were for breaking
the rule, the less it would apply to you. Yet concerns with trust and
the abuse of trust must manifestly be at the heart of the disposition.

We want people to have a disposition of Sincerity which is centred
on sustaining and developing relations with others that involve different kinds and degrees of trust. Reflecting on that disposition, they
will think about the kinds of trust that are implicit in different relations, and how abusing them may resemble other, perhaps more
dramatic, forms of manipulation and domination, inasmuch as it imposes the agent's will in place of reality—the reality which all the
parties equally have to live within. The disposition itself enables the
agent to think clearly and without self-deceit about the occasions
when deceit is required, and to keep a sense of those among them
when something is lost by it. Much of one's thought, if one is such
an agent, looks outwards, to the other people involved and to the
relations they have to one, but at the same time, and without any
paradox, it involves a sense of oneself and of the respect one might
have or lose from people one can oneself respect.

That structure, of mutual respect and the capacity for shame in
the face of oneself and others, is a traditional, indeed archaic, ethical
resource, but it is still very necessary. Some of the ideas to which it
is directed and which give it substance in the disposition of Sincerity
also have a long history, such as the idea that some people deserve

more in the way of the truth than others—an idea which in the world of Odysseus, for instance, took the simpler form of a distinction between friends and enemies. What the disposition needs to be for us, however, involves a modern understanding of what people deserve, thoughts which did not exist in its earlier days. In part, that understanding must respond to social relations as they are constantly redefined in commercial society, those of privacy and intimacy as much as those of professional co-operation and rivalry. In part, the understanding must shift in philosophical space. We should hold on to Kant's insight that we need to understand the deeper implications of trust, and its value, in terms of individual freedom and the avoidance of manipulation, but we should resist his obsession (which indeed conflicts with that insight) that those concerns should speak to us in the form of an exceptionless and simple rule, part of a Moral Law that governs us all equally without recourse to power. There is no such rule. Indeed, there is no Moral Law, but we have resources for living with that fact, some of them no doubt still to be uncovered.

6

❖　❖　❖　❖　❖

ACCURACY: A SENSE OF REALITY

1. *The Elaboration of Accuracy*

We left the fictional genealogy, and moved toward real history, in considering what happens under more realistic conditions to the virtue of Sincerity. We must now follow a similar route with the virtue of Accuracy. At the very beginning of the State of Nature story we assumed that the people in the story were capable of reflection; we could not understand them as people, and in particular as having even a minimal virtue of Accuracy, unless they were capable of thinking, to some extent, about what they were doing. However, at the most elementary levels the demands on people's reflective ability were not very great. We should now allow the people in the story stronger and more sophisticated powers of reflection. The people who gather information and act as informants acquire a strategic sense. They were always more than reliable or unreliable information gatherers and transmitters (as artificial satellites are), but as they are granted greater reflective sophistication, their monitoring of their efforts becomes more complex. In particular, it comes to involve a conscious choice of policies of investigation. They come to assess the value of possible information against the cost of acquiring it. This can involve collective as well as individual decisions, which can be inserted into a more conscious process of the division of epistemic labour. It can become common knowledge that particular inquirers will think it worthwhile, or not, to try to acquire information of a certain kind.

The particular significance of this development is that for the first time in the story we are given a sense in which a price is set on acquiring information about a certain subject matter. This is the notion of an investigative investment. The language of "investment" admittedly does not capture very well all the reasons for carrying on inquiry. An individual who is conscientiously acting in circumstances of trust to inform other people will take trouble to make sure, to a reasonable degree, that the belief he passes on is true; this is equivalent to saying that an investigative investment can be made on behalf of someone else, or on behalf of the group. But it is also true, and it will be a particular concern of this chapter, that the interest in coming to know the truth may lie much further away than this from reductive conceptions. The satisfaction of curiosity can itself come to count as the reward of investigation, and not just as giving practice in inquiry, or as a speculative investment against future practical needs. (Of course, if one thinks of such rewards in terms of cost-benefit analysis, they will prove hard to weigh in with other sorts of rewards, both privately and publicly, but that is true of many considerations.) As with Sincerity, we should not suppose that because we start with very simple decision-theoretical considerations, it follows that, at every point of cultural elaboration, there is (or ought rationally to be) a reductive route back to the primitive basis. That is simply false of human historical and cultural development, and it is a virtue, as I have already said, of a genealogical method that it helps to remind us of this, by not confusing explanation with reduction.

The idea of an investigative investment, and related ideas of investigative strategies, imply that inquiry will encounter obstacles. There are inner obstacles to truth-discovery as well as external obstacles, and even the external obstacles have an inner representation and imply inner attitudes toward dealing with them. This is the basic reason why Accuracy can be properly treated as a *virtue*, and not simply as a disposition to pick up reliable information—just as Sincerity is a virtue, and not just a reliable disposition to express inner informational states, because it operates in a space that is structured by motivations to conceal or dissimulate. (A. E. Housman said that accuracy in scholarly work was a duty, not a virtue. As Gloucester says in *King Lear*, "And that's true, too.")

The external obstacles to truth-discovery are an example of the world's being resistant to our will. It is, of course, resistant to being changed in various ways, but equally it is resistant to being discovered, interpreted, or unravelled, and these two kinds of resistance—to being changed, and to being discovered—are intimately connected with one other, as can be seen particularly in the idea of an experiment.[1] The fact that there are external obstacles to the pursuit of truth is one foundation of our idea of objectivity, in the sense that our beliefs are answerable to an order of things that lies beyond our own determination. There is also another sense of "objectivity," in which it is a virtue of inquirers, and in this sense it is connected, rather, with internal obstacles to discovery and true belief. Self-conscious pursuit of the truth requires resistance to such things as self-deception and wishful thinking, and one component of the virtue of Accuracy—which, once again, is why it is a virtue and not merely a disposition of reliability—lies in the skills and attitudes that resist the pleasure principle, in all its forms, from a gross need to believe the agreeable, to mere laziness in checking one's investigations. The virtues of Accuracy include, very importantly, dispositions and strategies for sustaining the defences of belief against wish, and against one of the products of wish, self-deception.

There is a consideration here that is relevant to the ways in which we should think about self-deception. It is a well-known question, whether what is called "self-deception" can be seriously seen as a species of deception at all: since standard deception involves the deceiver's knowing things that the victim does not know (including his own deceitful intention), how can one person be both deceiver and victim? Let us jump over that problem (though it is worth remarking that we are familiar enough in other cases with the idea that when an action is applied reflexively, some of its usual implications are lost—as with "self-taught," for instance, or "self-employed").[2] Let us accept for the sake of argument that someone can, more or less literally, deceive himself. We then encounter another, and less discussed, question: where the fault in this transaction is to be found. The standard picture is that the fault lies with the self as deceiver—which means, in effect, that we should concentrate on self-deception as a failure of Sincerity. But if we consider the ordinary interpersonal operations of deceit, we know that when there are deceivers around, trying to convert them to better behaviour is not the only relevant project. It is at least as important to improve the caution of the people who may be deceived, and it is probably more important, particularly if we suspect that some of the deceivers are incorrigible. If there is such a thing as self-deception, the same, surely, should apply to it. Our failures as self-deceived are to be found at least as much in our lack of epistemic prudence as victims as in our insincerity as perpetrators.

This is very important when we are thinking about self-deception as one of the faults that an agent has to avoid when it is a matter of giving himself or others who rely on him true information. But when we consider, as we shall in this chapter, the further development of Accuracy that consists in the desire for truth "for its own sake"—the passion for *getting it right*—then we must remember equally the role of Sincerity in one's dealings with oneself. As Nietzsche said with regard to that passion, "here we stand already on moral ground,"[3] meaning precisely that to insist on getting it right can be a matter of conscience, honour, or self-respect; and these qualities operate in much the same way in this connection as, we saw in the previous chapter, they operate to form and sustain the virtue of Sincerity in one's dealings with other people.

2. Methods and Obstacles

From the beginning, I have called Accuracy and Sincerity equally "virtues of truth," and the discussion up to now has shown why this is appropriate. Each of them, at the most primitive level, gets its point ultimately from the human interest, individual and collective, in gaining and sharing true information. So far as their point or purpose is concerned, they are equally related to the truth. However, there is this difference, that merely in defining Accuracy we have to mention *the truth*, whereas with Sincerity the reference to truth comes one stage later. We can define Sincerity merely by mentioning people's beliefs—it directly implies only that a speaker says what he believes. Truth comes into it because beliefs "aim at" the truth. Accuracy is directly related to that aim of beliefs: it implies care, reliability, and so on, in discovering and coming to believe the truth.

This feature of Accuracy involves two aspects. One of them concerns the investigator's will—his attitudes, desires, and wishes, the spirit of his attempts, the care that he takes. It involves his resistance to wishful thinking, self-deception, and fantasy. The other aspect of Accuracy involves the methods that the investigator uses. The two aspects are, of course, interrelated. We may be tempted to call Accuracy a virtue only with respect to the first kind of factor, but this would be a mistake. Inasmuch as Accuracy is prized, praised, cultivated, and so forth, it is taken to be effective, and attention to this must include a concern with the investigator's methods.

I have expressed this in terms of an individual's virtues, but this is too simple. There are collective enterprises which not only bring together the virtues of various individuals, but which display collective virtues, the virtues of a team or a group who share a certain culture or outlook. The relations between individual virtues and the common culture also have a political dimension: as we shall see later, an individual's commitment to the virtues of truth may stand opposed to a political culture which destroys and pollutes the truth. (Here, as often, intrinsic values turn out to have their uses.) In turn, that individual's sense of truthfulness may be sustained by his or her conscious sense of belonging to some other group—a scientific profession, for instance—whose practice is taken to embody those standards.

Accuracy implies the notion of effective investigation, and this itself implies that there is a genuine property which some methods of inquiry have and some others lack, the property of leading to true belief: we may say, summarily, that some methods of inquiry are *truth-acquiring*.[4] It may be asked whether there can be such a property at all, and, correspondingly, whether we are indeed right in supposing, as I am supposing, that the aim of our inquiries is to arrive at the truth. Though it need not detain us very long, we should consider a style of argument, more popular than it ought to be, which is supposed to show that there is something altogether wrong with this picture of inquiry and its methods.

The argument exploits an idea that if "truth" were in any substantial or interesting sense the goal of inquiry, inquiry would be hopeless, because "truth" would have to be inaccessible. Richard Rorty, for one, is fond of distributing polemical capital letters, turning simple truth into "the Truth" or "Reality," where these are supposedly metaphysical objects hidden from us by the screen of our experience or our language. (We may recall Nietzsche's early problems, which we encountered in chapter 1.) Since such objects will be by definition inaccessible, he concludes that we should not take seriously the idea that our inquiries aim at the truth, as opposed to their securing some social objective, such as the widest possible agreement.[5]

This line is perhaps most charitably understood as a version of an *indistinguishability argument*, which takes the following form. We suppose the goal of inquiry to be that of getting at the truth; equally, we commend some assertions and beliefs as being true and reject others as being untrue. When can we suppose that we have arrived at the goal of truth or are in a position to commend a particular assertion "P" as true? The answer must be: when we are in some psychological or social state, which we may call "being justified in believing that P" or "our all being in reasonable agreement that P." Rorty and his fellow pragmatists do not need to say that these expressions *mean* the same as "it is true that P"; indeed, they had better not say this, if they are going to urge us to care about agreement but not about truth. Nevertheless, the argument goes, if we (unqualifiedly) believe or (completely) agree that snow is white, there is no further for us to go in the direction of truth, so to speak. We cannot tell the difference between snow's being white and our (completely, etc.) agreeing that snow is white. So we might as well say, or would better say,[6] that our aim is to secure the psychological or social state in question rather than that we are aiming at the truth.

In considering this style of argument, we should bear in mind, first, how entirely general it is meant to be. There are of course many difficult questions about the relations between the truth-conditions of particular kinds of proposition and our best grounds for believing those propositions. This is the field of the theory of knowledge; in some part, too, of metaphysics, particularly when the relations between truth-conditions and the existence of proofs is systematically obscure, as in the case of mathematics. But the pragmatists' argument is not concerned with any such issues. It is supposed to show quite generally, for any proposition or belief whatsoever, that we cannot distinguish between its being true and our accepting or agreeing on it, and this will apply as much to the plainest and simplest truths as it does to anything else.

A second preliminary point: when it is said that *we* cannot distinguish between these two things, the most that can be claimed is that we cannot make this distinction with regard to ourselves at the present moment. I can make it with regard to you, and you can make it with regard to me, and each of us can make it with regard to our own past or future beliefs. It might be thought that the proper generalization from these facts is not that *we* cannot make the distinction but that *we* can.

There is a basic objection to the argument. If the social or psychological states in question are called such things as "being justified in believing that P" or "our being in reasonable agreement that P," there is an immediate problem, that these descriptions already call on the notion of truth. A justified belief is one that is arrived at by a method, or supported by considerations, that favour it, not simply by making it more appealing or whatever, but in the specific sense of giving reason to think that it is true. This comes out when we consider beliefs which are not arrived at in these ways. Although there are indeed questions about what it is for a method of acquiring beliefs to be favourable to those beliefs' being true, we certainly have some clear ideas about ways of acquiring or agreeing on beliefs which are not favourable to their being true—taking hallucinogenic drugs, for instance, or being brainwashed, or agreeing by vote to a hypothesis drawn blindfold from a hat. When we consider the state of the question with regard to "P," beliefs or agreements reached in these ways do not count. "Why not?" is a question to which the pragmatist owes us an answer.

Moreover, this raises a question about the indistinguishability argument more generally. Those who acquire beliefs in some such way may be just as convinced that their beliefs are true as others are; either they will not know how they acquired them, or, more radically, they may be convinced, contrary to the rest of us, that those methods are perfectly sound. Are we to say that because, being as they are, they cannot tell how their beliefs stand to the truth, we, being as we are, cannot tell how our beliefs stand to the truth? This is to rely on an old and discreditable device of philosophical scepticism, the symmetry assumption, to the effect (for instance) that since I cannot standardly tell that I am dreaming when I am dreaming, I cannot tell that I am awake when I am awake; a pattern of argument which might as well show that since I cannot tell that I am dead when I am dead, I cannot tell that I am alive.[7]

Pragmatists often say that it is precisely their way that can lead us out of philosophical scepticism: once you see that there is no further question about truth, beyond agreement, solidarity, and so on, you see that there is nothing to be sceptical about. They will reject the idea that we can wonder, as I just put it, "how our beliefs stand to the truth." But this is to miss the point. The indistinguishability argument comes into the discussion earlier than the pragmatists' claim to have overcome scepticism; it is used to convince us in the first place that there is no question of how our beliefs stand to the truth. The pragmatists will agree that if there are two parties with conflicting beliefs, each may try to convince the other. They can distinguish as a matter of sociological fact some methods of doing this from others—discussion, argument, experiment, and so on, as opposed to extended brainwashing. The rest of us have stories to tell about why those distinctions matter, to the effect that some methods are better than others in leading to the truth. The pragmatists reply that these stories themselves are simply a part of what one party believes, and the most that can be said at the very end of the line is that the party which tells these stories is in charge (or something like that).[8] But why should we agree with that? It is here, already, that the indistinguishability argument will be used: the brainwashing party thinks that its beliefs are true, and we think that our beliefs (including our beliefs about the brainwashing party) are true, and there is no advance on that, because the situation is symmetrical. It is a very bad argument, and one reason for thinking that it is bad is that the same form of argument can motivate unconvincing, even absurd, forms of philosophical scepticism. The fact that pragmatists themselves do not like philosophical scepticism does not rule out their making some of the same mistakes.

We can leave the quite general argument against the idea that some methods of inquiry have the property of being truth-acquiring. There are still serious questions about what this property can be. The Romans used augury as a method of acquiring some kinds of information about the outcome of a battle. Chickens, for instance, were offered some grain, and if they ate it, this was taken as a favourable portent. The story is told of a Roman admiral who, when the chickens refused to eat, said, "Let them drink," and threw them into the sea. Augury is not an effective way of getting information about the outcome of battles, and the fact that, as it turned out, this admiral lost this battle may be thought to be bad luck not only for him but for predictive rationality. As a matter of real historical or anthropological understanding, we should not assume that those who used augury were simply stupid or misinformed. Rather, as with oracles and other such "supernatural" sources, there is some obscurity about what beliefs they legitimated and what exactly they did to legitimate them. Certainly, a favourable augury did not mean that you would win the battle without trying to do so.[9] It would be seen, rather, as encouraging to the troops, and if you proceeded in the face of a bad augury, you were more likely to be blamed for failure. But to the extent that practices such as augury can be understood as predictive methods, they were poor methods, and we can explain why.

This looks like a good example of a bad predictive method. But what is a good method? What characteristic does a method have if it is disposed to generate true belief? This question seems to require an answer that is at once general and substantial, and this may be thought to present a problem. The answer has to be general, because the idea of being truth-acquiring is univocal: we can understand the claim that a certain method is truth-acquiring with regard to some subject matter, without being told what the method and the subject matter are. At the same time, the answer has to be substantial, because it is clearly an informative judgement that, for instance, augury is not truth-acquiring with regard to battles. These demands taken together might suggest that there should be an account *of truth itself* which is both general and substantive enough to yield these conclusions, and it would be at the very least unwise to assume that there is such an account. But we do not have to assume this. While we need an account of what it is for a method to be truth-acquiring, the level at which that account has to be substantive is not the same as that at which it has to be general. It has to be substantive because the efficacy of the method is related to the content of the propositions or classes of propositions in question. If a method is a good way of finding out whether "P" is true, then it is a good way of finding out whether P; and the question whether a method is a good way of finding out whether P depends centrally on what the content of "P" is. At the same time, the account of being truth-acquiring is also general because of the formal point that we can generalize over various such schemata (as in fact we have done, by using the dummy "P").

Some general things that one might be tempted to say about methods of finding out the truth turn out to be trivial. We might think that we could usefully say the following: no method will have the desirable property if its efficacy in generating the belief that P would extend equally to generating the belief that not P. But this is no help. In many cases, the method that will generate the belief that P (if P) *will* generate the belief that not P (if not P): the same method answers the question "P?" whether the answer is yes or no. We shall have to say, rather, that what lacks the desired property is a method that will generate the belief that P *even if not P*, and conversely. But this simply says that it generates belief without regard to the truth, which is to say that the method is ineffective, and this gets us nowhere. Nevertheless, there are some relevant properties common to many methods of inquiry and many subject matters. For instance, it is a highly general truth, if not a very interesting one, that nothing is a method of acquiring true rather than false beliefs which randomizes over the selection of beliefs; and there are some very general features that make for randomization, such as picking hypotheses out of a hat, or guessing.

The real problems about methods of inquiry, and which of them are truth-acquiring, do not lie at this very general level but, as I have already suggested, belong to the theory of knowledge and metaphysics: for a given class of propositions, how are the ways of finding out whether they are true related to what it is for them to be true? (One important kind of question will be what counts as a particular class of propositions in this perspective.) These problems are not the present concern. Our concern is with the virtues of truth, and this leads us to a different question: granted there are methods of inquiry that are, for different kinds of proposition, truth-acquiring, what are the qualities of people who can be expected to use such methods reliably? One immediate consideration is that they should actually want to find out the truth on the question at issue. (This does not mean that the idea of finding out the truth on this question gives them pleasure; we shall consider in a moment cases where it does not.) So we should look more closely at what is involved in really wanting the truth on a question, and at the qualities that go with having that desire and seriously trying to satisfy it. If someone seriously wants to find out the truth on an issue, we can say that this is equivalent to his wanting to get into the following condition:

if P, to believe that P, and if not P, to believe that not P.[10]

It is an advantage of this formula that it makes it clear that the project of seriously pursuing the truth is one of controlling the formation of belief; and because of its schematic form, it can remind us that the appropriate ways of acquiring beliefs will depend on the subject matter.

If one wants the truth on a subject, then what may be needed is persistence, effort, and so forth. The truth may be hidden or hard to find—which means, in the first place, that it is hard to come by a belief which one has good reason to think is true. This will be a matter, as we may say, of external obstacles. In some ways, external obstacles to finding the truth are like external obstacles to carrying out other tasks, and to that extent, while they are of course exceedingly important in practice, they may not raise any particular issue of principle. However, there is a special feature of external obstacles to finding out the truth—that, typically, one does not know exactly what they are. There are, perhaps, very simple cases in which there is an absolutely determinate physical obstacle to answering a question, as when I know that the truth (in a waterproof container) is at the bottom of this well. But, generally, when I do not know how to answer a question, I do not know fully determinately what is stopping me doing so. This has in fact some consequences with regard to external obstacles more generally: dealing with them will often involve problems of finding out the truth, even when this is not the agent's primary aim. The crevasse stands between me and my goal, and so much is obvious, but part of my problem is that I do not know what alternatives there may be to crossing it. The practical obstacles to reaching some goal may themselves be indeterminate because it is indeterminate what questions one needs to answer in order to get round them.

If we do not know exactly what obstacles there may be to answering a question about a given matter, this means that there are other questions to which we need answers, and we do not know exactly what those questions are. This has an important consequence for the economy of inquiry. Inquiries in the real world about questions that are at all difficult do not typically yield certainty, and the pursuit of certainty would be either impossible or absurdly expensive in terms of effort and time.[11] So, very often, we leave various avenues unexplored; and this means, also very often, that we do not know exactly what avenues have been left unexplored. This means, further, that it may be hard to decide when one has invested enough effort in finding out the truth on a given matter, with the result that it is easy to convince oneself that one has taken enough pains, when the situation is that one has some other kind of reason for not taking more. So it is that the external obstacles to finding out the truth turn out, often, to be in alliance with internal obstacles—at the most obvious level, laziness, but, more interestingly, the desires and wishes that are prone to subvert the acquisition of true belief.

We have noticed, more than once, that Accuracy has to include resistance to self-deception and wishful thinking and so forth, but now we need to look a little more closely at what it is that is involved in a desire that something other than the true belief should be true. How can there be such a desire? It can take two different forms. One of them is that I want a certain belief or theory to be true, not directly because of its content, but because of some other feature that the belief or theory has—in particular that it is *mine* (declared by me, published by me, or whatever). This first possibility is particularly important in relation to the idea that scientific activity is supposed to be disinterested, an idea that we shall come back to later.

There is a second form that the desire can take, and this is both more basic and more familiar. This is the case in which I want the belief that P to be true because what I want or wish is that P. Not able to have the truth that P, I may notoriously make do with the motivated belief that P.[12] Of course, as we have already seen in chapter 4, I cannot bring it about that I believe that P by directly willing to believe it. The basic reason for this is simply that my beliefs are answerable to the world, and if I were conscious that I had formed a belief on the basis of my wishes, I would in that very consciousness know that this belief was not responsive to the world. My beliefs aim to be true, and, just for that reason, I must take them to be independent of my will. When my beliefs are motivated, the product of wish-fulfilment, they are not independent of my will, but that fact cannot itself be obvious to me.

Of course there is another, and innocuous, sense in which the truth of some of my beliefs is not independent of my will. This is the sense in which some actual states of affairs are dependent on my will.[13] If the states of the world that make my belief true are under my control, then, in that indirect and uncontentious sense, my beliefs will follow the changes that my will can produce. What the inquirer must have in mind, as a condition of getting himself and his beliefs in the right relation to the world and to his will, can be summed up in these terms: some things in the world he can affect and most others he cannot; with regard to what he cannot affect and knows he cannot affect, a want can only be a wish; and a belief cannot properly be dependent on a wish.[14] All of this adds up to a sense of reality, where this offers a contrast with fantasy. Self-deception, which is one thing that the accurate agent must avoid, is a homage that fantasy pays to the sense of reality.

3. *Realism and Fantasy*

I argued earlier, against the pragmatist deniers, that we should accept the everyday idea that inquiry, and the virtue of Accuracy, are directed to *the truth*. However, it may be thought that what has now been said, in relation to belief and the will, implies not just an idea of truth but a specifically *realist* idea of truth, in the sense of an independent order of things to which our thought is answerable. We must ask how far this is so. The most primitive cases of plain truth imply a simple kind of empirical realism; for instance, the objects mentioned in such statements can have causal relations to us and play a causal role in the formation of our true beliefs, while, conversely, our thoughts about them and, specifically, our wishes do not affect the objects' existence unless those thoughts are mediated by causally effective interventions.

It has often been recognized that the idea of a reality independent of us can involve an implication of resistance, resistance to the will. In the case of physical objects, this is classically connected with the notion of "obstance," the capacity of physical objects to resist and impede our movements. It was this that was being exploited (rather optimistically) by Dr. Johnson when he sought to refute Bishop Berkeley's idealism by kicking a stone. In this case, resistance to my will means resistance to me, resistance to my body's efforts. Moreover, in this case, resistance to the will typically means that I can try to do something (to move something, to move through it), and its resistance is what prevents my being successful. But if we are to get a broad enough connection between reality and resistance to the will, the notion of "obstance" is too restricted. In many cases, it is not that the world presents an obstacle when I try to do a certain thing: rather, the resistance to my will goes so deep that there is not even anything that would count as trying. If someone says, "Be on the moon in thirty seconds' time," and I protest that I cannot, it is no good his saying, "You can always try"—there is no direction in which I could set out even to do that much. (How would I try? Give a leap? Pick up the telephone to call NASA?) There are cases that seem even more radical than these. Suppose that he invites me to change the result of an experiment that took place yesterday. Here, with the idea of changing the past, we seem even further away from conceiving of what would count as trying.

But now it seems that any case of necessity will be an example of radical resistance to the will. Equally, we cannot change the truths of mathematics—indeed, their necessity may seem a paradigm of unchangeability. The idea of resistance, however, came into the discussion in explaining a notion we have of a reality to which our beliefs are answerable. Must we say that, simply because the truths of mathematics are not subject to our will, we should in some sense interpret their truth realistically? Surely not. Realism in the philosophy of mathematics, the question whether we should understand mathematical beliefs as being answerable to an order of things that exists independently of our thoughts, is a much disputed issue. Whatever the status of that question, it cannot be right that a positive answer to it follows immediately from what everyone agrees, that mathematics is not subject to our will.

Some philosophers cut off the move in that direction by asserting that our ideas of realistic truth are paradigmatically associated with empirical objects that possess causal powers to affect us and each other. Others respond that this is merely an arbitrary restriction.[15] There are complex questions here, of explaining what it is to construe a class of truths in a realistic manner. They include the question of how, and how much, our sense of a state of affairs' being resistant to the will is indeed related to metaphysical issues such as the independent existence of mathematical objects. The present discussion is not intended to answer those questions. I should like to suggest, however, that inasmuch as there is a connection between our conceptions of reality and the idea of resistance to our will, what can be expected to present us with the idea of an independent reality is a state of affairs *to which there is a conceivable alternative*. What this means in metaphysical terms is a further question, but at least we can explain our impressions, I think, in terms of what may be called a phenomenology of the wish. This might even contribute to a diagnosis of those metaphysical questions, and if it did, this would be one of the places at which reflection on the virtues of truth can, indirectly, help us to understand problems associated with truth itself.

We start from the idea of the subversion of rational belief by a wish (which is, of course, precisely one of the things that Accuracy has to guard against). We ask what wishes have the power to subvert belief, and to generate a motivated belief which may serve, eventually, as a surrogate of reality. Suppose that "Q" is some truth about the past—for instance, that I missed the train to Venice. I can understand the idea that not-Q; I can coherently, and poignantly, wish that not-Q. I cannot properly understand the idea of *bringing it about (now) that not-Q*. Can I wish that I could bring it about now that not-Q? In a way, one might say; but not in very determinate terms. Some blend of merely wishing that not-Q, and wishing that I had brought it about (then) that not-Q, and some unfocussed fragment of a fiction of time travel, constitute about the best that I can achieve.

Suppose now that "M" is a mathematical truth. In this case, again, *bringing it about that not-M* is inconceivable, but now for the more radical reason that not-M itself is inconceivable; one cannot clearly or determinately conceive of what would be involved in not-M's being the case. This seems to baffle even the wish that not-M; neither the wish that not-M nor the wish that I could bring it about that not-M has, it seems, anywhere to go. It is possible to have a wish which *seems* to be of that sort. So a mathematician might have taken himself to have proved some mathematical result which was then shown to be false, and he might wish (it could be said) that the result which he thought he had proved was true. But the focus of his wish is surely something different, something that is entirely intelligible: he wishes that he had given a proof of a correct result. Similarly, he might have given a proof of what was indeed a correct result, but his proof was unsound (as, recently, with Wiles's first version of his proof of Fermat's Last Theorem). Here he wishes that he had given a correct proof—and this does not mean that this very proof, identified in mathematical terms, should have been valid (which is impossible), but that his work should have issued in a valid proof.

But leaving aside the wishes of frustrated mathematicians, can I really not wish that a particular, determinate mathematical truth were otherwise? I have to pay a bill for $3,000 and have $2,500 in my account and no overdraft facility. Can't I wish that 2,500 minus 3,000 were not a negative number? I certainly have many wishes in such a case, but the wish for that very abstract impossibility is surely not one of them. My wishes concentrate on a disjunction of the contingent features of the situation, the factual matters which, if they were otherwise, would mean that I had more money. They give wish a grip, as a denial of a mathematical necessity does not. Since wish does not get a grip there, fantasy does not either: wishful thinking has to do its work in the densely covered ground of the merely factual.

Perhaps there are some more exotic cases in which wishes might extend to the content of a mathematical proposition itself. The Pythagoreans, we are told, were very distressed to discover that the length of the diagonal of a square could not be expressed as a whole number ratio of the length of its sides (as we would now say, that $\sqrt{2}$ is an irrational number). It offended their conceptions of the world's harmony, and they presumably wished that it had turned out otherwise. A condition of their having that wish was that they should not think in a determinate or focussed way about what it involved; if they had done so, they would have found themselves wishing that the same natural number should be both even and odd (that is the point on which the relevant proof turns). This means that there was very little room for their wish to subvert belief. Once the proof that $\sqrt{2}$ is irrational has been discovered, the belief that it is not so cannot survive in a society where it is an issue what one should believe in mathematics, as seemingly it was for the Pythagoreans. They might, of course, have suppressed and forgotten the proof altogether, which would have meant that they stopped asking this question and others related to it; perhaps they would have had to give up mathematical inquiry altogether. After a while, at least, that would have been a substitute for wishful thinking, rather than an example of it.

In other cases in which it is more tempting to say that I can wish for a logical or metaphysical impossibility, the explanation of how my wish can have an object is often that there is a surrogate of the impossible which is conceivable, and which embodies some elements of the attraction. A man I knew used to say that he wished that he were monogamously married to each of four women at once, and one sees how he could get to that wish. In general, the more plausible the surrogate of the impossible is as the object of a wish, the more room for effective fantasy, and the greater the chance of fantasy's subverting the formation of belief.

In psychoanalytical theory, our deepest wishes and fantasies are said to involve logically impossible contents, those that figure in the processes of the Freudian unconscious. But this does not really affect the present issue. When fantasies at that level subvert rational behaviour, whether with regard to belief or otherwise, they can do so only via some symbolic transformation: their influence is necessarily indirect. But the fantasies and self-deceptions controlled by the disciplines of truth operate at a much higher level, the level, as one might say, of the subconscious. Fantasies at this level, the everyday items with which the virtue of Accuracy has to deal, are much more nearly homogeneous in their conceptual content to what they are trying to replace. Indeed the wish itself—though not the fantasy process by which it generates belief—may present itself openly to consciousness, as when the bereaved mother knows in the first place perfectly well that she wishes that her son had survived the crash; what needs a subconscious indirection is the transition from that to the motivated belief that he did survive the crash. In the case of the deep fantasy wishes of the Freudian unconscious, they cannot present themselves in any such way to consciousness.

My speculation is, then, that it is the sense of a conceivable alternative that is particularly associated with realism. Realism invokes the idea of an order of things that is independent of us, where that means, in particular, independent of our will. One paradigm of this is the familiar phenomenon of "obstance," where material reality simply obstructs our attempts. But the idea reaches beyond that, to a wider range of cases in which something turns out in fact not to be possible: we can coherently, perhaps vividly, wish that reality were otherwise, and the wish can marshal a process that subverts true belief. This possibility is so significant that one of the two basic virtues of truth, Accuracy, aims to encourage resistance to subversion by the wish. This, precisely, is one of the things that is involved in keeping a hold on reality. But this is called upon only in the cases where there is a possible wish and so a possible subversion induced by that wish; and, although we can, in some circumstances, wish for the logically or metaphysically impossible, the subversive effects of wish, of the kind that Accuracy is there to guard against, are most significantly present with determinate and focussed wishes, and focussed wishes are those that grow out of a well-defined alternative to the actual.

4. *Truthfulness and Freedom*

The virtue of Accuracy plays an important part in guiding and sustaining a collective division of epistemic labour. This was already so in the State of Nature, and there is of course a genuinely historical story, a hugely complex one, of the cultural and eventually industrial sophistication of this idea into what is now called "science." One important feature of that process has been the way in which the understanding of nature itself affects what counts as an appropriate and effective division of labour. We can imagine already in the State of Nature a certain degree of specialization; it is not merely that two people go in different directions, but they recognize that one person is better at looking for fish while another excels with game, or one has a nose for the scent of game while another has a sharp eye for its traces. There is a long but entirely intelligible route from this to the discovery of the structure of DNA, in which the basis of the fact that animals resemble their parents was uncovered through an understanding of crystallography.

Another significant part of this process is that it has generated refinements in the virtues of truth themselves, in the form of a dedication to science and to standards of scientific truthfulness, which involve not just Accuracy but Sincerity, both with others and with oneself.[16] Under this transformation, the notion of an investigative investment becomes more abstract, and the motivations associated with wanting the truth for its own sake (about a significant or interesting question) become more important. The search for truth becomes in these respects an intrinsic good. As with Sincerity, the fact that Accuracy can be coherently treated as having an intrinsic value contributes in important respects to its having an instrumental value: not just in the well-known sense that technologically useful scientific truths very often emerge from "pure" research, but in the more personal connection that, as we shall see, the desire of a scientist to discover and hold on to reality can stand against such forces as political corruption and terror.

Many have thought that the motivations of the scientist stand for an ideal of personal disinterestedness, in contrast to the place-seeking and self-assertion of business or politics. This traditional, Platonic, conception may raise a smile now when (among other studies of unsaintly scientific motivation, and indeed a growing sociology of the subject) James Watson's account of his and Francis Crick's discovery of the structure of DNA[17] has gleefully admitted, indeed exaggerated, the desire for fame, the hope for the Nobel Prize, and the uncomplicated desire to do down Linus Pauling that inspired their work. Watson's story certainly reveals the spirit of much research, and one can be sure that the spirit is not an entirely modern development. But so far as truthfulness is concerned, to make a lot of the fact that scientists' individual motives are more worldly than the Platonic myth suggested is significantly to miss the point. Their goal is fame, above all fame and prestige in the scientific community itself, and that will come from the recognition that they have done good science.

To despise them for seeking fame is itself to suffer from a Platonic misunderstanding. A desire for fame does not corrupt or undermine the search for truth, if what one will be famous for (if all goes well) is having found the truth; just as those who in the ancient world or in the Renaissance sought fame through writing notable verse recognized that they would not achieve it without the notable verse. Here, as always, self-respect and respect from other people whom one respects are linked to one another. Science may perhaps be more unyielding about what counts as a notable achievement than verse has always been, or best-selling novels now are, but that is just the point. It is a point which would of course lose its force if scientific recognition itself—in particular, the acceptance of new theories or models as correct or as better than their predecessors—were itself a function of social position, power, eloquence, capacity for intrigue, and so on. Some programmes in the sociology of knowledge give the impression that they would like to deliver that conclusion, but, if that is their aim, they certainly have not delivered it or anything like it.[18]

There is a subtler version of Platonism, which suggests that the reason why the more abstract kinds of natural science can offer a sense of purity and liberation is that their content and their interest to us transcend human affairs altogether. Their content aims to be a representation of nature which abstracts to the greatest possible degree from the perceptual and other peculiarities of human beings.[19] Such an inquiry can give the sense that in abstracting from our epistemic condition, it also takes us away from the squalid and repressive limitations of our social and political life. If one has an absorbing interest in such a content, then that certainly will take one away from the confines of politics, but perhaps it will take one too far away—too far away, anyway, to express a sense of liberation that has anything to do with politics. In itself, it offers liberation from humanity, rather than expressing liberation for humanity. It gives no particular sense of the powers that might be better used in everyday life by people who were not subject to a corrupt political order.

Plato himself was caught in precisely this ambiguity. In the famous image of the Sun and the Cave in his *Republic*, he offers the picture of an escape from the darkness and superficiality of everyday life and in particular politics, to an intellectual world of clarity and light. There is an ambiguity, as there must be, in the dualist image itself. It contrasts a metaphysical promise with the everyday, but the content of the promise is represented, inevitably, in terms of the everyday. In invoking the sun, it reminds us that there is already something here in the natural world that we value. All the works in which Plato offers the promise of his dualism are shaped by this implicit conflict. Sometimes the suggestion is that real beauty and value are not to be found in this world at all, and that what is here is only some image or association of them; it is as though the world contained a photograph in place of a lover, or no love and only a madeleine. But elsewhere, and more truthfully, he suggests that what we need is here, but only in an incomplete, never entirely satisfactory, form.[20]

With respect to the Cave, the *Republic*'s conflict also presents itself the other way round: why do the imperfections and cruelties and compromises of the world concern the philosopher (as the inquirer is for Plato) who has looked outside? It was only because Plato had some hope that the authoritarian rule of reason could improve things in the everyday world that the student of intellectual reality could have any reason to go back there. Even if the dualistic dream could yield a politics, it would not be a politics of freedom. More-over, the hope that the dream could offer any politics at all is likely to fade, and many philosophers in the ancient world after Plato (and after the collapse of the city-state) indeed concluded that the right reaction was, to the greatest possible extent, withdrawal. The in-quirer stays out of the cave and leaves the political world to its natu-ral and incurable influences of greed, force, and fraud.

Primo Levi recalled how he spoke to his colleague Sandro in 1939 of the "new dignity and majesty" that the study of chemistry and physics had acquired in that time; it was an antidote to "the filth of fascism which polluted the sky," because "they were clear and dis-tinct and verifiable at every step, and not a tissue of lies and empti-ness, like the radio and newspapers."[21] It was certainly not a Platonic route that he had in mind: science may have been a relief and an encouragement, but it was not an escape. The point lay not in the fact that natural science dealt with what was more, or less, than human, but in the fact that it embodied honesty in a peculiarly ro-bust form. The answers were hidden, the work was hard, and the virtues of truth were called upon all the time. So long as you were really doing science, you could not fudge the results: you had to get it right.

For the inquiry to mean what it meant to Levi, it had to be a struggle with nature. Although Levi spoke to Sandro in rather ele-vated, Platonic, tones of clarity and distinctness, Sandro listened to this rhetoric, as Levi puts it, with a certain irony, and indeed he learned from it, but he equally taught Levi something from his experience as a peasant. "Did I know how to light a stove? Wade across a torrent? Was I familiar with a storm high up in the moun-tains? The sprouting of seeds? So he too had something vital to teach me." The encounter with the obstinacy, the unanswerability, of natural fact was something they were to share in the experience of mountaineering: "A piton goes in or it doesn't, the rope holds or it doesn't: these were the sources of certainty." There would have been no point in Levi's spending his time on acrostics,[22] even very difficult ones, or on sophisticated chess problems. What was needed was something in which the effort was not arbitrary, and in which the struggle was not one against another will. Science is, in game-theoretical terms, not a two-party game: what confronts the inquirer is not a rival will, and that is a key to the sense of freedom that it can offer.[23]

To be free, in the most basic, traditional, intelligible sense, is not to be subject to another's will. It does not consist of being free from all obstacles. On the contrary, freedom has any value only if there is something you want to do, and if, moreover, the want you have is not one that you can change at will for another want. A central form of freedom, then, is not to be subject to another's will in working toward something that you find worthwhile. Levi was working toward something that he valued—discovery—and part of that value itself lay in this, that the difficulties and obstacles were not produced by anyone's will, and no strategies of conciliation or evasion, no bargaining, could get round them. That is why fudging the results would have been simply beside the point. The task was directed to the truth, which as an object of pursuit is entirely unresponsive, and elusive only in the sense that the inquirer may be going in the wrong direction. So the virtues of truth do not need to be limited by the calculations of competition with another will. Levi's scientific inquiry could express freedom in contrast with arbitrary will, and truthfulness in contrast with deceit, and both for the same reason, that the truths of nature have no will, and in discovering them the virtues of truth are on their own, together with insight, experience, and luck.

Primo Levi was a scientist, and science made his point. As Levi himself puts it, there was a significance in the impact of experimental results, which bring it home with special force that the struggle is with something other than oneself. Might similar meanings be found in scholarship? Perhaps the same significance could be found in an activity which mobilized the sense for small, obstinate, inconvenient, perhaps philological facts, to which Nietzsche referred: "The ancient world: all the presuppositions of a scholarly culture ... were already there: the great, the incomparable art of reading well had already been established ... the *sense for facts*, the last and most valuable of all the senses."[24] Philology indeed deals in obstinate fact, and it notably calls on the virtues of truth in dealing with them. So do other kinds of historical research. Can they express what Levi found in experimental science? The detailed facts, the hard grit of discovery, are equally there, but an interest in finding facts, any old facts, merely for their own sake, makes no more sense than it does in the sciences; antiquarian or literary curiosity has its charms and its uses, and it can sustain an individual life, but in a larger scheme of things historical research will not make sense unless it is driven by some question, and ultimately by the prospect of some interpretation. Are the constraints on interpretation (I mean, on any large scale, not at the level of words, sentences, or even individual works) so problematic in the humanities that a sophisticated inquirer will find it hard to sustain, as Primo Levi could, a sense of straightforward discovery? It is obvious that varying interpretations, such as differing historical narratives, can be the product of rival schools or ideologies or idiosyncrasies. Even if that is not necessarily a bad thing and it is appropriate to these subject matters, does it mean that such studies can never offer quite the kind of liberation and significance that Levi found in natural science, because at this level, above the obstinate philological facts, shadows are cast by rival wills, even if they are quite a long way off—and particularly so in a season when, in the humanities, the sun is low in the sky? That is one question from which the present study started; we shall come back to it finally in the last chapter.

The sense of freedom that Levi found in his inquiries was grounded in their truthfulness: the "dictates" of nature are not the product of anyone's power. For just the same reason, it is a very basic exercise of power over another person to induce beliefs in that person without regard to their truth or falsehood; intentionally to induce false beliefs, for instance, just because they are false. This is a point that Orwell made in *1984*. The character Winston writes in his diary, "Freedom is the freedom to say that two plus two equals four. If that is granted, all else follows." It is significant that what matters is that one should be able to *say* it: freedom to believe the truth must be shared. Orwell says elsewhere that mere "inner" freedom is not real freedom because our beliefs are never entirely our own (this is an idea for which the State of Nature story leaves room, and we shall see more of it in chapter 8). It does not matter here that the belief in question is a piece of arithmetic; the issues about

realism that concerned us before are not involved. All that matters
is that the belief is as manifestly true as any belief can be; and since
there is no world in which two plus two does not equal four, to come
to believe that this is so is to be driven out of one's mind—or perhaps
one might rather say, out of the world into one's mind.

The Party boss, O'Brien, through torture makes Winston believe
for a while that twice two equals five. In an interesting discussion of
the book,[25] Richard Rorty has claimed that it does not matter to the
ethical or political point of this story that it is true that twice two
equals four—it is the freedom to say it that matters, and, equally, if
O'Brien made Winston believe something true by these methods, it
would have been just as bad. In one sense, what Rorty says is correct;
torture is no way to induce any belief. But it cannot be right to go
from this to saying, as Rorty does, that "truth and falsity drop out."
He means that the account we should give of the values involved
here need not mention the distinction between truth and falsehood,
and this is doubly wrong.

In the first place, we need to distinguish, not merely torture from
other methods, but more generally between acceptable and unacceptable ways of inducing belief, in particular between various kinds
of persuasion. There is no reason to think that we can do this without mentioning *the truth*. We need, for instance, to be able to describe those authoritative forms of persuasion that are legitimated
under the title of "education," and we have no reason to think that
we can do this without using the notions of truth and falsehood. As
we have seen, we have to mention *the truth* in making sense of the
virtue of Accuracy, and the same applies to education, which is, after
all, a rather straightforward example of the division of labour. The
only alternative to incorporating notions of truth and falsehood into
an account of education will involve, as it seems to me, the assumption that legitimate, educational, forms of persuasion can be distinguished from others simply by their methods: for instance, they are
supposed to be specially rational, or to be uniquely directed to the
interests of those being persuaded, where neither rationality nor the
pupils' interests are understood in terms of a concern for the truth.
Some educational practices may have tried to base themselves on
such ideas, but we do not need much reflection to see that appealing

to methods simply in this sense gives no results, or unacceptable results; if they do draw the required lines in the right places, they do so because they in fact rely on ideas of truth and falsehood.

There is a second reason for rejecting Rorty's surprising account, one that relates directly to Orwell's point. Many exercises of power *confront* their victim with a necessity, a necessity that can be understood by the victim within the framework of truths that helps to constitute his sense of reality. The torture that Orwell imagines, however (and the same will be true of many kinds of persuasion), does not do this. Rather, it subverts true belief so as to destroy the victim's relation to the world altogether, undoing the distinctions between fantasy and reality. It puts Winston into a fantasy which is O'Brien's, or the Party's, creation. This is a final affirmation of power, as Orwell saw, and Rorty, in letting truth and falsehood "drop out," disables himself from understanding it. He writes of Winston's "pain and humiliation"; such things are part of what Rorty has in mind when he says "cruelty is the worst thing we do." He explains this pain and humiliation simply in terms of one belief's being imposed in place of another. But this cannot be enough, because we need the idea that some of a person's beliefs are true, and that the possibility of this being so is connected ultimately with some things being and some things not being in his power. Without that, we have no adequate idea of his freedom, nor, in the end, of what counts as his humiliation.

Rorty, in rejecting the value of truth as itself central to the liberal ideas that he is trying to articulate around Orwell's text, has missed its point, and this is further shown by his taking O'Brien's remark "the object of torture is torture" and explaining it as though it meant "the object of torture is pleasure." It is very important that this is not what it means. It means in *1984*, as torture means in fact, that the object of torture is the assertion of power. This is why it is deeply appropriate that O'Brien should direct it against the sense of reality and the capacity for true belief.

7

❖   ❖   ❖   ❖   ❖

WHAT WAS WRONG WITH MINOS?

1. *Introduction*

In the two previous chapters we have moved in more than one direction from the State of Nature story into real history. In the case of Sincerity, the main point has been that a disposition to express one's real beliefs would not be robust enough to perform even the function identified for it in the State of Nature unless it were seen, to some extent, as having an intrinsic value, and it could not be coherently seen as having this value unless it were allied to or expressed some other disposition that had a value. What this disposition was, and hence in a sense what Sincerity itself has actually been, has varied from time to time and place to place. I have tried to follow, to a limited extent and very much in outline, some of that history, and I have criticized some of the forms that dispositions associated with Sincerity have taken (and, more particularly, the forms that some theorists have tried to impose on them), in particular because they did not yield a reasonable interpretation of Sincerity's fundamental connection with trust.

I suggested that when Sincerity is understood in a reasonable relation to trust, this also affects the value given to Accuracy. If others are to rely on what you tell them, you need, as well as not misleading them about what you believe, to take the trouble to make sure that your belief is true. This may affect the investigative investment you think appropriate. To the degree that you owe them the truth—in the everyday phrase that I suggested was right for these relations—to that degree you owe them an appropriate effort to get hold of the truth. In one sense, this already gives Accuracy a more than instrumental value. If one's relations to certain people are of the right kind, the felt need to make sure you tell the truth can be elicited simply by their expectations, and not simply or necessarily by a mutually understood division of labour.

Yet the division of labour, I suggested, can itself make the needs and passions of Accuracy take off from the purely instrumental: in the form, for instance, of the standards, the honour, and the mutual esteem appropriate to a scientific profession. Individuals, whether as members of such a profession or not, will display this kind of commitment to Accuracy when, concerned with some significant matter, they find it shameful to fudge it, to make do with a bad answer when without obsessional or unreasonable trouble they could have had a better one, or to make themselves think that the answer they have is better than they know it is. This disposition has, just in itself, a powerful political significance. These developments of Accuracy have a real history—the history, in part, of the sciences, but also more generally the history of intellectual integrity. In this case, unlike perhaps some of the more luxuriant elaborations of Sincerity, the seeds of what has actually grown can be picked out fairly clearly when we look back at Accuracy as it already appeared in the State of Nature. Yet it is also true that, looking simply at the State of Nature and the considerations that went into constructing it, no-one could predict the special ethical, psychological, and organizational structures that have in fact come about in association with an ideal of Accuracy.

I want now to go back once more to the State of Nature story, and to set out again in an altogether different direction. In the last section of chapter 3, I suggested that we should not assume that the people in the story had what I called an "objective" conception of the past, according to which every past event had a fixed place in a temporal order. We should not make this assumption because there is good reason to think that this conception itself had an historical origin. In this chapter I shall try to describe that origin (at least in the West) and to locate it at a specific point in the development of Greek thought in the fifth century B.C. I shall claim, too, that this change was intimately connected with a new conception of what it is to tell the truth about the past (or rather, as we shall see, about the remoter past).

If I am right, this is a kind of case that introduces a relation between the State of Nature story and real history different from those that we have already encountered. In this case, we may find it hard to imagine people who could do without a conception that seems to us quite basic to our idea of past time. Since, moreover, this is a respect in which the description of the people in the State of Nature applies straightforwardly to many actual human beings in the past, and perhaps to some who exist now, the question arises of how from our standpoint we see those human beings. This is not simply a case in which real historical developments offer elaborations or more specific determinations of something sketched in the State of Nature story. The historical emergence of an "objective" conception of the past adds a distinct element to what was offered there. Moreover, to some people this looks like progress from a less rational to a more rational process of thought, from confusion to clarity; others take a more relativist view of it. Whether the development should count as an increase in rationality is a question we shall come to at the end of this chapter, though I hope that it will be clear by then that it is not any one question.

2. Thucydides

David Hume wrote: "The first page of Thucydides is, in my opinion, the commencement of real history. All preceding narrations are so intermixed with fable, that philosophers ought to abandon them, in a great measure, to the embellishment of poets and orators."[1] It is a familiar judgement, but what exactly does it mean? In a footnote, Hume says, "In general, there is more candour and sincerity in ancient historians" (he means, they are less partisan) "but less exactness and care, than in the moderns," adding that the commonness of printed books in modern times has "obliged modern historians to be more careful in avoiding contradictions and incongruities." In the light of this, what exactly, on Hume's view, did Thucydides do in order to start real history? The suggestion is, roughly speaking, that he was the first to tell the truth. Does that mean simply that he was the first to do so, to succeed in separating fact and fable? Or does it mean further that he was the first even to try? Was he perhaps the first to possess the concepts, fact and fable, that would enable him to try?

There are certain characteristics of Thucydides' style which are very obvious and to which Hume was doubtless responding—with respect not only to his historical methods, but to the displayed unsentimentality and political realism, in the sense of the expression that applies to Thomas Hobbes, who was of course an admirer and translator of Thucydides. These characteristics are part of Thucydides' compelling effect, an effect that can seem startlingly modern, or at least startlingly familiar to modernity. He himself carefully organized that effect, in part by deploying a set of contrasts between his own work and the looser, more obviously congenial, writings of his predecessors (including, for certain, Herodotus, though Thucydides never mentions him by name). Among the contrasts that he draws is indeed one between, as Hume put it, fact and fable, or as Thucydides himself said, the true and the mythical. He represents himself as making a new start in telling the truth. We need to consider what this might mean.

It is generally accepted that there are significant methodological differences between Herodotus and Thucydides; fewer critics now would say that these made Thucydides the first real historian.[2] It used to be said that Thucydides secured his effect, and earned our respect, by being the first *scientific* historian. This was a theme of a former colleague of mine, a veteran Marxist, who used to permit himself the remark that it is true, as people often say, that Herodotus was the father of history, granted that it means that history started in the next generation.[3] The crudest view in this style combined an admiring view of Thucydides as scientist with a positivist view of science. On this account, Thucydides led the way in writing history which consisted of bare factual statements together with causal explanations. It is not very hard to see that whatever Thucydides' work consists of, it is not this—if only because of the crucial role played by the speeches. The positivist interpretation of Thucydides can presumably be pronounced dead. It is widely recognized that his effects, and indeed the effect of an austere objectivity itself, are the product of art, an art which structures his story in terms of powerful underlying contrasts, between *gnômê* and *tuchê*, for instance, reason and fortune, and between *logos* and *ergon*: the complex contrasts between what people say, plan, think, and hope, and the often hideous and unpredictable outcome of events.[4] It is in a certain sense a tragic vision. It was not to a positivistic scientist that one writer could apply a phrase drawn from Yeats's *The Fisherman*, "as cold and passionate as the dawn"; and Nietzsche, who wrote of Thucydides' "strong, severe, hard, factuality," also mentioned him in the same context as Sophocles.[5]

There is a danger that, in rejecting this old story, we may be swept away by an idea in a more fashionable style, that Thucydides no less than Herodotus is a rhetorical teller of tales, and it is merely that the fictions he offers are less superficially charming. But this is no more helpful. It suffers in a rather more subtle form from the false opposition that F. M. Cornford deployed when he, in one of the first reactions against the positivist interpretation, claimed that Thucydides wrote an Aeschylean tragedy because he lacked the resources to construct a proper positivist history.[6] The more recent version of this does not suppose, as Cornford did, that there could be a proper positivist history, but it shares his assumption that if history cannot be that, there is nothing for it to be but some version or another of myth, some fictive performance. But even if we grant some of that vocabulary—not "myth," indeed, but "story," and even perhaps "fiction"—we are still left with all the interesting work to do, of trying to understand what kind of story it is that has the special character of history.

Anyone who was ingenuously unspoiled by the critical literature would say that it was a kind of story that had something specially to do with telling the truth. This innocent answer must surely be right, so far as it goes. The reason why Thucydides is so interesting in these connections is not merely that he comes near the beginning, in the West, of the activity of constructing such stories (near the beginning, indeed, of telling any story in prose), but because the style that he contrived and the objectives that he set himself express in a specially sharp way some of the most basic relations that historical narrative cultivates with the truth, and helps us to understand them. The old positivist interpretation of those relations—that they are a matter of *wie es eigentlich gewesen*, and that's that—got it seriously wrong, but it got *something* wrong.

The style that Thucydides self-consciously adopted differs markedly from that of, in particular, Herodotus, and in more than one way it contributes to the effect that he aimed to give, of simply telling the truth. It is widely agreed that the significant shift in outlook between the two writers was connected with the fact that Thucydides was firmly located in a literate culture, while Herodotus was in "the situation that results when literacy first becomes an important tool in a still essentially oral society."[7] However, there is much less agreement, or clarity, about what this shift involved or how it may be best described. I am going to suggest that underlying these differences is a move from what I called in chapter 3 a "local" conception of the past to an "objective" conception of it,[8] and that this was, most basically, a shift in conceptions of what it is to tell the truth about the past. My aim is not to add to the extensive literature about the relations of orality to written history, but to offer an account of the shift that we can detect in this particular case, an account that will link time, truth, and causal explanation.

Everyone everywhere has some idea of the past. At a certain age the child can recognize that the grown-up has just gone out; at a later age, that she went out a while ago; later still, that she went away yesterday. These are constants of cognitive and developmental psychology, and we can see why they should be. For us, in addition, the time series consists of intervals that can be indefinitely iterated. Those who are old enough to remember Gian Carlo Menotti's opera *The Consul* will recall a character who went around singing, "yesterday, and the day before yesterday . . . ," and we know that he could have gone on indefinitely with that formula. So long at least as there have been days (and there were days, certainly, a long time before there were human beings), each day (roughly speaking) has had a day before it. Moreover, everything that has really happened to a human being happened on one or more of those days. So we tend to think that anyone who can think at all in terms of "yesterday"—and that is every relatively mature and capable human being—must share those conceptions. But is that so?

3. *"Legendary Times"*

The crucial text I want to consider is a passage of Herodotus (3.122.2). He is talking about Polycrates, ruler of Samos (who died in 522/521 B.C.), about whom he says that he was

> the first of whom we know to have aimed at control of the sea; apart from Minos the Cretan or someone earlier than he who may have ruled the seas. But out of what is called the human race, Polycrates was the first.

The central question about this passage is what is meant by the strange phrase (*tês de anthrôpêiês legomenês geneês*) which I have translated as "what is called the human race"; and the point of asking this question is to determine what it is about Minos which means that, whether he had a fleet or not, for Herodotus he does not count. What was the matter with Minos?

In what is now the standard treatment, the phrase is not translated as I have rendered it, but in terms of time. A recent writer, fairly typically, offers, first, "the 'human epoch,'" and later "'the properly denominated age of men'"; fifty pages later it has become "in ordinary human history."[9] But there is no reason to think that it can mean any such thing. The most frequent use of the word *geneê* in Herodotus is indeed connected with time, but as standing for a chronological unit, a generation, which is not what is needed here.[10] Elsewhere the word means such things as "birth," "descendants," or "pedigree," and in one passage, the seven classes or castes of Egyptian society.[11] The expression that Herodotus uses here can only mean "the human race." But then it is quite unclear what is being done by *legomenês*, a form which standardly refers to what something is "called" or "is said to be," when either there is a doubt whether it should be so called, or the name in question is something like a title or nickname.[12] Why should Herodotus find anything at all questionable or notable about calling the human race "the human race"?

Minos, king of Crete, is of course the figure who has given his name to the Minoan culture. There was a doubt even in antiquity whether he was supposed to be merely human or not. He was standardly said to be the son of Zeus and a mortal woman, Europa, and so semi-divine, but a verse ascribed to Hesiod calls him "the most kingly of mortal kings."[13] It remains controversial whether there is an historical basis to the stories about him. After a long discussion, the most authoritative reference work judiciously concludes: "So there seems to be nothing in all the significant features of the picture of Minos (kingship, mastery of the sea, law-giving and state adminis-tration, military campaigns) which is so fantastic that it could not have a historical basis."[14] But whatever exactly he was, his times were supposed to have been earlier than ours, and earlier than Polycrates, as this passage makes clear. Elsewhere Herodotus, saying nothing about his status, assigns him to "the old days," to "ancient times," and once gets nearer to locating him in time, saying that the Trojan War happened in the third generation after him.[15]

So if Minos was semi-divine, there was an earlier time when there were such figures on earth. However, Herodotus has no clear idea of when this was, and if he is pressed, he seems to contradict himself. "I hold that the Egyptians did not come into being with the making of what the Ionians call the Delta," he writes, "but have always ex-isted since the beginning of the human race" (2.15.3). He conjec-tures that the Egyptians moved northwards, occupying the Delta as it was gradually formed by alluvial deposits (2.11), and he estimates that this process stretched over a period of ten thousand to twenty thousand years or more. He was, famously, impressed by the antiq-uity of Egypt, and by the records of its kings, which suggested that between the first king and his own time 11,340 years had elapsed: "in all of which time, they said, they had had no king who was a god in human form," though gods did rule Egypt before men did (2.144). Herodotus certainly regards the chronology of Egypt and of Greece as forming one system, and he is very interested in connections be-tween their histories. He has an elaborate argument to suggest that the Greeks are wrong in thinking that certain of their gods were recent: if they did arrive relatively recently, they were probably human beings who were named for old gods from Egypt. There is also a lot of material, in relation to the more recent history of Egypt, about the Trojan War. If you put all his calculations together, it looks as though Herodotus is committed to thinking that three generations before the Trojan War, when Minos was supposedly around, the world had for a very long time been exclusively in the hands of human beings.

The scholar I have already mentioned in connection with the translation of Herodotus's phrase says, to quote him more fully:

> Herodotus . . . does not consider the legendary histories of most of the Greek city states worthy of inclusion, nor does he tarry over stories about the gods, because they and semi-legendary beings such as Minos are beyond the evidence that history can deliver or explain. They are generally obscure in their workings and not part of the "human epoch."[16]

This is, to put it bluntly, a confusion. It runs together what are for us now two different answers to the question about what was wrong with Minos: on the one hand, that he was legendary or semi-legendary, which is a matter of the status possessed by him and the stories about him; on the other hand, that it is merely too obscure what we can assert about him, because it was too long ago, which is a matter of our possible knowledge. Of course, the second matter can extend to the first, in the sense that we may know so little that we do not even know whether a given figure was legendary: and that is indeed the case with Minos. Nevertheless, these are two very different considerations. There are thousands of people in classical antiquity whose names we know, and who are certainly not legendary, but about whom we can assert very little; there are others who are legendary and about whom we can assert a great deal, such as Zeus. Since these are, for us, two different matters, to run them together, as this scholar does, is, for us, a muddle. But Herodotus himself did not make this muddle, because it was not yet possible to do so. In his outlook, there was, rather, a certain kind of indeterminacy about the past, an indeterminacy which we should try to describe without ascribing the muddle to him, or falling into it ourselves.

The question of what we can know is certainly connected with time, and particularly so for Herodotus. He makes a display of relying on oral evidence when it is not a matter of things that he has seen himself.[17] He claims to put more trust in matters for which there is a reliable oral tradition, and he typically relies more on testimony about events that occurred in the century or so before his investigation, signalled as an appeal to the *mnêmê anthrôpôn*, the memory of men: a practice that has a sound rationale in a pre-literate culture, as it takes one back, very roughly speaking, to things remembered by the oldest person one can meet.[18]

Time has been thought to be involved also in the other idea, that the trouble with Minos is not his obscurity but his legendary status. This suggestion, in relation to Herodotus's words, goes back at least to Ph.-E. Legrand, who wrote in 1932: "Les générations 'que l'on appelle humaines' s'opposent aux générations mythiques, les événements 'humains' . . . aux événements fabuleux." It has been deployed by many subsequent scholars, for instance, by Moses Finley: "Effectively, Greek thinking divided the past into two parts, two compartments, the heroic age and the post-heroic (or the time of gods and the time of men)."[19] Those last words consciously echo a famous phrase used by Pierre Vidal-Nacquet, "temps des dieux et temps des hommes."[20] This way of putting it implies that the legendary or fabulous figures are gods, or closely related to the gods, and this is, strictly speaking, a further step, since there can be myths or legends with no divine content, but in the present context that does not matter. The world of Greek myths was certainly full of gods, and if Minos was legendary, he was, as we have seen, probably also semi-divine.

Vidal-Nacquet's formulation is misleading, in more than one way. It encourages one to think of the difference between human beings, on the one hand, and divine or semi-divine beings, on the other, too exclusively in terms of eras; Vidal-Nacquet is indeed prominent among those who mistranslate Herodotus's reference to the human race as a reference to time.[21] It might suggest, too (though this is not what Vidal-Nacquet intends), that the two classes of beings were separate from one another in time, but of course the world in which the gods still acted and revealed themselves was also a world of human beings, and this is shown by the presence of figures with one divine and one human parent: even in those old days, copulation required some degree of simultaneity. Moreover, those semi-divine beings, and the shifting stories about the status of a figure such as Minos, remind us that while there were some who were purely gods, and some who were purely human, there were others who were in many varying degrees connected by birth with the gods; and, significantly, Minos and those like him were often divine in some contexts and not at all so in others.

Another recent writer, influenced by Vidal-Nacquet, has said: "Herodotus found himself able [on the basis of his work in Egypt] to extend backwards by thousands of years *le temps des hommes* to a period when gods mingled with men, a time so remote from the present as to be unimaginable, and one that challenged *le temps des dieux* accepted by the Greeks."[22] There is something in this, but I think that it also expresses a misconception implicit in this approach, a misconception which goes deep. Such formulations make Herodotus's work sound like an exercise in palaeontology—as though another type of hominid, *Homo semi-divinus*, had walked the earth at one time, and it was a question of dating the era when it did so. But this scholar herself reveals in the phrase "so remote as to be unimaginable" that she is uneasy with this way of relating time and the mythical. Once again, we are seeing signs of a tension between two different answers to the question of what was wrong with Minos, our ignorance or his status; there are signs, equally, of an anxiety about the way in which those two answers are supposed to be related to time. I suggest that Herodotus was beginning to be anxious about it himself.

There is, certainly, a sense in which Herodotus, above all in his work on the Egyptians, extended backwards the territory of history, in the sense of what could be asserted as true on the basis of reliable testimony including, now, written records.[23] But it is a misconception to think that Herodotus had a point of view from which, in Finley's words, he "divided the past into two parts, two compartments." This is to read into this earlier mode of thought the kind of abstract and unsituated classification schema which precisely does not suit it. Herodotus does not think in terms of a boundary between two worlds, the world of history and the world of myth, related to which there are two times, historical times and what play-scripts and libretti used to call "legendary times." In order to think of such a boundary, and to think of himself as having moved it backwards, he would require a view of both sides of it, and there is no place from which he could have had such a view. He and most of his contemporaries, and the generations before them who told these stories about gods and men, essentially started from where they were, and, to understand them, we must see what this involved.

In Herodotus's time, many things were said, many tales were told. Of some, many of them relating to recent times, he had good reason to say that they were simply true, in the sense in which all human beings everywhere have understood that some statements about what has recently happened (for instance, what has *just* happened) are true. Other stories, in similar terms, were simply false. As the stories went back in time, they became vaguely related to each other; there was little known about how they came to be told; they rarely referred to any determinate past time. Their times were merely earlier, a long time ago, the old days. Moreover, many of them did have, relative to the present, a rather strange content: they were stories about gods, heroes, monsters. The fact that the stories with this strange content, or most of them, were about the past was a feature of the Greek world and of course does not apply to all myths elsewhere: the Greek gods were supposed to have gone away, which is why the "time of the gods" has come into the discussion at all.

About such stories, people could say that they were told, and they might tell them themselves. They could compare them, even try to reconcile them, as Hesiod tried to do.[24] It could be important to ask whether a given version of a story was the story that was usually told, or told by the most respected story-tellers, and this gave a sense to "Is this version correct?" But, fundamentally, the question, "Is this a story we should tell?" had the force "Is this a story to be told now, to this audience?" Would it—as we may put it—*suit* them? There is nothing in those people's practice to make us say that if they asked about such a story, "Is it true?" there was some *further* consideration that might be brought in: that question, if it was asked, was not an independent question. It is a question that indeed arises, everywhere, in relation to what is familiar and recent; relatedly, everywhere it is one possible reason for not telling some stories to some people that one knows them not to be true. But those considerations did not press on those stories about the old days, with their strange content and their indeterminate temporal remoteness. As Paul Veyne said, in one of his answers to the question that provided the title of his book, "Did the Greeks believe in their myths?": "These worlds of legend were believed to be true, in the sense that people did not doubt them, but they did not believe in them as people believe in the realities that surround them."[25] Such a practice is not inherently unstable; it can last for long periods of time. But it becomes unstable if the kind of question that is appropriate to the everyday begins to encroach on the stories about the old days, and there ceases to be a natural and unreflective way of moving from one way of taking or offering a story to the other. This began to happen in Herodotus's time.[26] In the traditional practice, within which he still for the most part moved, the fact that a story related to a long time ago was enough to separate it, in a spontaneous and unreflective way, from questions that certainly arose about what was done yesterday by the woman next door; but his own and other people's inquiries, in particular, his researches in Egypt, made it increasingly awkward to continue that practice. A story is offered, and it is said to be about a long time ago, but now, for the first time, the question "What difference is that supposed to make?" begins to need an answer. Herodotus does not formulate that question. But it is the next question after many he has formulated, and the ground that supports the old practice which is still his practice, one in which that question does not present itself, is moving under his feet. I think that this is what explains the strange phrase "what is called the human race." The question is to hand, "What excludes Minos?"; and if Herodotus were to face it, he would not have an answer.

4. *The Past and the Truth*

Near the beginning of his own history, Thucydides also considers the question of Minos and his fleet. He briskly says, "Minos was the earliest among those of whom we know by hearsay . . . who ruled

over most of what is now the Hellenic sea" (1.4). "Of whom we
know by hearsay" (*hôn akoêi ismen*) is a Herodotean phrase, and Herodotus's editors say that Thucydides is probably "by implication
correcting Herodotus." They add: "Herodotus for once is more
truly critical than Thucydides."[27] But this misses the point. It may
be that Thucydides should not have unqualifiedly asserted the existence of Minos's sea power. But Herodotus did not assert it quali-
fiedly, or decline to assert it, either: as we have seen, he did not *count*
it, for reasons which, in our perspective, are inherently unclear. Our
perspective is already Thucydides' perspective. For him, as for us,
there is a fact of the matter whether some given years ago there were
or were not ships controlling a certain area of sea,[28] and similarly
that there was or was not a real person at that time corresponding
to the Minos of whom the tales were told—someone possibly,
though not necessarily, called "Minos." If it is said that Minos was
a legendary or mythical figure, then Thucydides will say that you
may of course tell a story about him, but you cannot tell that story
in just the way you assert what happened yesterday; the story is a
myth or legend, and if you assert it in just that way—where it remains to be seen what "just that way" involves—you assert something untrue. Thucydides, unlike Herodotus, understood this perfectly well, and unless someone earlier than either of them had the
same thoughts, which is unlikely,[29] we can say that in coming to
understand it Thucydides invented historical time.

Historical time provides a rigid and determinate structure for the
past. Of any two real events in the past, it must be the case either
that one of them happened before the other or that they happened
at the same time.[30] This does not hold for the mythical, or, more
generally, for the fictional or the imagined. Just as there is no answer
to the question of how many children Lady Macbeth had (and yet
it is not correct, either, to say that she is a Shakespearian character
with a vicious temperament and an indeterminate number of children), so, of many events in myth or legend, there is nothing to be
said about when they are supposed to have happened. For this reason, there is an intimate relation between historical time and the
idea of historical truth. To say that a statement about an event is
historically true is to imply that it is determinately located in the

temporal structure; if it is not, historical time leaves it nowhere to go, except out of history altogether, into myth, or into mere error.

When someone—I think it was Thucydides—for the first time worked clear-headedly and confidently within this outlook, it was not that he introduced a new definition or theory of truth. In the first instance what he did was to insist that one should put just the same questions to stories about the remoter past as people put in everyday life to stories about the immediate past: Is it true? Is it just a story? Everybody everywhere already has a concept of truth; indeed, they all have the same concept of truth. (The fact that they may have very different theories of truth just shows how much people's theories of truth misrepresent their grasp of the concept.)[31] However, they do not all have the same ways of applying the concept of truth to the past, or at least to the remoter past: to the extent that they do not, we may say that while everyone everywhere has some concept of the past, they do not all have the same concept of the past. Thucydides imposed a new conception of the past, by insisting that people should extend to the remoter past a practice they already had in relation to the immediate past, of treating what was said about it as, seriously, true or false. I have called this a shift from a "local" to an "objective" view of the past. This is still a view *of the past*: it is not a question of stepping outside the past-present-future series altogether and thinking only in terms of one event's being (time-lessly) before or after another. The point is that when we have the objective view, we do not think only in terms of *the* past; we can think also of *our* past, not in the sense of our own life, but in the sense of what is past relative to us, or to now. We become conscious of our being, in temporal terms, some people among others, and with this comes the idea that some of our past was other people's present, that our present was other people's future, and so on: in particular, that what for us, now, is the remote past, for past people was the recent past or the present. Given this idea, that however long ago a day of human life may have been, it must have been somebody else's today, it has to be recognized that one cannot implicitly treat the remoter past as a peculiar area in which indeterminate happenings and people could exist. If one can say only indeterminate things about them, then that is a matter of our relation to them. Either there was no time at which they existed, so they did not exist at all, and are mere stories; or they were real, and as determinate in their time as similar things are in ours, and we simply do not know enough about them.

This is the metaphysical substance, so to speak, of the change from the local to the objective view of the past. But of course it did not announce itself in those terms, as a metaphysical discovery. It was expressed, rather, in a change in people's practice (indeed, unless it were expressed in that way, there would be nothing to possess a metaphysical substance). So what was involved in this new practice? Here it is essential that there is more to it than merely a change in the way people talk. It is not just that they now apply words that can be translated as "true" and "false" to statements about the remoter past, including stories about the gods. They did that before.[32] What matters is the force of such words, what turns on saying "true" rather than "false." Moreover, it cannot merely be that after this development there will be two styles of narration about the past: that in some cases people just come out with stories about the past, as they come out with other things that they intend to assert, but in other cases they bracket their narration with some disclaiming formula suitable to myth, such as that natural legacy from the Herodotean world, "once upon a time." They may well come to do this, but these distinctions among speech-acts are not self-sufficient: both we and they need to know what turns on telling stories in these different modes, how the social consequences differ. What responsibilities does one take on by telling a tale in what, at this stage, we may call the mode of truth rather than in the mode of myth?

Those responsibilities are entirely clear to Thucydides. In the famous two chapters near the beginning of his book in which he declares his methods (1.21–22, the so-called preface), in Greek that is characteristically knotted and unlovely, he uses the notion of the "mythical" (*to muthôdes*). He contrasts the account he has already given of earlier times with those given by poets, and also with those of the so-called logographers (who are often thought to include Herodotus),[33] "who, aiming more at attracting their audience than getting at the truth, have put their accounts together from materials which cannot be checked and which, in many cases, owing to the distance in time, command no belief and are consigned to the status of myth" (21.1). What this implies comes out in the next chapter (22.4), where he says of his own account that the fact that the mythical is absent from it may make it seem less pleasant to a listener, but that it will be good enough if it is of interest to people who want to have a clear view of these events.[34] And in the unforgettable words which have indeed made themselves true: "It has been composed not as a competition piece for the moment, but as a possession for ever."

These sentences do not just offer a comment on his style and a boast about his purposes. They help us to understand what the mythical is. A myth, or at least a Greek myth, is, among many other things, a good story, one that can entertain, warn, remind, strike home.[35] This does not mean that the subject matter of every myth is pleasant, or that every true story is about something unpleasant: not even Thucydides thought that. But it implies that in the mode of myth, the question whether the story should be told is just the question whether the story is appropriately directed to its audience, whether, as I put it before, it will suit them. Truth, as I said earlier, is a different matter, and in the mode of truth, there are always two questions possible about whether the story should be told: in the practice of the logographers, Thucydides says, you could not count on there being more than one.

Truth is not audience-relative. In particular, the truth of a statement has nothing to do with whether a given audience will be pleased to hear it.[36] This is a special case of something that everyone implicitly and pre-theoretically understands about truth (even if their behaviour, quite often, does not make this very obvious). Everywhere, there are wishes, and, among them, unfulfilled wishes; it is the pathos of the unfulfilled wish, in fact, that makes wishes obvious, and it registers the gap between wishes and truth. Just because the gap can be so painful, true belief, as we have seen in earlier chapters, has to be protected against subversion by the wish, and this is why both the virtues of truth typically include defences against the pleasure principle, whether it is a matter of finding out the truth, and the protection is against such things as laziness and self-deception, or one is concerned, as we are at this point, with the announcement or rehearsal of the truth, and the defences must be against such things as cowardice, ambition, and the desire to be loved. The fact that Thucydides starts his history in such terms represents one way in which he gave substance to the distinction between the mode of myth and the mode of truth. It is entirely appropriate that he sees the virtues of truth as also political, and that later in his history he condemns the leaders of the Athenian democracy because (he claims) they, unlike Pericles, spoke to please the crowd. There is a connection, too, with the uses of literacy. When the Athenian general Nicias needed to communicate his situation to the Athenians, Thucydides says,

> He was afraid that the messengers might not report the facts as they really were, either through lack of ability in speaking, or bad memory, or a desire to say something that would please the general mass of opinion. He therefore wrote a letter, thinking that in this way the Athenians would know what his views were without having them distorted in the course of transmission, and so would have the truth of the matter in front of them to discuss.[37]

There is a second way in which Thucydides does not just announce, but enforces, a difference between the mode of myth and the mode of truth, and in doing so makes clear the kind of responsibility that the mode of truth brings with it. If someone is going to be taken seriously, by himself as much as by others, as wanting to tell the truth about the past, he has to have some reason to believe that a certain thing happened rather than not. He will have such a reason only if it makes sense, in terms of the evidence he has and the other things he believes about the past, that it should have happened. But there is no way in which it can make sense unless, at some level of generality, that *sort* of thing makes sense. If we are to place events in the framework of the past, on the strength of present evidence, then we must be able to relate them to each other and to ourselves in terms that make them intelligible. Indeed, this is implicit to some extent in the use of general terms over different times: if we say that there was in past time a battle, or a king giving orders, or a fleet, then what we believe to have happened to people then must resemble in relevant and intelligible respects the way things are now if such things exist among us. In virtue of that, we can, often, explain them; and if we cannot explain them, then at least we have to explain why certain evidence exists, and why it gives us reason to think that this inexplicable thing happened. This general requirement is interpreted in very different ways by various historians and in different styles of history, but the fact that there is some such requirement follows simply from two substantive demands on telling a story about the past in the mode of truth. They are demands which are entirely transparent in themselves, and, yet again, they are familiar to everyone everywhere with regard to statements about the recent past: you cannot just make the story up, and it is not necessarily a good enough reason for telling it, that someone else has told it.

Thucydides himself interprets the explanatory requirement in a very strong way. In the chapters about the earliest times, he addresses the most famous of all Greek stories, the *Iliad*, and makes some hard-headed military, economic, and geopolitical assessments of what must have gone on in the Trojan War. Once again, he has been chided by modern historians[38] for a naive use of poetic material, but once again, the principle is stronger than the example. What we claim to have really happened in the past must make explanatory sense, and at some level of generality, the explanations must be the same as they are of things now. The principle serves also, and indispensably, to link past with present, yielding the idea of a trace that constitutes evidence, such as the ruins of ancient buildings (1.10). Herodotus had also shrewdly discussed the material remains of past times, such as the many wonderful things he saw in Egypt. But there is a special, and very typical, twist in Thucydides. Assessing the remains of ancient Mycenae that were to be seen in his time, he compares them with the remains that he supposes might be left to future generations by contemporary Athens and Sparta. Here the explanatory unity of the world binds not just the past and the present, but the present and the future as well; and concrete expression is given to the idea that our today will be someone else's distant past.

Thucydides in fact tends to favour, though by no means exclusively, tough explanations of social and political happenings in terms of power, but the principle he is using is not restricted to these.[39] If a happening in past time is explained, for instance, by a person's having a certain intention, then we should be able to understand such an intention operating in our own time; or, if not, then we need an explanation of that—for instance, that our situation is culturally different from theirs. We ourselves are much more impressed by the importance of cultural variation than most people were before the nineteenth century, and in other ways, too, different causal forces and kinds of event come into play, but the question of how specifically similar the explanations may be between different times and cultures is secondary to the idea that at some level the world is explanatorily homogeneous.

However, once we allow the world to be importantly different between different times, and do not require the explanations of actions and events to be always very specifically similar: might there not after all have been a time of the gods? Just as the theory of evolution by natural selection, a theory which applies at all times, allows us to believe that at one time there were dinosaurs and there are no dinosaurs now, so perhaps our explanations should, in principle, allow us to think that it is at least possible that gods once walked the earth and now do not. Perhaps there is some very abstract and airless level of principle at which that could be right, but in fact it is not so. Those gods are given to us through those stories, and once we accept the idea of historical time, it is quite clear that the gods are essentially indeterminate, in many respects, and could have no fixed or clear relations to it. Once the structure of historical time is in place, the gods will eventually bow out. Of course, they do not disappear altogether, because the stories about them become fully acknowledged myth, and in myth they have a hold on us, but myth is not a time or place.

Mythical or otherwise fictional characters have a hold on our thoughts and feelings; indeed, they can have a hold on our beliefs. It is true that Zeus took Leda in the form of a swan, that Anna left Karenin for Vronsky, that Sherlock Holmes lived in Baker Street. It is not true that Odysseus stopped his ears so as not to hear the Sirens' song.[40] When we answer questions about such things, and try to recall, for instance, what it was that M. de Charlus said about the conduct of the War, or which of Antigone's brothers it was that she made a fuss about, they are like events and figures of the past, and our frame of mind does approximate for a while to the outlook of a world in which myths were not clearly distinguished from history. That outlook is familiar to us, and we should not find it hard to recover it. But our outlook taken as a whole is very different from that because, living in a culture which takes for granted the presence everywhere of written fictions, we instantly come back to the recognition that what can be truly said about such characters is controlled by the relevant texts, texts which we can look up in the full consciousness that they are fictions.[41]

There is another difference as well, which is a direct expression of the Thucydidean outlook. We know that it is true of Sherlock Holmes that he lived in Baker Street, and we could win in an easy quiz by saying so, but we know just as well that it is not true of Baker Street that Sherlock Holmes lived in it. Or rather, to go more carefully, there is a sense in which that is indeed true of Baker Street; it is the sense appropriate to the quiz, and it is, as we might say, written all over the place (the Underground railway station there has the profile of the sleuth on its walls). But what we understand just as well is that if we are writing the history of London, we will not list him among its residents, and indeed we will not find his supposed address. We can move with great ease between these ways of talking, and reflecting on one of them can help us to grasp what the old attitude to myths was like. But we have to remember that there were not two distinct ways of talking, or a definite way of moving between them, before Thucydides invented it.

The account of this significant change that took place in the fifth century B.C., the invention in the West[42] of historical time, may help to persuade philosophers of something that some find it hard to believe, that human beings can live without the idea of historical time. Equally, it may persuade cultural relativists that there are reasons why such an idea should emerge, and that when developments such as literacy have occurred, it becomes inevitable that human beings should, in this respect, come to see the world as Thucydides saw it. Here we meet those questions I mentioned at the beginning of this chapter. Did this change represent intellectual progress? Did it come with, or perhaps from, an increase in rationality? There are, needless to say, several questions.

Was the change inevitable? No: very little is inevitable, not even the invention of writing. Was the change inevitable, given the invention of writing? Surely, yes, granted an interest in the past and hence in explaining things left behind from it. Did the change bring with it an increase in explanatory power? Surely, yes; and this was so in terms of *anyone's* conception of explanation. It is not simply a matter of taste or fashion whether one prefers an explanation in the Thucydidean style of those ancient structures that were called "Cyclopean" walls, or the explanation which said that they were built by a race of giants. There is of course a cultural difference between a situation in which the second sort of explanation still has currency and one in which it does not, but there is also a period of cultural change, in which one of these situations gives way to the other, and in that period it becomes quite clear that to many Thucydidean questions and answers the traditional story has no response at all. The traditional story falls silent on such matters, and so do the declining number of people who stick with that story.

Is that a matter of power? Yes, and it has social expressions: the questions to which the old outlook has no responses are now the questions that are asked, and the old style looks feeble, is associated with the old-fashioned, and moves to the margin.[43] But this is not opposed to what is sometimes called "the power of reason." If there is to be a power of reason, it had better recognizably be a power, and if it is, it will work through the ways in which some people affect other people's behaviour.[44]

So does that mean that those who operate in the new style, who have the "objective" conception of time, are more rational or, again, better informed than the others? No, if that implies (as it is usually meant to imply) that those in the traditional practice were confused or believed something false. The later practice expresses the belief that (as I have put it) anyone's remoter past was once someone else's present, and people will come to formulate this belief explicitly, in one way or another, as a truth, which indeed it is. But the earlier practice did not deny this truth; it merely did not address it. The fact that it did not address it, moreover, does not mean that the people living in that practice were confused. In particular, we should not say that they believed something necessarily false, that the difference between the real and the mythical is a difference in time. The invention of historical time was an intellectual advance, but not every intellectual advance consists of refuting error or uncovering confusion. Like many other inventions, it enabled people to do things they could not conceive of doing before it happened.

8

❖ ❖ ❖ ❖ ❖

FROM SINCERITY TO
AUTHENTICITY

1. *An Ambiguous Invention*

The invention of historical time in the fifth century B.C. brought
about a conception of the past that had not been available earlier.
Equally, it was not anticipated in the State of Nature story, though
it can be seen, when we look back, as virtually an inevitable exten-
sion, given the invention of writing, of ideas that exist universally
and are represented in the State of Nature. The invention, with its
new conception of what it is to tell the truth about the past, was a
new development in the conception of Accuracy.

In this chapter I turn to another and very different invention—
an invention, this time, in the dimension of Sincerity. It consists of
an idea, or a set of ideas, which associate Sincerity with personal
authenticity, an association that first came into distinct existence in
the eighteenth century. This invention stands in a different relation
to the State of Nature. It cannot be seen as a development of human
needs, concerns, and interests which was (given certain technical
developments) inevitable, or even particularly probable. It is separated from the State of Nature, and from the universal considerations that are represented in that fiction, by a much denser and more
complex set of real historical contingencies. This does not mean that
there is no real genealogy of these ideas. It is simply that an historical
account of their origin would call on many more and more various
phenomena than are anticipated, even in the broadest sense, in the

State of Nature. The rise of these ideas has deeply affected our present conceptions of truthfulness and its relations to the self, and these conceptions are among those that notably give grounds for philosophical puzzlement and concern. So here again philosophy, in order to do its business, must move into history, but this time it is because of an historical development that is autonomous (as I put it at the end of chapter 2) relative to the abstract framework laid out in the State of Nature story.

The history of this invention is enormously complex. Both the circumstances that gave rise to it, and the forms that it has taken—the intellectual, social, and ethical developments in the past three centuries that have centred on these ideas—offer a dense and complicated story, and I can tell very little of it.[1] My main suggestion will be that the invention was ambiguous, and that underlying these new ideas of authenticity there have been two different conceptions of the self and of self-understanding, which imply different ideas of sincerity and its relation to society. These two different conceptions can be associated—certainly not exclusively or without qualification, but distinctively enough—with two very different writers, Rousseau and Diderot, who were contemporaries and, at one time, friends, but later became (as Rousseau, at least, felt) enemies, after a falling out that had at its heart, more than anything else, these two different conceptions of what it takes to be a truthful person.[2]

2. *Rousseau*

—Excuse me, I wanted to ask you, do you believe that Jean Jacques
  Rousseau was a sincere man?
  Stephen laughed outright . . .
—He was like you, I fancy, said Stephen, an emotional man.

—JAMES JOYCE[3]

Near the beginning of his *Confessions* Rousseau tells of an incident in his childhood when he was falsely accused of breaking a comb and found that his true denial was not believed. In his fascinating book about Rousseau,[4] Jean Starobinski makes this incident central to his account of the writer's psychology. "From that moment, paradise was lost, since paradise was the reciprocal transparency of consciousnesses, a total and confident communication between them." Starobinski sees all Rousseau's later efforts toward improvement as attempts to regain that lost transparency.

> It is enough to be sincere, to be oneself, and from then on natural man is no longer a remote archetype to whom I compare myself; he coincides, rather, with my own presence, with my existence itself. The old transparency came from the naive presence of men under the eyes of the gods; the new transparency is an interior closeness to myself, a relation of the self to the self. It comes about in the clarity of his view of himself, which allows Jean-Jacques to represent himself as he is.[5]

Rousseau was under no illusion that every statement about his past in the *Confessions* was correct. As he says at the beginning of Part II, "The first part of my book was entirely written from memory, and I must have made many mistakes in it. As I am obliged to write the second part also from memory, I shall probably make many more." However, this turns out not to matter much, in terms of what the *Confessions* is about.

> I may omit some facts or transpose them, or make errors in dates; but I cannot be deceived about what I have felt, or about what my feelings have made me do, and that is what I am mainly concerned with. The real aim of my Confessions is to make known precisely my inner state, in all the situations of my life. It is the history of my soul that I have promised to give, and in order to write it faithfully I do not need any other records; it is enough, as I have done up to now, to go back into myself.[6]

Given this clarity of view, and Rousseau's dedication to total candour, it should have been simplicity itself to explain his motives to others, but in fact his explanations were never a success, and his failures to explain himself were deeply built into his increasing paranoia: "No-one knows me except I myself. I see that people who live most intimately with me do not know me, and that they attribute most of my actions, for good or ill, to motives quite different from those that have produced them."[7] As Starobinski puts it,

> The *Confessions* is in the first place an attempt to rectify an error made by other people; it is not a recovery of "lost time." Rousseau's concerns start with this question: why the interior sentiment, which is immediately evident, does not receive an immediate recognition in which it can find an echo. Why is it so difficult to bring about a concord between what one is for oneself and what one is for others?

It may be that Starobinski exaggerates the significance in Rousseau's life, and in the *Confessions*, of the particular incident of the comb. It has been remarked that Rousseau tends to present each incident of his early life as decisive in his formation, and commentators have taken their choice of which to emphasize.[8] But however exactly he came by the project, the purpose of the *Confessions* was to reveal him to his readers. The prior task of understanding himself was already completed, or, rather, was hardly a task at all; in Starobinski's phrase, he was always close to himself. He took it to be entirely obvious to himself what he was like, and his aim was to make it clear to the world. As he wrote to Malesherbes, "I shall show myself to you as I see myself, and as I am, for since I pass my life with myself I am bound to know myself, and I see from the manner in which others who think they know me interpret my actions and my conduct that they know nothing about them."[9] And in the *Confessions* he says of his decision to write the book,

> Although it might not be at that stage particularly interesting for the facts of my life, I felt it might become so from the frankness that I was capable of putting into it, and I decided to make of it a work that would be unique because of its unparalleled truthfulness [*véracité*], so that once at least people would be able to see a man as he is within himself.[10]

When he looked back at the *Confessions* in his last, at times deranged, and very moving work of self-examination, *Les rêveries du promeneur solitaire*, he felt that he had underestimated the difficulty of the task: the "know thyself" of the temple at Delphi was a maxim which was less easy to follow than he had supposed, and the real and basic motives of his actions were not as clear to him as he had thought. His account of himself, though given in the utmost good faith, had no doubt been influenced by his wishes. In the fourth Promenade of the *Rêveries*, he admits that sometimes he may have involuntarily concealed some blemish by painting himself in profile; this is exactly what, in a preliminary draft of the *Confessions*, he had accused Montaigne of doing, and which he had been determined to avoid.[11]

In the *Confessions*, it had been a question of his telling the truth about himself, in the first place to himself, and then in order to make himself understood to others. But he recognized that in the course of his life, and even when he was supposed to be especially devoted to truthfulness, he told a lot of untruths to other people:

> But in examining myself with greater care I was very surprised by the number of things which I had invented but which I remember saying as though they were true, at a time when, proud in myself of my love for the truth, I was sacrificing to it my security, my interests, and my own person with an impartiality of which I knew no other example among men.[12]

He recalled various occasions on which he had lied to others, usually from shame or embarrassment, which came from a lack of social readiness. This social incompetence—with which, in itself, he was perhaps quite satisfied—provided one reason, he says, for his wanting to live in the country, where the demands of social life, particularly fashionable social life, would rarely affect him. His tortuous reflections in the *Rêveries* on lying and truth-telling come back to the action which he narrates in the second book of the *Confessions* (a mirror image, in effect, of the comb incident), when he stole a ribbon, and persisted in accusing a fellow employee, Marianne, of having taken it, as a result of which she was dismissed without a reference.[13] She had been a good friend to him. All she said was, "Rousseau, I thought that you were a good person. You make me very unhappy, but I would not want to be in your place." His remorse at this action had lasted all his life. He had told no-one about it, and the need to reveal it for the first time contributed, he says, to the decision to write the *Confessions*.

He expresses his remorse vividly, but he inserts a few mitigating considerations. Besides the suggestion that there is virtue merely in confessing the incident, and the claim that his remorse has kept him from any such crime for the rest of his life, he finds some extenuation in the fact that there was no spitefulness or malice (*méchanceté*) in his motivation: he was merely overcome by shame and embarrassment at the prospect of being found out. It does seem distinctly odd that he thinks that this will be either a surprise or a reassurance to his readers. Something else is even odder. He says that the roots of his accusing Marianne lay in their friendship—he had intended to give the ribbon to her, and that was why her name was the first thing that occurred to him when he was accused. Psychologically, it is a remarkable observation, but the suggestion, which seems certainly to be in the text, that this somehow reveals a benevolent and mitigating motive for his putting the blame on her, is a touching achievement of self-deception.[14]

David Hume said of Rousseau, "I believe that he intends seriously to draw his own picture in its true colours: but I believe at the same time that nobody knows himself less."[15] Paul de Man wrote, "Rousseau is one of the group of writers who are always being systematically misread," and he added that these misreadings are almost always accompanied by an overtone of intellectual and moral superiority.[16] It seems to me that Hume and de Man were both right, and that these two truths are connected to one another. It was hard for many of those who knew Rousseau to avoid the impression, not just that he was tiresome and temperamental and suspicious and ungrateful, all of which was certainly true, but also that he was somehow a fraud or a humbug, and this impression has been inherited by his later readers. The suspicion of insincerity is all the sharper, of course, because he was seen, and saw himself, as standing for sincerity before all things, and indeed for the idea that sincerity could in some way be *the* virtue. The picture of him as the apostle of sincerity was projected in his lifetime above all by the epistolary novel *La nouvelle Héloïse*, a best-seller which aroused, on a scale unknown up to then, an interest in its author as an individual. For later readers, the picture is most strongly associated with the *Confessions*, but the *Confessions* is itself a work that arouses doubts about the effectiveness of his supposed sincerity, and it can encourage the disapproving readings of itself and of the other works, to which de Man referred.

Leaving aside the ridicule he attracted by giving tireless advice about how to bring up children when he had refused to bring up his own, a major focus for the suspicion of Rousseau was his attitude to fame. He was supposed to have cut himself off from the corruptions and compromises of social life, installing himself in rural solitude, but he seemed to retain a flair for publicity. Saint-Lambert (the lover of a woman with whom Rousseau himself was passionately but unsuccessfully in love) said, "Do not be too sorry for him; he is travelling with his mistress, Reputation."[17] To some extent this was unfair: Rousseau was right when he said that he got a lot of attention he did not want. But at the same time this was no accident, and it stemmed from his own project. He was a writer who, reasonably enough, wanted his work to be widely read and his principles widely known, and his writings, even when they were not autobiographical, drew attention to himself as an individual, partly because they were unusual, partly because they spoke in general of individuality and authenticity. He never found a way of reconciling in good faith the consequences of his publishing his writings with what he claimed were the conditions of his producing them.

More generally, his critics have felt that he made himself out to be more virtuous than others, and more virtuous than anyone could be, including himself. This impression, too, is not entirely fair, but its roots, once again, lie deep in his project, and, specifically, in his conception of sincerity. This conception presupposes several things. It requires, as we have seen, the authority of self-discovery: the idea that sincere, spontaneous, non-deceitful declaration, the product of his presence to himself, will guarantee a true understanding of his motives. Moreover, what is revealed and understood in this way will represent a character, a whole person, and this implies that it will be coherent, or, as one might say, steady. True self-revelation will of course reveal conflicting moods and short-term feelings, and Rousseau is particularly clear about himself, that his emotional reactions were often violent and transitory. But under this there is assumed to be a real character, an underlying set of constant motives, in which his true self is expressed.

In his own case, he was sure that these motives were basically benevolent and well-disposed toward others. This impression is basic to Rousseau's project of reassurance, the removal of distrust by first-personal explanation. The result of the explanations is supposed to be that others will trust him, and this requires more than that they should trust what he says, in the sense of taking it to be true. What someone says, after all, may sincerely express malign and uncooperative self-interest. Of course, it is not so common that people will express this, since the malignly unco-operative have good reason not to display their motives. This thought gives some backing to an idea which Rousseau had not merely with regard to himself but as a general view of human nature, that sincerity (and this is to a great extent the Sincerity which has been our concern throughout) could in itself be at the heart of virtue. If one can speak frankly and spontaneously to others, then it must be that one has no reason to conceal one's motives from them, which usually means, at least if one is living with others and not as a savage, that these motives are ones that others can appreciate, share, or at least acknowledge without fear or insult. As Wolmar puts it in *La nouvelle Héloïse*, "one principle of morality can take the place of all the others, and it is this: never say or do anything which you would not want everyone to see or hear."[18] What we trustworthily declare must itself form the basis of our trusting each other, in the sense of providing the substance of living together. Since the motives that are honestly revealed must provide the basis of a shared life, they need to be basically moral or self-transcending.

There are great tensions here. Rousseau carefully crafted the *Confessions* to appeal to an interest in idiosyncrasy, the life and character of a particular person who was distinctly unlike others. This, he declared, would include his faults; in refusing to paint himself in profile, he was to offer himself warts and all. To some degree he did, and the book can be startlingly frank (and in its frankness about other people and his relations to them, particularly women, it was to cause great offence). But there are severe limits to this impulse, and his account of the incident of the ribbon, for all its self-laceration, clearly reveals them. The actions in which he harms others turn out to be mere episodes, not expressions of a settled disposition.

Moreover, what produces them is weakness, not an active desire to harm. Both these devices help to move these actions away from his real self, for which he expresses considerable moral esteem.[19] But in doing this, they undermine the project of reassurance through autobiography. The idiosyncratic peculiarities which were to be a major interest are, when they are unfavourable, relegated to the episodic and the superficial, and this suggests that the project must fail as autobiography: if real autobiography is to be the story of the real self, it will turn out, on these assumptions, not to be deeply particular and idiosyncratic after all, but at its heart much like the story of any other virtuous person. But equally his account of himself cannot succeed as ethical reassurance, since a person who is disposed to this kind of weakness is no more reliable than someone who is malicious, and in some ways is less so. This tension between the idiosyncratic and the ethical helps to make the *Confessions* a tricky book, and feeds the impression that one is dealing with a tricky author.

Rousseau's project is under tension, too, from what it implies about his view of others. His task, as Starobinski put it, was to overcome the obstacles he had met in trying to explain himself to other people. He had made it plain to them that he had honourable intentions, but they did not hear, or seemed not to understand, or did not believe him. How could this have been so? It is alarmingly easy to see the turns of thought in which Rousseau was trapped when he failed, as he supposed, to make himself understood. If self-understanding is immediately to hand, only sheer deceit, a wilful desire to mislead, would withhold it from others. Since he was not deceiving others, and only desired to reveal himself to them, their failure to understand him could only represent malice on their part. He could see no reason why they should be so malicious; but then that must have been because they had made it impossible for him to understand what they were doing, which proved that they were malicious. The alternative was to see others as mere automata, having no intelligible motives at all, and indeed this is an idea with which he briefly tries to comfort himself in the *Rêveries*.[20] But his settled conclusion in his last years was that those who systematically did not understand him were wicked, members of an evil conspiracy. He was inevitably left with the impression, which perhaps he did not really want but which certainly irritated others, that he was more virtuous than most people he had to deal with.

It followed that there was virtually no-one with whom Rousseau could live. His own sincerity would lay him open to others' malice, and indeed he would be laid open to violating that sincerity himself: one motive for his retiring from social life, as we saw, was that he wanted to avoid the encounters that, given his weakness and embarrassment, could lead him into lying. The sincere man of sensibility ends up alienated from society altogether, where "society" seems to mean, simply, everyone else. But sincerity was supposed to be at the heart of virtue, and to conclude unconditionally that sincerity must exclude life with other people would be a disaster. If the man of sincerity is, as things are, alienated from society, then there has to be an account of "society" that explains what is wrong with it, and how it involves a perversion of what people might otherwise be. This defines a task of discovering what form of society might make genuine sincerity possible, and this is a major aim of Rousseau's political theory. In the *Discourse on the Origins and Basis of Inequality* he particularly stresses the role of excessive inequality of property in corrupting society, the influence of luxury, and the development of *amour-propre*, competitive self-assertion. In *The Social Contract*, "taking men as they are and laws as they might be," as he significantly says at the beginning of the book, he tries to find forms of political organization, suitable to different places and peoples, that will allow the expression of a general will which is necessarily virtuous and transcends personal self-interest, and nevertheless allows every individual to be free. Such a polity implies that the real self, which will be sincerely revealed under its influence, will be virtuous. Freedom will consist in living in accordance with one's real self, so that laws which elicit that real self, allow virtue to express itself and not be suppressed by the distortions of a corrupt environment, will, in the famous phrase, "force one to be free."

It is not altogether surprising that Rousseau has sometimes been associated with the most coercive aspects of the French Revolution. The "citizenly virtue" strain in his ideas has been supposed to have encouraged the Terror; some who thought this, Leninists and others, have taken it to be a compliment to him, but most have not.[21]

His name was indeed often invoked in the revolution, and honours were extended to his memory; Robespierre gave a eulogy of him in his discourse on the Supreme Being on 18 floréal of the Year II (May 7, 1794). The story is told that Napoleon, visiting as First Consul a room at Ermenonville in which Rousseau lived at the end of his life, said, "He was a madman, your Rousseau; it was he who brought us to where we are now." Recent writers have made it clear that he was invoked as much by more moderate elements as by the most radical, and that the Jacobins knew very well that some of their most distinctive positions were at odds with his ideas. Nevertheless, it is agreed there is a general atmosphere or tone drawn from his writings that greatly influenced the thought and the rhetoric of the revolution; in particular it invoked the alliance that he sought, and was driven by his conception of sincerity to seek, between citizenly qualities and the sensibility of individual private life. With Rousseau, Bernard Marin has written, virtue "takes on at once the characteristics of Mucius Scaevola and those of Julie . . . the mingling of these two conceptions gives to Spartiate virtue the charms of subjectivity and sentiment."[22]

There is an obvious tension between these elements, and it is the same tension that is to be felt in the *Confessions*. If there is such a thing as the "real self" of an individual, what reason is there to think that it must coincide with an underlying character of honour, considerateness, and compassion? If real sincerity reveals the real self, that may not be, as Rousseau assumed, a citizenly self, and sincerity may not be what a shared political life requires, but rather the reverse, as cynics of the *ancien régime* took for granted. In any case—and this is a further question—what guarantee is there that sincere self-declaration will reveal the real self? As Rousseau himself eventually came to suspect, one may be in the dark about what one most wants or most deeply needs. If there is such a condition as having one's life or work coincide with these realities, then that may go beyond sincerity as honest self-declaration. Indeed, it may not get that far—as Lionel Trilling points out in his brilliant and still indispensable book on these questions, the shepherd in Wordsworth's poem *Michael*, stricken with grief by his son's desertion to the city, reveals this condition without statement or self-inquiry, in a way that makes any question of his *sincerity* indecently inappropriate. "[W]e are impelled to use some word which denotes the nature of this being and which accounts for the high value we put upon it," Trilling writes. "The word we employ for this purpose is 'authenticity.'"[23] However, authenticity does not have to be, as the shepherd's was, inarticulate. Indeed, the whole point of authenticity as a characteristically modern value has lain in the attempt to regain in some reflective form the unexpressed certainties which are supposed to have structured the pre-modern world. But, however authenticity is expressed as an ideal, it is clear that its demands will not necessarily coincide with the demands of anyone else, or of anyone else's authenticity.

It has been suggested that Julie, the heroine of *La nouvelle Héloïse*, embodies a recognition of this by Rousseau himself.[24] The interest of the book lies not very much in its lengthy and improbable philosophical excursions, but in the layered ambiguities that surround Julie's passion for her lover Saint-Preux, the demands that she accepts in giving him up and marrying someone else, and the relations of the after-life of that passion to her feelings for her drily virtuous husband, and to her religion. The letters between her and Saint-Preux in the last part of the book, including the one that she writes on her deathbed, leave it compellingly indeterminate how her feelings are to be described. The story, as it is put before us in the letters, suggests a reconciling and ennobling answer, but it insists on nothing. The question is certainly raised, of who Julie is. At the moment of her marriage, she says that the experience of the religious service has restored her from a "forgetfulness of herself" that was involved in her affair with Saint-Preux, and that "the helpful hand" of the Supreme Being has "given her back to herself despite herself."[25] This experience survives through the novel as a decisive moment of self-recognition, but at the end, all the same, room is left (if no more than room) for an idea that the "real" Julie was not the virtuous wife and household organizer, nor the moderately ecstatic *dévote*, but the bearer of a dangerously incurable passion for her former lover. That idea would divide authenticity not just from what is regarded as virtue, but from sincere self-declaration, for certainly we are to understand that Julie was as sincere as she could be in affirming that she was the first of these things and denying that she was the last.

For Rousseau there remained unresolved tensions between individuality and the demands of virtue, but he certainly wanted there to be a link between sincerity as authenticity, and virtue with its familiar implications of trustworthiness, honour, and benevolence. Trilling wrote: "The ideal of authentic personal being stands at the very centre of Rousseau's thought. Yet I think that its presence there ... is rather too abstract, or too moderate, to command the modern imagination"; and he referred to Rousseau's "abiding commitment to an ideal of patrician civility."[26] Some later ideas, however, offered authenticity in a more distinctive form, in which it represented an heroic ideal of coinciding with oneself and one's deepest needs or impulses, whatever they might be, to the exclusion of other demands. There is no reason for those needs or impulses to yield motives that are well-disposed to others—they are whatever they are. Moreover, by this stage authenticity no longer has a reason even to sustain a connection with sincerity as behaving truthfully toward others: telling the truth to other people has no more claim than anything else to constrain the demands of self-expression. In its grander and more literary forms, this was essentially and unsurprisingly a minority way of life, a kind of aristocratic, typically aesthetic, libertinism.

Authenticity survives as an individual ideal, if many of the forms it now finds are distinctly run-down. In those forms, it is often taken as a target by neo-conservatives who attack outlooks that abandon commitment, public service, and a sense of right, for a concern with "Me" and narcissistic satisfaction.[27] However, it is very unclear that what is being attacked by these critics is any one thing, or the same as the aesthetic antinomianism that was indeed a version of the ideal of authenticity. The outlook under attack has been said to involve the idea that hypocrisy is a specially significant vice, more significant than egocentricity. That idea has something to do with authenticity, and it certainly represents a modern ideal, one that I mentioned in chapter 1 as a starting point of this book. But *hypocrisy* is an offence in public or interpersonal relations, a violation of sincerity, and while an ideal that is opposed to hypocrisy is compatible with egocentricity (I can make it honestly clear to the other that what I am concerned about is myself), it involves a demand of truthfulness between people which certainly transcends mere narcissism or self-concern. In this it is true to its origins in Rousseau.

I shall try to get a better focus on authenticity as a personal ideal in section 5 of this chapter. I shall take up a question there that has been lurking in the discussion up to this point: how far can the demands of an authentic life be regarded as a matter for *self-discovery*? If it is a matter of discovery—as we might imagine Julie, for instance, realizing in her last illness that she had betrayed herself in giving up her lover for her virtuous life with Wolmar—what kind of discovery is it? What kind of truth is discovered? And how exactly is the discovery of this truth, if that is what is involved, related to sincerity—indeed, to Sincerity as it has concerned us up to now, as the virtue of the free declaration of belief? Authenticity, or at least the pursuit of authenticity as a reflective ideal, seems to turn on a notion of honesty that links sincerity and a courageous confrontation with the truth, and we need to ask how this can be. Before we can get to those questions, however, we have to consider another picture of the self, one that comes historically from the same world as Rousseau's but is very different.

3. *Diderot and* Rameau's Nephew

I mentioned in chapter 1 a certain image of the Enlightenment, in terms of the tyranny of theory, where theory is identified with an external "panoptical" view of everything, including society. There were of course such tendencies in the Enlightenment, and, in more narrowly political terms, some of its figures, notably Voltaire, were identified with despotism.[28] But it is only if the Enlightenment is identified with its own most scientistic images of itself, or, rather, with the typical nineteenth-century appropriation of those images, that these features should lead us to reject it. It is from nineteenth-century debates that we have inherited the dichotomies of mechanical vs. organic, instrumental reason vs. feeling, discursive description vs. expression, and so on. There are no doubt some connections in which we need to hold on to these dichotomies, in particular to assert their right-hand side, but certainly we should stop using them to assail the Enlightenment, a phenomenon which entirely transcends them.

If anything is emblematic of the Enlightenment, it must be the *Encyclopédie*. At the centre of it was Denis Diderot. He invented it and was its editor, along with d'Alembert, but he did most of the work; he promoted it and defended it from the censors, wrote a lot of it, plagiarized other books to put into it, went hungry and was sent to jail for it. The *Encyclopédie* was not, for all that, one man's work; it was an enterprise, and its organization and reception constituted a complex social fact.[29] But it is interesting what the man who had this relation to it was like: funny, passionate, disordered, sometimes sentimental and sometimes, as it would seem to a modern taste, cruelly malicious. Besides the many articles for the *Encyclopédie*, he wrote some very unsuccessful plays to which he was greatly attached; novels, including the story of catastrophic inconsequentiality *Jacques le fataliste*; several philosophical pieces; and some works which are formally related in a very original way to their content, such as the story called "This Is Not a Story," and the *Supplément au voyage de Bougainville*, a dialogue which deploys its participants as an essential part of what it has to say about sex, colonialism, and primitivism. With his *Salons*, he virtually invented the genre of art criticism. But what concerns us is in particular *Rameau's Nephew*, a masterpiece that is still perhaps less familiar, at any rate to philosophical discussion, than it should be.

It was not published in Diderot's lifetime and in fact first appeared in a German translation made by Goethe from a manuscript lent to him by Schiller, a manuscript which then disappeared. Only an imperfect French version remained until 1891, when a perfect copy in Diderot's hand was found by chance in a bookseller's box on the Quai Voltaire in Paris. It presents a conversation. One party is "Moi," the narrator, whom we can, if we like, take to be Diderot, so long as we do not make too much of it. The other, "Lui," is Jean-François Rameau, the nephew of the famous composer. Rameau is an extraordinary figure. As the narrator puts it,

> he is one of the oddest characters in this land of ours where God has
> not been sparing of them. He is a compound of high and low, good

sense and insanity. The notions of what is decent and what is not must be strangely muddled in his head, for the good qualities nature has given him he displays without ostentation, and the bad ones without shame.[30]

He keeps going by flattering and acting as a kind of court jester to the rich (he has just been thrown out of the household of a wealthy official called Bertin and Bertin's mistress Mlle Hus of the Comédie-Française, a ménage sometimes referred to as the Bertin-hus). His appearance, his clothes, and his build vary greatly from time to time depending on his fortunes. He is resentful and envious, particularly of his famous uncle,[31] but also maniacally cheerful. He has wild swings of mood even in this one conversation. He has a deafening voice and amazing powers of mimicry, and in the course of the dialogue he goes into several turns, toward the end rendering all the parts of several pieces from French opera. Between these performances, the dialogue moves with great ease and freedom over all sorts of topics—virtue and vice, sincerity and hypocrisy; philosophy and scientific materialism; French and Italian opera.

Rameau's Nephew has caused critics a lot of anxiety. There has been a question of what the dialogue is supposed to be about; but it is not clear why there has to be any one thing that it is about. Critics are worried, too, about the point of view we are supposed to adopt. But it is already clear from the surface of the conversational drama that neither Lui nor Moi is an authority figure. Moi, though he makes various interpretative and sometimes condemnatory remarks in asides, is a real collaborator in some of Rameau's more outrageous opinions. Lui has had some encouragement from Moi when he gets going on the psychology of virtue:

> [Y]ou think that happiness is the same for all. What a strange illusion! Yours presupposes a certain fanciful [*romanesque*] turn of mind that we don't all possess, a special type of soul, a peculiar taste. You dignify this oddity with the name of virtue and you call it philosophy. But are virtue and philosophy made for everyone?[32]

> . . . why do we so often see the pious so hard, so tiresome, so unsociable? It is because they have imposed on themselves a task that is un-

natural to them. They are miserable, and when you are miserable yourself you make others miserable as well. That does not suit me, or my patrons. I have to be gay, adaptable, agreeable, amusing, odd. Virtue commands respect, and respect is not fun.[33]

A recurrent theme is that Rameau is not inconsistent:

Devil take me if I know at the end what I am. In general, I have a mind as round as a ball and a character as straight as a willow: never false if I have the slightest interest in being true, never true if I have the slightest interest in being false . . . I have never reflected in my life, before I say something, or while I am saying it, or after I have said it.[34]

And the narrator says of him in summary:

In all this there were many things that people think and on which they act, but which they do not say. That indeed was the most striking difference between this man and most of those that we meet. He owned up to the vices he had, and which others have—he was not a hypocrite. He was neither more nor less abominable than they; he was simply more open and more consistent, and sometimes profound in his depravity.[35]

As Wilma Anderson has said, *Rameau's Nephew* is a text that each reader has to process for himself or herself.[36] That this should be so is entirely true to it. One thing we can do with it is to turn it to the interests of philosophy, and there are no doubt many ways of doing that. I hope that my way of doing so will at least give it fairer treatment than it received in its most famous encounter with philosophy, when it turned up, though not explicitly by name, in Hegel's *Phenomenology*.[37] Hegel is contemptuous of Moi, whom he takes to stand for conventional and unreflective morality, while he sees in Lui the historically higher phenomenon of the unhappy consciousness, which embodies modern reflective subjectivity and separates itself in irony and division from accepted circumstances of social power. In setting Lui entirely positively against Moi and representing him as the more reflective of the two, Hegel's reading is simply untrue to the character as he appears in the dialogue: Lui is to a significant degree more open and spontaneous, less given to crippling reflection, than Moi. Hegel is not in fact interested in making such a discrimination within the dramatic texture of the conversation. His purpose is to use Lui in order to illustrate a stage in the history of consciousness, and the two characters are read simply in terms of the contrast, which Hegel saw as an historical succession, between "the honest soul" and, in Trilling's words, a "disintegrated, alienated and distraught consciousness."[38] This is bound to lose the sense of what it is for the narrator to be engaged with Rameau and to conspire with him in generating this conversation. By neglecting this aspect of the work as a piece of writing, Hegel's reading also loses a view of some of its major philosophical ideas, and that is a loss which affects his own purpose: the ideas might contribute to an understanding of the history of consciousness.

Some of the ideas that I recover from it are these. Rameau is true to himself in at least this sense, that he is conspicuously not self-deceived. We might say that he *possesses* a lot of truth about himself. He is also to an unusual degree sincere. He certainly flatters and lies, but he is unusual in the degree that he admits that he does so. He *reveals* a lot of truth about himself. In these qualities, he offers an exceptionally clear example of sincerity in its basic form of uninhibited expression or enactment, rather than in the form of reporting the findings of self-examination. He is unguardedly spontaneous, too, in his second-order or reflective comments. The model of sincerity as uninhibited spontaneity even applies to his flattery and deceit. In those activities, as he makes clear, the expectations of his audience make him actually become, to order and for a while, what they require; his availability to them takes the form, not of a systematic misreporting of his states, but rather of an instantaneous impersonation, a improvisation of another short-lived personality. What he is not is a unity, all of a piece. He is, to a greater extent than Moi, "disintegrated."

These characteristics of Rameau immediately raise those questions to which Rousseau, most of the time, assumed such optimistic answers, of how much morally and socially is secured by either sincerity or authenticity. The example of Rameau certainly shows that those qualities cannot be guaranteed to serve the purposes of virtue—co-operation, self-transcendence, social dignity. But it raises a more radical question, how far the self can be expected to be receptive to morality at all. One's relations to other people's interests will be a matter of temperament, and for many temperaments this can be a strain, a matter of rather desperate contingency. (On this theme, there is in the dialogue a refrain from Moi of reassurance in the style of Hume, about the pleasures, to people like him, of virtue. The reader will ask, as Rameau asks, how reassured he or she feels.)

Further, it is not simply a matter of a character that is revealed once and for all in sincere self-disclosure. There is no self that is revealed on the spot. Rameau, we have been told, is consistent, always the same, but that is because he freely and unashamedly expresses very different things at different times. Diderot was always attracted to a picture of the self as something constantly shifting and reacting and altering; as a swarm of bees; as a clavichord or harp or other instrument, with the wind or some such force playing on it. It is near to a picture that Nietzsche offers, of our desires and needs groping around and reaching out inside us, as though they formed a kind of polyp.[39] This means that the declaration at a given instant of self can be only a declaration of self at that instant. As Rameau, Lui, reminds us, feelings, needs, passions, identifications actually come and go: in some people less than in others, and in most people less than in him. Those people are, as one might say, steadier. But what is it to be steadier? How is it brought about, and what are its workings?

The fact that we can ask this question shows that there is more than one level on which we need to consider Diderot's outlook. On the one hand, Rameau is indeed a remarkable and unusual individual, "one of the oddest characters in this land of ours." Hegel took him to be emblematic or representative of a disintegrated and unhappy consciousness that was peculiarly modern, not because Hegel supposed modern people to be typically just like Rameau, but because that character could be seen as an extreme enactment of what modern culture involves, a self-consciousness which can no longer feel unreflectively at home in its social environment. On this showing, Rameau is historically and not just individually special, because he represents a special cultural phenomenon. However, below any such differences, whether individual or historical, there must be a general human psychology in terms of which we can understand these variations. (We may recall the idea discussed in chapter 2, that cultural variation implies an underlying psychology capable of being acculturated.) On Diderot's view, as I understand him, it is a universal truth, not just a special feature of modernity, that human beings have an inconstant mental constitution that needs to be steadied by society and interaction with other people. Different people, and people in different circumstances, are steadied by these forces to a greater or lesser degree; modernity, perhaps, makes it specially hard, or hard in a special way, to steady them. This picture of the mind implies that it has relations to other people and to society that are quite different from any imagined by Rousseau, and this implies different conceptions of both sincerity and authenticity.

4. *Steadying the Mind*

What Rameau declares at one time may be markedly different from what he declares at another, and his declarations may all be sincere: at least, he spontaneously and uninhibitedly comes out with what is in his mind. But if his declarations are too whimsically inconstant, there comes a question of what kind of thing is in his mind. With regard to beliefs, in particular, it is not simply that a person will seem inconsistent or contradictory or hopeless if they change too often; rather, if they change too often for internal reasons, they will not be beliefs but rather something like propositional moods.

With many states that count as beliefs, such as memories of particular experiences, knowledge of standing states of the world, and the retention of pieces of information, it is their relation to their subject matter, their mere semantics and epistemology, that requires them to be steady if they are to count as beliefs at all. They could not be understood as containing and offering information about those states of affairs unless they were relatively unaffected by the weather of the mind. This is why, in the State of Nature story, in emphasizing the exchange and pooling of factual information, we could take for granted that the dispositions of belief were relatively steady. But there are other states that may be counted as beliefs or opinions—narrative understandings of the past, for instance, or estimates of people, or evaluative outlooks. With these, we do not always find what philosophers often seem to demand, an unchanging dispositional state, steadily ready to be activated in declaration or action. As Diderot says elsewhere, in the *Conversation between d'Alembert and Diderot*, "our real opinion is not one in which we have never wavered, but the one to which we have most regularly returned."[40]

Nevertheless, our declarations do need to be patterned in some ways rather than others if they are to count as declarations of *any* sort of belief or opinion. When we leave those relatively straightforward cases, such as the retention of information, where the identification of a person's beliefs is strongly controlled by the subject matter and the person's relations to it, we need some other assurance that for the most part sincerity in the form of spontaneous declaration will have some validity over time. For the most part, in characters steadier than Rameau, we have it, but we have it in a form that is socially shaped and supported. The assurance rests in the practice which socializes people into having such beliefs. If what I uninhibitedly declare at a given moment can be taken by myself or anyone else as a declaration of something which I believe, that is because there is a practice that firms up the expression of the immediate state into something that has a future. It is what enables us, most of the time, coherently to make such declarations as declarations of belief, and to read them in what other people say.

The basic mechanism depends on the fact that there are others who need to rely on our dispositions, and we want them to be able to rely on our dispositions because we, up to a point, want to rely on theirs. We learn to present ourselves to others, and consequently also to ourselves, as people who have moderately steady outlooks or beliefs. This picture of course does not represent a calculation that individuals make. As we have seen in developing the State of Nature, it is not, and could not be, a matter of working out from egoism; except in very desperate circumstances, everyone is brought up in a world in which he or she shares such needs with some others. When we have learned to have such beliefs, and we are asked what our belief is, we may simply come out with an expression of one that is sincere in the most basic sense of its being spontaneous and uninhibited, and that fact itself will encourage us to stand by it, to present ourselves and go on presenting ourselves as people who have that view. Sometimes, of course, nothing may present itself in that way; or if it does, we may hesitate to let others rely on it, that is to say, to commit ourselves to it. It can be unclear to us even at the instant what we think we believe. One possibility then is to interpret ourselves in much the spirit that we interpret others or others interpret us, with the small but real advantage (one of the many denied to us by behaviourism) of having a sense of what at the instant we might be disposed to express, and of what expressions at that instant we might be disposed to inhibit. So we must leave behind the assumption that we first and immediately have a transparent self-understanding, and then go on either to give other people a sincere revelation of our belief from which they understand us (or, as Rousseau bitterly found, misunderstand us), or else dissimulate in a way that will mislead them. At a more basic level, we are all together in the social activity of mutually stabilizing our declarations and moods and impulses into becoming such things as beliefs and relatively steady attitudes.

I have started with what I called "beliefs and opinions" in the sense of such things as evaluations, and narrative and personal understandings. But the same point stretches, as one might say, both backwards and forwards from there: backwards into straightforwardly factual beliefs, and forwards even into our desires. Many factual beliefs, as I have said, are simply controlled by the conditions under which they are acquired and, in relation to that, their semantics. The immediacy with which an assertion presents itself—its degree of spontaneity "with regard to *what*," as I put it in chapter 4[41]—is reliably linked, a lot of the time, to the truth of the assertion, or at least to the warrant that the speaker has for it, in the sense that if the belief turns out to be false, there is an epistemically convincing explanation of how he came by it (an explanation, that is to say, which is consistent with his having exercised on this occasion those powers that make him in general reliable in acquiring and retaining information about such matters). This is not to say that the speaker himself decides whether a given assertion is true by relying on the spontaneity with which he is disposed to come out with it, though there are cases in which that is so. The system works in general by the speaker's being disposed to come out with an assertion which is in fact likely, in virtue of that fact, to be true. However, this by no means always works. Leaving aside the cases in which the speaker is convinced but merely wrong, there are cases in which an assertion readily presents itself, but he has some reason to wonder whether it is true. Again, there are, very importantly, cases in which no definite *assertion* presents itself, but some proposition, a thought or content, does. (We shall see a further significance in this possibility later on.) Here, the speaker may reflect on other reasons that bear on the matter, to decide whether he does believe it—where that means, in such a case, whether it is true. He may simply want to know whether it is true. Very often, however, there is another reason why he should reflect in this way, that he is engaged in trustful conversation with another who relies on him, and the question is whether he can give that person to believe the proposition. In doing that, he may well, in such a case, give himself to believe it as well. It is the presence and needs of others that help us to construct even our factual beliefs.[42]

It is a further implication of Diderot's picture of the mind that similar factors can help us to construct our desires. If we consider what is involved in this, it can give us, also, a deeper insight than we have had so far into the nature of wishful thinking.

Ever since Plato, there has been a tendency to suppose that the irrational agent is to be understood in terms of a conflict between elements in the mind which act, at least to some extent, as separate agencies. These agencies may themselves be described as "irrational," but this means merely that they are the cause of irrationality in the person in whose mind they live. Desire, for Plato, was irrational because it was the enemy of the rational principle. If one looks at things simply from desire's point of view, it is far from clear that it is irrational in trying to extend its hold over the system as a whole; from that point of view, it is in rather the same position as Dawkins's "selfish" genes.

There are well-known problems in modelling the individual agent in this way, on the lines of a quarrelsome council. There is a persistent difficulty that the various internal agencies demand a more elaborate intentionality than the model can allow—they tend to turn into people, whose behaviour itself needs to be explained. But there is another objection, which is less often heard. The divided, conflicted, and confused agent is not always, or even typically, one in whom several different and equally organized voices make conflicting claims. Rather, his states of mind are themselves unfocussed or variably directed, and they have differing influences on his behaviour at different times and in different conditions. The political picture of the soul implies identifiable members of the mind's assembly, but in the typical case, as Diderot recognized, the agent is awash with many images, many excitements, merging fears and fantasies that dissolve into one another. To sort things out to a point at which they seem like an assembly of definite and identifiable voices is already an achievement. A deeper account will offer a less organized state of affairs than is given in the political analogy, and Diderot's images can lead us to that account.

There is a difference between desires and mere wishes. In our dealings up to now (particularly in chapter 6) with wishes and wishful thinking and the disciplines that are needed to counter their subversions, we have used the idea, which is sensible enough, that if one knows that one cannot possibly bring about or affect a certain thing, then that thing can be matter only for a wish. There is a complication in this idea, however, which has not mattered up to now: that what is possible for an agent, in the sense of what is practically possible for him, is in part a function of his desires. Many things are indeed absolutely impossible for any agent, or for a particular agent. Leaving those aside, however, what I *can* do is going to depend on constraints set up by my other aims, my commitments, and my patterns of life. When a person says that he *cannot* take a winter sports holiday in January, he may well not mean that there is simply no way in which such an outcome is accessible to him given the laws of nature; he may mean, entirely reasonably, that in order to take such a holiday he would have to give up his job, sacrifice his savings, abandon his family, or generally rearrange his life to an extent in which the idea of placing a winter holiday into it would become entirely meaningless.

Consider the context of a particular deliberation. A desire will be a state of an agent, the content of which he can regard at various stages of the deliberation as being potentially satisfied by the actions that will flow from the deliberation. A (mere) wish will have a content that cannot be satisfied in that context. Now since the process of deliberation itself decides what can and cannot be satisfied within that context, there will be some states that start in the deliberation as desires but end (for the time being, at least) as wishes. Others, such as the standing aims against which the agent measures all the possible courses of action, remain desires throughout; yet others are never more than wishes. In addition to all these, there must be states of mind that have neither been definitely advanced as candidates for satisfaction nor definitely dismissed, and these too can be called "wishes," but without the implication of a *mere* wish, that is to say, something with a content which at least in this context is not going to be satisfied.

Desires may be said to involve "commitments" in this sense, that the agent, in a given context of deliberation, is committed to considering a desire as a candidate for satisfaction in the outcome of that deliberation. Rather similarly, an agent's beliefs are states (or rather their content) which he is committed to holding true in the context of his deliberation. These truth-commitments themselves will often not all be in place at the beginning. In the course of considering what to do, the agent will inquire what is possible, and what the consequences and conditions of various actions may be; he may do this in reflection or by further investigation, but in either case he will entertain the ideas of various outcomes or processes as possible or relevant. Just because this is a practical deliberation, he will have some attitudes toward these outcomes and processes, attitudes which are themselves a function of the desires and wishes that shape the deliberation. Among his states of mind will be fears or hopes. If the agent simply does not know whether P, but he recognizes that it would be very good for the satisfaction of his desires if P, then it is presumably one of his hopes, and his fears have much the same structure, running in the opposite sense. What he hopes or fears he does not yet believe; rather, he entertains the idea of the outcome or the process with a positive or a negative attitude, and, whatever degree of probability he assigns to it, it is less than enough to warrant his belief in it. In this sense, he is not committed to it.

Hopes and fears seem to involve at least some rudimentary kind of probability estimate, but there is a further state that is more primitive than this and even less committal. A state of affairs, an outcome, or a process may come before the agent's mind, either on the way to being assessed, or, perhaps, merely as passing through, and since it comes through in the context of desire and deliberation, it will very probably carry with it an attitude; indeed, its coming through is likely to be explained by an attitude. If the attitude is favourable, such a content seems itself to be indistinguishable from a wish. If this is right, it seems that the wish can play a role both in the register of desire and in the register of belief. To put it more accurately, a content, relating to an outcome or a process which is relevant to the deliberation and to the affective state in which the deliberation is conducted, comes before the mind, carrying with it an attitude that is part of the affective state. This does not represent, yet, any commitment of the agent, in the sense that I have used the term: it is not yet either a belief or a desire. *But it may be on the way to becoming either.* As a result of one kind of process, this picture may come to embody a belief of the agent's about an outcome, for instance, that it is genuinely possible; as a result of another, it will come to express a desire that the outcome should occur. Those different processes will typically include some conscious reflection, different in the two cases, but they certainly consist of much more besides. There are two routes, leading respectively to committed belief, supported by evidence, and to clear-headed desire, articulated with reasons, and the boundaries between the two routes are not sustained merely by conscious processes, still less simply given in advance.

If this is on the right lines, it has significant consequences. First, it suggests that wishful thinking is not at all mysterious. It turns out, in fact, to be precisely well-named: it is thinking full of wishes, and since all practical thinking is full of wishes, in the most general sense of the term in which wishes can occur on the route both to belief and to desire, there is no mystery about the fact that (to put it crudely) an agent may easily find himself committed to their content in the wrong mode. Second, it is a misunderstanding of one-person practical reasoning—one encouraged, certainly, by political models of deliberation—to think of it in terms of a set of formed and committed desires adjudicated in the light of formed and committed beliefs. Rather, the process of arriving at a practical conclusion typically involves a shifting and indeterminate set of wishes, hopes, and fears, in addition to the more clearly defined architecture of desire and belief. If we think only in terms of desire and belief, we may well overlook subtle problems within the economy of desire itself, notably the fact that to distinguish between a desire and a mere wish is an achievement, and, to a significant degree, a cognitive achievement. For that reason, and more generally because of the discipline that is involved in maintaining the barriers between the route to desire and the route to belief, we can recognize that the virtues we need in considering what to do coincide at deep levels with the virtues that we need in inquiring into anything, the virtues of truth.

Individual deliberation is not a peculiar kind of internal many-person deliberation, and of course it is not ordinary many-person deliberation, in which we get together to decide what *we* shall do. But the fact that it is inherently open to wishful thinking, and that it needs the virtues of truth as much as purely factual inquiries need them, helps to explain the very obvious truth that thinking about what one individual should do can usefully involve more than one person: we can think about what I should do. This is not just because you may have experience and knowledge which I lack, but because your wishes are not mine—possibly not in their content, certainly not in their effects. In practical reasoning as much as elsewhere we can help to sustain each other's sense of reality, both in stopping wishes' becoming beliefs when they should not, and also in helping some wishes rather than others to become desires. Of course, necessarily, there can be a negative side to this same process: in helping you to decide, I may reinforce your fantasy, and we may conspire in projecting wishes into a deceptive social hologram.

5. *Authenticity and Other People*

Even though some forms of delusion are collective, this does not mean that one best keeps a hold on reality in solitude. The quarrel between Rousseau and Diderot started when in February 1775 Diderot sent Rousseau a copy of his new play *Le fils naturel*, in which one character says to another who, like Rousseau, had decided to live by himself in the country: "Look into your heart, and it will tell you that the good man is in society, and that only the bad man is alone." Though Rousseau claims in the *Confessions* to have sent Diderot a mild and friendly letter, he misrepresents Diderot's apologetic, if rather breezy, reply to it, and he makes it very clear that the incident rankled. From then on, he felt only growing suspicion and dislike.[43]

The occasion of the conflict was deeply appropriate. The perversities of Rousseau's conception of sincerity did lead to his solitude. It was not that his views in themselves entailed a solitary life. It was of course his own self-deceptions and psychological peculiarities that drove him away from others, but what Diderot understood and Rousseau did not was that Rousseau's picture of the world did not allow the right place for his own or anyone else's weaknesses and idiosyncrasies. He wanted each person's life to be authentically his or her own, a life with which that person was fully identified, and he needed that life to coincide with the demands of virtue. But his idea that sincerity could in a way guarantee the other virtues, together with his conception of it as simply the spontaneous declaration of what was immediately evident to oneself, inevitably led to disappointment and self-deception, and explained more than anything else the general suspicion that his rejection of the world aroused; it came to represent not just a personal limitation or a determined insistence on the conditions of doing his work, but a crisis of moral egoism.

The threatening political theory of civic virtue that is presented in *The Social Contract* only reinforces those fears and suspicions. It claims in the strongest terms to reconcile individuality and the demands of social co-operation, but its attempt to do so rests in the end on a desperate assertion, that I will coincide with myself only if I coincide with others, and this is a mere fantasy, a triumph of the wish. As Huyghens brilliantly described Descartes's scientific theory, with its hopeful projection of pure geometry onto the world, as "ce roman de la physique," one might say that *The Social Contract* is a political romance, except that it is less truthful than some of Rousseau's own fictional writings.

Because Diderot's picture of the mind, and hence of sincerity itself, makes better sense of idiosyncrasy, it can actually help us to make better sense of social and political co-operation. It installs a social dimension into the construction of beliefs, attitudes, even desires. These are the materials of idiosyncrasy, and the lesson is that we need each other in order to be anybody. There is indeed no straight road from that lesson to the demands of social co-operation. As we have seen several times before in this study, and *Rameau's Nephew* should dramatically remind us, such theoretical considerations, whether about the constitution of the mind, the nature of assertion, or whatever, get us as far as they get us and no further. If the impact of the social world has made some man into an idiosyncratically uncooperative and self-centred figure, there are no reasonings drawn from this process that can rationally require him to be something else. What they may be able to do is to give us ideas of how to make him into something else, and perhaps to discourage others from being like him, to the extent—and this is a real question—that we really want to discourage everyone from being like him.

Steadiness, as *Rameau's Nephew* reminds us, has its costs, sometimes in hypocrisy, frustration, and bitterness, but some degree of it is so important to human interaction and to a manageable life that it is not surprising that much effort should be devoted to constructing relatively steady beliefs and outlooks out of the shifting sounds of Diderot's psychic musical instruments. In different historical and social circumstances, various structures may serve to build a self that will at once make sense of episodic feelings and thoughts—render the subject, as I have put it, steadier—and also relate the person to others in ways that will serve the purposes of co-operation and trust. Since this aim took on specifically modern forms in the eighteenth century, it has come to involve two problems that are particularly acute in their combination. One is a political problem, of finding a basis for a shared life which will be neither too oppressively coercive (the requirement of freedom) nor dependent on mythical legitimations (the requirement of enlightenment). The other is a personal problem, of stabilizing the self into a form that will indeed fit with these political and social ideas, but which can at the same time create a life that presents itself to a reflective individual as worth living; in particular, one that does so by reinventing in a more reflective and demystified world assurances that were taken in an earlier time (or so we imagine) as matters of necessity. Rousseau foresaw the need, but at the political level he provided not much more than a mere assertion to meet it, linking in one gesture sincere self-declaration, morality, and the politics of the general will.

At the political level, one powerful bearer of the idea of authenticity has been, and very much remains, the politics of group or national identity. An identity in this sense is something that a person individually has, but it is something that is essentially shared: it is a group identity, such as an ethnic, a religious, or (in certain cultural surroundings) a sexual identity. People who think of themselves in such terms think of their affiliation, their relations to the group, as representing in some sense what they really are, and they might indeed say that it is what they essentially are. Yet it is important to the ways in which these thoughts run that this idea of one's essence is not related in any very simple way to one's diachronic personal identity. An essential property in the standard metaphysical sense—the property of being a human being, for instance—is something that those who have it cannot possibly lack if they still exist; if I am around in the world at all, then I am in it as a human being. It is sometimes said that if an ethnic culture or way of life is destroyed, the people who earlier lived under it will have lost their identity: it may be said that as a people, they have ceased to exist. But this cannot mean that each of them has ceased to exist, and this is not a mere philosophical quibble, for the complaint about the destruction of their way of life precisely implies that the individual people will exist: the complaint is directed to the way in which they will exist, as culturally impoverished and robbed of the expression of their identity.

An identity in this sense is standardly understood by social psychology as a social categorization to which value is attached, but this is something of an understatement. Someone may set great store by his membership of the golf club, but he would be in a bad way if such a thing came to constitute his identity. To form an identity, the social category has to be rich enough to permeate and affect many of the most important aspects of life—at the limit, to form the structure of a whole way of life. Rather as a "natural kind" is not an arbitrary classification but represents a significant and explanatory grouping of properties, so an identity can be seen as a social or cultural kind.

It is related to this that an identity within a group cannot simply be a matter of the individual's decision. If I could join some group merely at will, that in itself could not constitute an identity. As befits something that comes close to being my essence, it must be something that I can discover, but mere factual discovery will not be enough, either. I might agree that as a matter of fact I did belong to some ethnic group, but be quite indifferent to the idea that it gave me, or contributed to, my identity. The narrator of Philip Roth's *The Human Stain* says of Coleman Silk, the principal character:

> At Howard he'd discovered that he wasn't just a nigger to Washington D.C.—as if that shock weren't strong enough, he'd discovered at Howard that he was a Negro as well. A Howard Negro at that. Overnight the raw I was part of a we with all of the we's overbearing solidity, and he didn't want anything to do with it or with the next oppressive we that came along either. You finally leave home, the Ur of we, and you find *another* we? . . . No. No. He saw the fate awaiting him, and he wasn't having it. Grasped it intuitively and recoiled spontaneously. You can't let the big they impose its bigotry on you any more than you can let the little they become a we and impose its ethics on you. Not the tyranny of the we and its we-talk and everything that the we wants to pile on your head. Never for him the tyranny of the we that is dying to suck you in, the coercive, inclusive, historical, inescapable moral *we* with its insidious *E Pluribus Unum*. Neither the they of Woolworth's nor the we of Howard. Instead the raw I with all its agility. *Self*-discovery—that was the punch to the labonz.[44]

If in good faith and without evasion someone can live with such a rejection (and whether Coleman Silk could do so is in part the subject of the novel), then that identity is indeed not his. A relevant notion here is acknowledgement. Someone may come to acknowledge a certain affiliation as an identity, and this is neither a mere discovery nor, certainly, a mere decision. It is as though he were forced to recognize the authority of this identity as giving a structure and a focus to his life and his outlook. There are circumstances in which what was earlier a mere recognition of fact may come to compel acknowledgement, as when many assimilationist Jews in the 1930s came to acknowledge a Jewish and perhaps a Zionist identity under the thought that there was no way in which without evasion they could go on as though it made no difference that they were Jewish people.

How are these recognitions or acknowledgements possible? What truths am I discovering about myself? This is a question that is raised not merely in the political dimension of a social identity, but in the matter of a personal attachment, loyalty, or style of life, such as the question that hangs, as we have seen, over the end of Julie's story. As Rousseau sensed, but to more compelling effect in the purely personal than in the political case, the demands of authenticity require more than decision. Only some kind of recognition or acknowledgement can carry the weight that is needed to take the place, in a modern context of freedom and self-consciousness, of the old social certainties: or rather we should say, of what we think of as the old social certainties, for there is no need to assume that the standard contrasts between modernity and the old world are unqualifiedly correct. Those images of a pre-modern world are doubtless shaped by a general nostalgia which, in one form or another, has been part of Western consciousness right from antiquity. Nevertheless, it is still a special characteristic of modernity that nostalgia should take this particular form and should project onto the past this specific type of contrast between certainty and uncertainty, solidity and flux.

In trying to understand the questions raised by the search for authenticity, we will be better served by the models of sincerity and commitment that we have drawn from Diderot than by Rousseau's own. In the social or political case, where the presence of other people is vital, sincerity helps to construct or create truth. Drawn to bind myself to the others' shared values, to make my own beliefs and feelings steadier (to make them, at the limit, for the first time into beliefs), I become what with increasing steadiness I can sincerely profess; I become what I have sincerely declared to them, or perhaps I become my interpretation of their interpretation of what I have sincerely declared to them. The sense that I am contributing to this, that it is a project, fills out the idea that acknowledgement is more than mere factual discovery, while at the same time the sense that there is discovery involved is related to the need to resist fantasy in making sense of my beliefs and allegiances in this way. Much of this carries over into the purely personal case. Here the presence of others is not so insistent or essential. Julie, in her last reflections, need not declare herself to anyone, though she might have done so in her last letters to Saint-Preux (indeed, there is a question for the careful reader whether she has not done so). But even if there were reasons that would prevent her from saying to anyone what she would say with most conviction, there is always a question of what she would say if she could do so. The sense of being constrained by something that lies outside the will is the same. The resistance to fantasy, the consciousness that I cannot merely make things as I would wish them to be, a feature of all genuine inquiry, lends a sense of the objective to these acknowledgements, in the personal as much as in the political case. It is all the more so because there is an element of hope or prediction involved, that I will be able in fact to steady my beliefs in this way, and live under the social or personal consequences of this identification. What I have to ask myself is how far I can live without fantasy under these understandings. How heavy this commitment may be turns on several things. There is a question of how widely and deeply these understandings reach into one's life. There is also the question of how long, even when they are acknowledged, they are expected to last. Presumably the original idea of such an identity was of something that lasted a lifetime, but in some places now, certainly, an identity may itself represent only a shorter-term project of stabilizing the self, and it may be possible to take a Rameau-like attitude even to it.

The politics and psychology of authenticity will face further questions: whether there is a social identity that stands in an intelligible relation to my needs and my self-understanding as they already are; whether the political, social, and institutional expressions of that identity operate in good faith; how far the social forces that are moving me toward acknowledgement of this identity are coercive; whether the people with whom my relations will be defined by this identity are as I imagine them to be. There is an element of prediction—one that can operate counterfactually when, as finally for Julie, there is no future—and the prediction need not be simply of happiness or unhappiness. Some happiness may come about in ways that are irrelevant to the project of the authentic life, and some disappointments, equally, do not count as a rebuff to it: a project of living a life that is authentic either in social or in purely personal terms may come to grief for extrinsic reasons, which will not falsify the idea that it would have been an authentic life. But there are circumstances in which that idea may be falsified, and then the agent's hopes for a meaningful and satisfying life will be not just negated but refuted by what happens.[45]

The search for an authentic life is always questionable, and it is not a secret that it can lead to ethical and social disaster. The structure itself shows where the risks are likely to be. Since sincerity here has to create truth, and one's present self-understanding has to be extended into a life that will continue to be satisfying and will make enough sense, the risks of wishful thinking and self-deception, the dangers that the virtues of truth at their most flexible and resilient will fail one, are evident, and this applies to both the social and the purely personal case. The dangers are evident, that is to say, abstractly, within these pages. Given an actual situation of choice or reflection in which the pursuit of authenticity needs the virtues of truth, one reason why they may fail is that there, in the nature of the case, the need for them may be concealed.

9

❖   ❖   ❖   ❖   ❖

TRUTHFULNESS, LIBERALISM,
AND CRITIQUE

1. *Truth and Politics*

What are the most general relations between truthfulness and politics? Few or negative, the saloon bar cynic will reply, and he has a case. It applies most familiarly to governments' deceit of the citizens and to candidates' deceit of the electors, but also when sincerity and authenticity supposedly generate their own politics, as I suggested they do in the case of the politics of identity. Diderot warns us, in effect, that it will be exceptional if the politics of identity can be lived wholeheartedly, without self-deception and without strain; the communitarian self can usually, and often creatively, be subverted by spontaneity. Many have come to know that the way into the politics of identity is often coercive (people turn out to need some vigorous help in discovering their identity). Even when it is functioning, it by no means solves all the problems of trust. The sense of a shared social identity does not guarantee openness between people, even if it creates some channels for it, and the problems of trust still need to be negotiated within the politics of identity. Moreover, and notoriously, the politics of identity is not necessarily a friend of plain truthfulness. It breeds, almost inevitably, its own myths or, not to put too fine a point on it, lies.[1] It may be very important to rescue from the authenticity of communal attachment the more elementary virtues of truth.

Why does truthfulness in politics matter? We can start with the narrower question: why does it matter in government? One argument for truthfulness in government is the simple argument for truthfulness: if it is a good thing, other things being equal, for people to be truthful, it is good thing for people in government to be truthful. But this provides a rather modest basis. It follows a general pattern of argument for governmental virtue, against which there stands a moderate version of Machiavelli's thesis: the responsibilities of government are different enough from those of private individuals to make governmental virtue a rather different matter from the virtue of individuals—in particular, as he rightly pointed out, from the virtue of individuals who are being protected by a government. Any government is charged with the security of its citizens, a responsibility that cannot be discharged without force and secrecy. It will be lucky if it can discharge it without deceiving someone, and if that does not already include the citizens, it is very likely that it will come to do so.

However, Machiavelli's reminders themselves surely provide an obvious argument for truthfulness, *the anti-tyranny argument*: precisely because of their peculiar powers and opportunities, governments are disposed to commit illegitimate actions which they will wish to conceal, as they also want to conceal incompetent actions. It is in citizens' interests that these be checked. They cannot be checked without true information. At first sight, this yields only the conclusion that someone other than the government should have information, not the populace at large. In some areas, this is a practical point: in many states, non-executive legislators, senior members of opposition parties, and others outside the administration may be privy to security secrets, for instance. But the argument can be run again to suggest that this is not in general enough: there is a risk that either these other groups are sufficiently distinct from the government for the government to have an interest in deceiving them, or they are close enough to government to form part of the threat of tyranny (that of an élite or political class). This argues for truth's being available, with restrictions, to all the potentially tyrannized.

To the extent that the anti-tyranny argument is an argument, it is obviously one of the best, because it relies on such a modest basis.

It is of course an "instrumental" argument, but in this connection that is not a disadvantage, particularly because both the ends and the means apply universally. Everyone needs not to be tyrannized; everyone knows what tyranny is likely to bring with it; everyone has the idea that governments are less likely to get away with it if it is known what they are doing. It is also well known, of course, that truthfulness is not enough. A tyranny that persecutes a minority which is unpopular or which it is making unpopular may well court publicity, especially if there is not too much risk of international interference. Nevertheless, truthfulness is usually necessary or helpful in the restraint of tyrants. The trouble with these truisms about corruption and tyranny, and the reason for doubting whether they add up to an argument, is that just because everyone knows them, there is a question of who could possibly be listening to such an argument and in what circumstances. Tyrants will not be impressed by it, and their victims do not need to be impressed. As so often in political philosophy, the question needs to be asked: Who is supposed to be hearing this? Is there anyone who both needs to be told it and is in a position to make use of it? Political philosophy can no doubt offer reminders, but reminders are useful only where something is likely to be forgotten.

What may be forgotten is that it is a luxury to be able to discuss the precise value of truthfulness in politics and its relation to other political values. Political, particularly governmental, truthfulness is valuable against tyranny, but you will get it only as associated with other values and expressed in a set of institutions and practices that as a whole stand against tyranny. For us now, this takes the form of liberalism. Liberal societies are more successful in the modern world than others in helping people (at least in their own territories—their influence elsewhere has been less benign) to avoid what is universally feared: torture, violence, arbitrary power, and humiliation. This is the basis of the outlook that the late Judith Shklar eloquently and persuasively advanced as the least ambitious and most convincing justification of liberalism; she called it "the liberalism of fear."[2] It is indeed worth asking how, more precisely, truthfulness is related to practices and other values in the liberal complex, and that can lead to important practical questions of what liberal institutions should be and in what terms we should understand their value. But the value of the whole enterprise, political truthfulness included, is to be measured against the evils that it resists.

I shall try to say a little about the supports and the effects of truthfulness within the internal economy of liberalism. It is a large subject, and many of the most significant questions I shall have to pass by, particularly because they would require complex empirical discussion. I shall also leave aside a particularly interesting topic, the role of truthfulness in the transition from authoritarian to democratic rule. Such institutions as the Truth and Reconciliation Commission in South Africa mark a new and significant development. In earlier times, the start of a new and better political life was typically marked by "amnesty," forgetting and putting the past behind one, but now the demand is that past outrages should be confronted and recorded, and not necessarily in the interests of punishment. Why this should be so and what exactly it means are good questions.[3] One question is how these practices relate to justice. In South Africa, at least, as the reference to "Reconciliation" suggests, it seems that a particular conception of forgiveness is at work, one that involves confrontation with the truth. There is a question, too, of how far the process is intended to preserve memory of the victims of the past regime, and in this connection the idea of "bearing witness," powerfully associated with the Holocaust, has an influence. These questions are deeply tied into our conceptions of confronting the truth and living an honest political life, but they would take us too far into territory I cannot claim to understand.

In the next section, I shall take up one or two general points about the relations between truthfulness and other liberal values as they are expressed in modern conditions. My aim will be to bring out some ways in which the demand for truthfulness, though it should be an ally of other aspects of liberalism, can nevertheless run into conflict with them. In later sections of the chapter, by contrast, I turn to a particular way in which the demand for truthfulness can be an instrument of liberalism, by serving as the sharp end of a critique of injustice.

2. *Democracy and Liberty*

Liberal societies are democracies, and it may look as though it is the *democratic* element in the liberal complex that has a particular connection with a demand for governmental truthfulness. The people are the source of the government's authority and (under various substantial restrictions) even of its policies. Government is in some sense a trust; there is a special relationship between government and people, and it is a violation of this conception for secrecy or falsehood to come between trustee and people.

It is a feature of democracy, obviously, that the citizens are supposed to be able to trust the government. It is a question, however, to what extent the relationship of people and government in a democracy offers any distinctive considerations in favour of truthfulness, over and above those implicit in the liberalism of fear. Democracy (in the sense, at least, that the electors are guaranteed opportunities to dismiss the government) is itself justified by that conception, which already implies an ideal of trustworthiness. If the argument from democracy is to go beyond this, it will have to give special reasons why the value of truthfulness is, in a democracy, built intrinsically into the relations between the government and the people. In doing so, it will rely on some particular conception of democratic legitimacy. Is there any conception of democratic legitimacy that will yield this result? Or rather: is there a conception of it that both yields this result and can realistically be supposed to apply to modern democracies?

One relationship that by its nature excludes deceit is agency, in the sense of an agent's doing things on behalf of or in place of a principal, things that the principal is poorly placed, for instance, or too occupied to do for himself. But to understand the government in a democracy as an *agent* of the people implies an exceedingly strong model of democratic government as self-government, which cannot be applied literally to any modern democracy. We can indeed construct a model of democratic legitimacy in which "the People" may be said to authorize the government's acts, even acts that would be opposed by many citizens, perhaps by a majority of them. We can express this model in terms of a relation between government and a fiction, the People, such that, when various elaborate conditions are satisfied, the People can be said to have authorized the government to act. These conditions refer to acts by actual citizens: for instance, there is an electoral system under which a government is appointed after certain contests have been won by candidates who get a majority of votes cast by the appropriate set of citizens, and so on. In this model, to say that the People has authorized the government to do certain things does not imply that all or even a majority of the citizens have chosen those things.

One of the conditions we will include in the model is that the government should not deceive the People, and whatever exactly that means, it must imply, reassuringly, that the government should not (regularly, except for special cause, etc.) deceive ordinary citizens. There is nothing wrong with the conclusion. The trouble is that no extra argument for the conclusion has been supplied by the model or by the relations that it defines between the government and the People. Those relations, and the fiction of the People itself, are constructed so as to embody our conceptions of democratic legitimacy, including the requirements of truthfulness, and we have to decide what those requirements are before we can construct the model. There are complex relations between the ideals of democracy and truth in politics, and we shall come back to some of them in the next section, but it is not clear that demands for governmental truthfulness flow specifically from a definition of the basic democratic relation between people and government.

Democracy (in its modern, constitutional, forms) is valued, to an important extent, in the name of liberty. Rather than appealing specifically to the democratic element, we may argue for governmental and more generally political truthfulness by relating it directly to liberty, which for many people is the central element in the liberal complex. The falsification or suppression of information is an important limitation of liberty in itself and impedes the exercise of liberty in many areas. The appeal to liberty comes in stronger and weaker versions. The minimal version insists merely that government should permit maximum freedom (compatible with other goods, especially others' freedom), and that to deny people information and the right to spread information both violates liberty directly, in particular the freedom of speech, and devalues liberty in other areas, since effective action requires knowledge. A stronger version of the appeal calls, as J. S. Mill did, on the value of individuals' exercising and developing their powers. Both versions of the appeal to liberty raise an important question: how far are we concerned with liberty (above all, the freedom of speech), and how far are we concerned with truth? The standard liberal assumption is that the two objectives go together, and to some extent this is true. Self-development has been understood as development in the light of the truth, and liberties do get their point, in good part, from the possibility of effective action, which implies true information. However, it does not follow that all liberty, and specifically the freedom of speech, is necessarily helpful to the spread of the truth. We cannot take for granted Mill's optimistic conclusion that maximal freedom of speech must assist the emergence of truth in what has come to be called "a marketplace of ideas."

Before we come to the general question of how far freedom of expression encourages public truthfulness, it is worth looking at a specific application of the question, one that has perhaps been less discussed.[4] We noticed in chapter 5 the truism that secrecy may be justified where lying is not: people may have a right to be told (if anything) the truth, but often they have no right to be told anything. This applies to politics, and government is allowed by everyone to have secrets, though it is not supposed to lie, at least to its own citizens. Journalists have an obvious professional interest in confusing this distinction and standardly do so with their favourite phrase, "the public's right to know." This is rhetoric, but behind it they do have a further truism on their side, that we cannot rely on the government's judgement of who has a right to what truth—that is already to trust them too much. However, at this point yet another truism lowers itself into the discussion, in the form of the adage "Who asks no questions gets told no lies": the question of how many lies have to be told is, to a significant degree, a function of how insistent the inquirer is on being given an answer. This leads to the correct conclusion that suspiciousness about government tends to be self-justifying.

There are further complications. The government's behaviour in information-management depends not just on the degree of curiosity but also on the public's expectations of government (which themselves can affect the degree of curiosity). It makes a difference whether the public expects the government to behave badly, and also what it counts as "badly." The best results with regard to truth-management are not likely to follow from unlimited intrusiveness combined with unlimited righteousness (no doubt, on the part of the media, feigned) about how government can be expected to behave. This attitude, shared by many newspapers, is often what is being defended under the title of "the freedom of the press." Government management of the press, certainly, is not going to improve the situation. But some restrictions need to be observed by the media themselves if their activities are not going to be counter-productive—counter-productive, that is to say, if their aim is taken to be to encourage truthfulness in government and true belief among the citizens, and not simply to promote their own activities and (in a phrase of R. H. Tawney's) to sell pieces of paper with nonsense printed on one side and advertisements on the other.

3. *The Marketplace of Ideas*

The appeal to liberty in its minimal version suggests that anyone can say or ask anything; the most influential interpretation of it offers a strong presumption against intervention in a marketplace of communication. I argued in chapter 6 that it is a factual question what systems favour truth-discovery in a given area (it is a matter of the content of the truths in question), and the same point applies to the transmission of truth. People need to select what is worth considering and what is worth believing. This involves coherent discussion, and what has been accepted may need to be kept alive in the public consciousness, or, again, reconsidered. It is obvious that the demands on an effective system for accepting, sharing, and transmitting beliefs of various kinds are complex. It is very doubtful how effective an economic market can be in meeting these demands, with regard to many kinds of truths that are politically relevant.

It is sometimes said that the "marketplace of ideas" can be understood either literally or figuratively. Taken literally, it is presumably an economic market *in* ideas, a set of institutions through which communications expressing ideas are bought and sold—a market in books, newspapers, television programmes, and so on. What is the figurative contrast to this? Let us say that an *idealized* market is a structure in which the success of a given idea is measured not by its being bought but by its being accepted. The competition will be not a commercial interaction between entrepreneurs but an intellectual interaction between people advancing various ideas, and the "market forces" that operate on the ideas will consist of processes that are truth-acquiring relative to the question at hand. Abstracting from particular subject matters, these processes will standardly be such things as careful argument, attention to empirical inquiry, sifting of evidence, and so on. With regard to an idealized market, unlike a commercial one, it will not be a substantive question whether its operation tends to favour the acceptance of the truth, because the model is designed to embody just the processes that will favour the truth. However, the structure should not be idealized too much. We need not assume that the operation of these forces is frictionless, so that investigative investments are necessarily optimized; we should allow for the possibility, which exists in real life, that more time spent in investigating a given question may make it less likely that one will find the truth, not only about other questions but, in some cases, about that very question. The model should be of real people working within a structure that could be socially realized, working in a way that brings about competition between theories, suggestions, and so on (which may or may not be also a competition between people). The substantive question will then be, what actual structures approximate in a reasonable degree to an idealized market. A set of scientific laboratories in communication with one another are a favourable example; it is less clear how far criminal trials under the adversarial system are.

The idea of a free market in ideas as leading to truth has played an important role in the jurisprudence of the United States, and indeed it was first formulated in those terms by Oliver Wendell Holmes in one of the earliest and most influential contributions to

First Amendment doctrine.[5] When Holmes said that "the best test of truth is the power of the thought to get itself accepted in the competition of the market," he cannot simply have meant an idealized market, since he was arguing for not regulating certain kinds of speech in the actual social context of political and commercial activity, and the doctrine has been continually invoked ever since in the interest of not interfering with actual markets. The assumption of this approach is that, at least with regard to truths relevant to politics (and that reservation itself raises questions of First Amendment interpretation), the literal commercial market approximates to an idealized market. The trouble is that there is very little reason to accept this assumption. It has been convincingly argued that it is false in terms of economic theory, and at an empirical level the reasons for doubt are very familiar.[6] The literal market generates a high level of noise. Everyone knows that in modern conditions of communication messages compete for attention and cancel each other out, and that they are picked out for reasons that need have nothing to do with their truth. Moreover, the system fails to provide, typically, any structured context for understanding messages. The hearer may know at some level what message each sentence conveys, but not what the messages mean.

In accepting that these are consequences of modern communications, one should not be too impressed by the idea that things used to be better. It is true that there was a time, in the nineteenth and earlier twentieth centuries, when in well-ordered European states and the United States some newspapers gave more space to detailed news and heavy-weight debate of public issues than they do now. But these were far from fully democratic states, and even among people who were fully citizens, such papers did not appeal to everyone. To the extent that they appealed to a narrower section very much engaged in public matters, call it "the political class," there is no reason to think that such a section is less informed now, while it may be that a wider range of people are, if fragmentarily, better informed. However, there is more colour to a different pessimistic belief, that things are going to be worse. In many liberal democracies, and above all in Great Britain, newspapers have increasingly become more and more useless in these respects. In some countries the project of giving intelligible structure to the news and directing attention to public matters has to some extent been sustained by television. This varies very much from place to place, with more suspect *étatisme* in some places and more cringing consumerism in others, but in many countries major TV organizations have retained some sense of responsibility for offering relevant and true information. The international multiplication of TV channels may well reduce that effect. Many channels will offer no news of any sort, and those that do so may well offer either very local or blandly unstructured news.

Moreover, the Internet shows signs of creating for the first time what Marshall McLuhan prophesied as a consequence of television, a global village, something that has the disadvantages both of globalization and of a village. Certainly it does offer some reliable sources of information for those who want it and know what they are looking for, but equally it supports that mainstay of all villages, gossip. It constructs proliferating meeting places for the free and unstructured exchange of messages which bear a variety of claims, fancies, and suspicions, entertaining, superstitious, scandalous, or malign. The chances that many of these messages will be true are low, and the probability that the system itself will help anyone to pick out the true ones is even lower. In this respect, post-modern technology may have returned us dialectically to a transmuted version of the pre-modern world, and the chances of acquiring true beliefs by these means, except for those who already have knowledge to guide them, will be much like those in the Middle Ages. At the same time, the global nature of these conversations makes the situation worse than in a village, where at least you might encounter and perhaps be forced to listen to some people who had different opinions and obsessions. As critics concerned for the future of democratic discussion have pointed out, the Internet makes it easy for large numbers of previously isolated extremists to find each other and talk only among themselves.[7]

The merits of the market as a means of spreading true belief have been exaggerated because liberal historiography tends to treat the spread of expert knowledge itself, in particular the history of natural science, as a triumph of the market over restrictive practices. But this is very misleading. The emergence of scientific inquiry from restrictions exercised by the Church involved a change in the legitimation of belief with respect to physical nature. This change improved truth-discovery, and it involved free scientific inquiry. International scientific inquiry offers an approximation to an idealized market, but it does this only because its actual social structure is in important respects an example of a managed market: it involves such things as an increasingly high entry fee in terms of training, and also, necessarily, a powerful filter against cranks. The orderly management of scientific inquiry implies that the vast majority of suggestions which an uninformed person might mistake for a contribution to science will, quite properly, not be taken seriously and will not find their way to discussion or publication. Very rarely the cranky view turns out to be right, and then the scientists who ignored it are attacked for dogmatism and prejudice. But, they can rightly reply, there was no way of telling in advance that this particular cranky idea was to be taken seriously; the only alternative to their practice of prejudice would be to take seriously all such suggestions, and science would grind to a halt. The point can be generalized. Critics of the marketplace approach to First Amendment doctrine have pointed out that in institutions that are expressly dedicated to finding out the truth, such as universities, research institutes, and courts of law, speech is not at all unregulated. People cannot come in from outside, speak when they feel like it, make endless, irrelevant, or insulting interventions, and so on; they cannot invoke a right to do so, and no-one thinks that things would go better in the direction of truth if they could.[8]

If the problems of the literal, commercial, market system are taken seriously, how well does it do by the test of the various arguments for public truthfulness? It does not do too badly by a short-term interpretation of the anti-tyranny argument, since tyrannical outrages have quite a good chance of making themselves known through the market, but it does less well in sustaining the complex of attitudes and institutions that as a whole stand against tyranny.[9] It does well, of course, by the minimum appeal to liberty, but this is because that argument, in itself, is more interested in liberty than it is in truth. In terms of the "strong," self-development, appeal to liberty, the market system is disappointing, if, at any rate, the aim is not just a narcissistic self-construction out of commercially available materials, but (as Mill took it to be) cultural progress through experiments in styles of life that are conducted in the light of an emerging class of significant truths. The type of liberal position that combines both the stronger and the weaker appeals to liberty runs the risk of being inconsistent, granted the effects of the market system.

If we ask how the literal market stands in relation to ideas of democratic legitimacy, more than one answer can be given, and they interestingly conflict. Within United States jurisprudence, other approaches to First Amendment doctrine, co-existing uneasily with the marketplace tradition, have explained the significance of free speech in terms of democratic participation. One of them, particularly influenced by Alexander Meiklejohn, understands the rules governing free speech in political connections in terms of their contribution to the conditions for fruitful and orderly democratic debate. Meiklejohn took as his model a town meeting, in which speech is regulated by a chairman in order to facilitate informed and reasonable deliberation; as he put it in a famous formulation, "What is essential is not that everyone shall speak, but that everything worth saying shall be said." This approach, which has powerful contemporary support, naturally leads to allowing more interventionist policies, favouring such things as constraints on campaign finance, requirements of balanced discussion on TV networks, and the withdrawal of protection from racist and other kinds of prejudicial speech. It could also encourage positive initiatives in support of public service broadcasting and so on. To some extent, the proposals that would naturally go with this approach overlap with what might be needed for a closer approximation to an idealized market in truth: this is hardly surprising, granted that one requirement for orderly and fruitful democratic debate is accurate information.[10]

However, the Meiklejohnian theory itself has been criticized from the point of view of democratic legitimacy, as relying on an impoverished notion of participation. On this view, the model of the "orderly conduct of business" wrongly takes for granted a consensus about what the business is, and does not allow for the fact that one aim and effect of political intervention can precisely be to change the agenda. A function of the town chairman is to exclude disorderly and offensive expression, but speech in that style is certainly part of the political process and has traditionally been defended by the United States courts as such.[11] Other democratic societies take various views of these issues of principle and their practical implications. Unlike Americans, they do not have the questionable advantage of discussing them in terms of First Amendment jurisprudence, but they are all faced with similar conflicts. It is not simply that the marketplace theory of free speech is deceptive because it elides the huge differences between a commercial and an idealized market. Even if we give up the idea that a literal market in communication approximates to an idealized market of ideas, there will still be serious conflicts between the demands of truth transmission, on the one hand, and some implications of democratic legitimacy on the other. What the conflicts will be, and how extensive, depends on the prevailing conception of democratic legitimacy and how it interprets ideas such as participation. No liberal democracy can afford to be too discouraging of expressive, disorderly, and even prejudicial speech, or too fussy about who publishes it or how, and it cannot force people to think about public or political matters. At the same time, the basic rights of liberal society and democratic freedoms themselves depend on the development and protection of methods for discovering and transmitting the truth, and this requires that public debate embody in some form an approximation to an idealized market. Squaring this circle must be a prime aim of institutional invention in liberal states.

4. *Critique*

In the previous section we have been concerned with the internal economy of liberalism, and, in particular, the relations between truthfulness and liberty. Truthfulness is also connected with another political value, distributive justice. Here the idea of truth figures in a certain kind of critique, and this applies, very significantly, outside the range of questions that liberalism directs to itself. It is a critique that can be directed to institutions in non-liberal societies. I believe that if it can be made to work, it is one of liberalism's most powerful weapons, because it does not depend on merely asserting liberalism's own set of values against a rival set but mobilizes the values of truth in a distinctive political interest.

Liberalism has typically applied its universalist outlook not only to rights (there are basic human rights, and they are everywhere the same) but to the good. Distributive justice requires a currency in which it can assess the goods that are distributed in society, whether equally or otherwise, and liberalism would like that currency itself to be universal. A traditional candidate for this currency has been "welfare," as that notion is used by Utilitarianism. John Rawls, in his theory, gives a list of basic "primary goods," including liberty and the materials of self-respect; and there are other proposals.[12]

However, it is very reasonable to suppose, against these universalist tendencies, that what counts as advantage and disadvantage in a given society depends to some extent on the culture of that society. Social goods (which are what are in question) are goods that have a social meaning, and social meaning depends on local understandings. This point has been pressed by Michael Walzer in his work on distributive justice, and he must be right in insisting that we need to be sensitive to what counts locally as advantage and disadvantage if we are to protect ourselves against the charge that in accusing other societies of structural injustice, we are merely exporting modernizing liberalism as one ideology against others.[13]

However, we cannot simply rely on the locally accepted valuations. If we do that, we are likely to submerge our thought in some inert mixture of relativism and conservatism. Some critique of the local understandings must be possible, but we need to distinguish one sort of critique from another. Thus some society may be structured by a religious hierarchical order, and we may reject the story that legitimates this order. This does not necessarily imply that we regard the existing arrangements as unjust. We may think that no-one is being treated unjustly as things are, but rather that all the members of the society are caught up in a picture of the world that is untrue. (Of course, if they ceased to accept this picture, and yet the present distribution of advantages and disadvantages remained, then it might well be unjust, because there would no longer be a story to legitimate it. In those circumstances, moreover, the hierarchical system might come to be imposed by open coercion, and then it would be manifestly unjust.)

So even if the legitimation of an accepted hierarchical system is unsound, this does not necessarily mean that the system is unjust. But there are some circumstances in which a hierarchical system is accepted, in particular by the disadvantaged, and the system *is* unjust. Leave aside external critics who attack the system as unjust simply because they do not share its values and do not accept its legitimations. Other critics of it as unjust mean something more interesting than this: that even while the system is accepted, *the acceptance of it* already approximates to a paradigm of injustice, unmediated coercion. These critics suggest that the system is unjust because the supposed legitimation of it is accepted by the disadvantaged only because of coercion. This test of injustice offers a kind of critique that is not based simply on the values of the critic. It rests on a genuinely universal principle, that coercion in itself cannot constitute legitimation, and it deploys the idea that some methods of belief-formation are simply coercive. This is the style of argument that will concern us. Acknowledging the role that such an idea has played in social theory, we may call it the *Critical Theory Test*.

How should the test be expressed? What counts as a situation in which the social understandings in question are accepted in a way— a coercive way—which means that the supposed legitimation, even though it is generally accepted, will not defend the society against the charge of injustice? The following Critical Principle might be thought to provide a sufficient condition of this being so:

> Suppose that of two parties in the society, one is advantaged over the other, in particular with respect to power; and suppose that there is a story which is taken to legitimate this distribution, a story which is at least professed by the advantaged party and is generally accepted by the disadvantaged; and suppose the basic cause of the fact that the disadvantaged accept the story, and hence the system, is the power of the advantaged party: then the fact that they accept the system does not actually legitimate it, and *pro tanto* the distribution is unjust.

In any interesting case these parties (it is of course a simplification that there are only two of them) will be classes, social orders, or some such formation; very notably, they may be the two genders. The Critical Principle says that the story is "at least professed" by the advantaged party. The Principle will certainly apply very forcibly to a society in which the story is not believed by the powerful party. This is the familiar example offered, for instance, in some eighteenth- and nineteenth-century interpretations of religion as a racket controlled by priests and kings, and it appears equally in vulgar-Marxist images of conspiratorial capitalists. In those examples, however, the coercive element is so blatant that one hardly needs the Critical Principle to make the point. The interesting case—the one that concerned less vulgar Marxists—is that in which the advantaged and the disadvantaged parties both accept the story. The Principle says, in fact, that the story is "generally accepted" by the disadvantaged party. This is designed to cover not just the case in which most accept it and a few do not, but also the case, which is the standard case, in which most of them mostly accept it: that is to say, they grumble quite a lot and may even offer a folk version of the Principle, but in the end they accept, they bring up their children to accept, and so on.

On the face of it, the Critical Principle seems plausible, and we recognize its force in dystopian literature such as *Brave New World* and *1984*, in which authoritarian rulers intentionally manage their subjects' beliefs by means that conspicuously do not preserve truth or rationality, such as conditioning, gross propaganda, and drugs. However, the Principle will not be very interesting unless we can apply it to cases in which the manipulation is not intentional and the methods are not so gross. The Principle is certainly hard to apply to these subtler cases, and we shall come back to this question, but I shall suggest that when we ask how much the Principle has specifically to do with truth, we shall find that in one respect, the presence of false consciousness, the subtler cases offer richer material for the Principle than the crude cases.

The conditions invoked in the Critical Principle include unequal power, and the first question concerns this idea. "Power" is not being used in such a way that power is *ex hypothesi* illegitimate, and we are not assuming it to be necessarily unjust that power should be unequally distributed.[14] I take it that very often in situations to which the Principle might be applied, no-one denies the unequal distribution of power: the local parties agree with each other about this, and the external critic agrees too. The difference is that the local parties try to justify the agreed difference of power in terms of the local considerations, and the critic does not. There are some cases in which the locals or their advocates do not agree with the critic about the unequal distribution of power but rather invoke different kinds of power. I have heard a woman (a woman from New Zealand, in fact) explain how in Iran under the ayatollahs women had at least as much (non-political) power as men—more power, she claimed, than women in liberal societies. However, even she was not going to deny that men had more power than women in interpreting the rules that determined how much power women might have.

The second question concerns advantage. The Critical Principle describes the situation in terms of advantage and disadvantage, but Walzer's point about local meanings reminds us that there may be disagreement between the internal parties and the external critic about what counts as disadvantage. Often, things are not clear-cut: there is, unsurprisingly, some overlap between what they and we count as advantages, and someone who is low down in the hierarchy, while he does not have the same view of his position as he would have if he did not accept the legitimation, nevertheless is likely to understand the idea that he is disadvantaged relative to others in the society. Sometimes the story that supposedly legitimates the arrangements will agree that there is an unequal distribution of some goods, but will define other goods in such a way that an apparently unequal distribution comes out as not unequal. Thus, on some traditional accounts, men have more career opportunities, but women have more personal satisfaction, less alienation, and so on. In a rather different version, the effect is achieved by a shift into another space or currency of satisfaction. According to one old story, the working classes had fewer goods, but they would not have appreciated more and more refined goods, so "satisfactions" were equal.

However, this could hardly stand by itself, since the Critical Principle could be immediately redeployed with regard to this lack of appreciation itself. It is hard, on modern understandings, to keep going in this direction, and if a justification is demanded at all, unequal holdings will more often be justified by arguments about efficiency, trickle-down effects and so on.

The Critical Principle will claim that some local legitimations do not count, both with respect to what everyone agrees to be differential distributions, such as of power, and also with respect to what the critics, but perhaps not the locals, count as advantages; and it will claim this because the pattern of the legitimation, and the identification of advantage that goes with it, are the product of the power of the advantaged group. This raises two problems. What is the content of the causal claim, and what is its critical force? In the crude *Brave New World* cases where the advantaged party is acting in an intentional and interventionist way, the causal claim may be as obvious as any hypothesis about social causation can be, but how will it stand in the more interesting cases? Often when the Critical Principle is applied in a subtler way, the judgement is based simply on the idea that the arrangement is to the benefit of the advantaged party, together with a functionalist analysis. The suggestion is that the society works like this in order to secure these people's advantages. But further argument is certainly needed to make this convincing; otherwise the functionalist claim, and in particular the fact that this functionalist claim is chosen rather than some other, merely begs the question.[15]

Even supposing that a causal judgement can be established, more seems to be needed if it is to have critical force. Certainly the mere fact that one party causes belief in another does not show that the belief is unsound. Indeed, the Critical Principle does not simply say that one party causes the other's beliefs, but that the *power* of the one causes the beliefs of the other. Nevertheless, some will press a "genetic fallacy" objection, to the effect that the soundness of the belief must be an entirely separate question from its causation: what matters is simply the merit of the supposed legitimation, and all the distinctive, causal, content of the Principle is irrelevant.

5. *The Critical Theory Test*

Habermas, in his model of an Ideal Speech Situation, has tried to preserve the traditional idea of Critical Theory, that the validity of a legitimating belief and the way in which the belief comes about can be properly linked together: he does this by approaching the causal question hypothetically.[16] He offers a thought-experiment in terms of a space that is *Herrschaftfrei*, free from improper normative power, and the idea is that if a belief is sound, then it could have been accepted in those circumstances. This supposedly allows us to identify, by comparison, a power-based distortion of belief-formation in an actual society. Because the model is used to construct a norm of acceptability for beliefs, it does offer a critique of, specifically, false consciousness. As Geuss has paraphrased Habermas, "what it means for a statement to be true is that it would be the one on which all agents would agree if they were to discuss all of human experience in absolutely free and uncoerced circumstances for an indefinite period of time."[17]

Habermas made a further claim about the model of the Ideal Speech Situation, that it is transcendentally presupposed by all discourse, since all speakers and rational agents are committed to the idea of the truth.[18] All speech, insofar as it is rational, "anticipates" the Ideal Speech Situation. We can agree that all speakers are in some sense committed to the idea of the truth, but the transcendental claim follows from this only given two assumptions, neither of which there is reason to accept. One is that our idea of what is meant by "the truth" is given regulatively by the Ideal Speech Situation. The other is the familiar assumption that if some condition, such as a commitment to the truth or restrictions on lying, is in general necessary to there being rational communication and deliberation among people, then every agent all the time has reason to accept the norm of acting in accordance with that condition. I have already rejected that idea.[19]

The model of the Ideal Speech Situation encounters a range of problems, but for the present purpose, I want to concentrate on just one of them. The very idea of a conversation that arrives at a result but does not involve power of any sort (such as persuasive power, and indeed the force of argument, as it is rightly called) is based yet again on the misconceived radical distinction, familiar from the Platonic and Kantian traditions, between reasons and causes, or reason and desire. Of course, Habermas wants the ideal conversation to be free only of *Herrschaft*, illegitimate or inappropriate power, and happily we all know of conversations that satisfy this condition. But there is no reason to think that the idea of illegitimate or inappropriate power could be adequately established in quite general terms in advance of the imagined conversations, and so function from the beginning as a condition on them.

We need a less abstract approach, a critique that is "contextualist" or "immanent," rather than in the Kantian style. If we are to retain the spirit of the Critical Principle at all, we do need to hold on to the causal element; the critique must still impugn a belief through the explanation of how it comes to be held. At the same time, it must avoid the "genetic fallacy" problem and accept that a belief is not discredited merely because it is caused by someone. Indeed it should accept that a belief is not necessarily discredited just because it is caused through the power of someone. The "force of reason" can hardly be separated altogether from the power of persuasion, and, as the ancient Greeks well knew, the power of persuasion, however benignly or rationally exercised, is still a species of power.[20] Even if we can separate rational from less rational *considerations* deployed in persuasion, there is little reason to suppose that we can separate a rational from an irrational *agency* of persuasion, which is what the Critical Principle would need if it were to offer its criterion in terms of excluding the effects of power. The point is very clear with education. Pupils enter education, most often, under some kind of coercion, and some of them stay in it and listen only for those same reasons. If they have a good teacher, those reasons fall away, but the good teacher will have substituted other powers of persuasion for those. Much successful education, after all, is a benign form of seduction.

So how might the Critical Principle be modified, to respect these realities? A useful element here is an idea which is indeed congenial to Critical Theory, that the references to causation should not treat the society and its members simply from outside, like a physical system, but consider the situation rather from their, possibly improved, point of view. We can introduce the following test of a belief held by a group:

> If they were to understand properly how they came to hold this belief, would they give it up?

Clearly many beliefs acquired in a way that involves somebody else's power—such as beliefs acquired as an unwilling participant in compulsory schooling—will, properly, pass this test. Moreover, the formula avoids the problems of isolating causes. We can tell a story, as expansive as we like, about the context of belief formation, and if there is an unacceptable element in the history, it can be assessed. There is a problem, rather, with "If they were to understand . . ." In rejecting the model of the Ideal Speech Situation, we accepted, in effect, that any such understanding must always come about against some background. If we are supposing that the background is simply these people's current set of beliefs, then almost anything will pass the test (except perhaps some cases of extreme internal incoherence). If we suppose, on the other hand, an entirely external frame of reference, then nothing very distinctive is achieved by the test. We need a schema by which we start with the people's current beliefs and imagine their going through a process of criticism, a process in which the test plays a significant part. We can think of the disadvantaged as asking a series of reflective questions about their situation. Our picture of this will of course be an artificial rationalization, but something like it does actually happen on a social scale. It is not surprising that often it is started by an influence from outside a society which up to that point had been relatively closed.

The disadvantaged party initially believe

> (1) The distribution of powers and advantages in the system is basically just.

They are then led to reflect that

> (2) They believe (1) only because members of the more powerful party (call them the instructors) give them appropriate training.

To see the force of this reflection, we can consider a contrast with the victims of a crude *Brave New World* system. They might not believe either (1) or (2), because the manipulations by the management had damped down reflection to a point at which neither of these matters ever occurred to the disadvantaged people. Their situation will be condemned by a version of the Critical Principle, but it will not be best condemned in terms of false consciousness (to use Critical Theory's traditional expression), since it involves so little in the way of consciousness. We are now assuming, however, that the question of the justice of the arrangements has arisen in the society, and that on the whole its members do believe (1). We assume, too, that almost everyone in the society recognizes (2) in some form, but not necessarily in quite those terms. Though they acknowledge that there are differences of power, they need not, at this stage of reflection, think of the instructors' authority directly in terms of power. If the critique succeeds, they will come to do so.

The disadvantaged can now reflect:

> (3) It is only if (1) is true that the instructors are in a sound position to claim that (1) is true; the basis for their authority comes from the system itself.

Once again, the exact form that this reflection takes will vary, and (3) as it stands is a notably rationalized version of it. But one way or another, they will come to see that the justice of the system, the authority of the instructors, and hence their own reasons for accepting the justice of the system all hang together. Suppose they now turn to asking whether they have any independent ways of assessing the instructors' authority (it is a familiar direction in which people turn, even in traditional societies with fairly stable legitimations). Granted the kind of thing that the instructors tell them, is there anything about the instructors that makes it more or less likely that they have got it right? The disadvantaged are already familiar, in some form, with the idea that the instructors belong to the party that is advantaged and more powerful. This idea becomes more vividly and densely articulated, and can readily yield the thought:

(4) There are perfectly good explanations of the instructors' belief in their own authority. This means, granted (3), that there are good explanations of their teaching (1) which do not imply that (1) is true.

The instructors may give all the signs of sincerely believing (1), but even if they do, the disadvantaged will not need any very sophisticated psychological theory in order to accept (4).

At this stage there is already a contrast with the power used in school to get people to learn mathematics or geography. In those cases there is not any obvious reason why these people would teach these things unless there was at least a good chance that they were true. Moreover, in those cases, the teaching itself will have suggested, at least in outline, ways in which people might come to know mathematical or geographical truths other than being taught them by such instructors. In the case of the critical reflection, the disadvantaged may well have reached this stage without having any definite idea, or any idea at all, of other ways by which anyone could come to know such things as (1). The instructors may be in the same position as well; their hold on (1) may have come just from their having been similarly taught. They may in some societies (where they are priests, for instance, rather than merely elders) claim to have a mystery, an esoteric source of knowledge not available to the others. Then the critical reflection asks the same question again: what authority have they to claim that they have such a source of knowledge?

In the Platonic and the Kantian traditions, the processes of critical reflection have involved the idea that there is another, genuine, way of establishing truths about justice and other such matters, a way that the reflection opposes to merely traditional sources. It is supposed to be the way of reason, and Habermas's method is an example of the same. But the process we are now following does not make such an assumption. It uses only the weak, negative, and entirely plausible claim that, granted (3) and (4), these particular processes of instruction do *not* have the authority that is claimed for them. But if the disadvantaged have no reason to accept what the instructors tell them about the justice of the system, they have reason to reject it. This is not a case for mere scepticism. They already had the idea that the instructors were in various ways better off than themselves. Now, without the legitimation, that fact becomes far more salient—with changing ideas of advantage and disadvantage, indeed, it becomes *the* fact. Moreover, the processes of instruction, deprived now of any claim to authority, appear as an exercise of power and not much else. The more that the instructors and others of their party resist the objections to the status quo, as they no doubt will, the more obvious it becomes that the system is unjust in the most basic terms, an exercise of unmediated power. To the extent that it is defended by overt coercion, this is what it will have become. But there is good reason to say also that this is what it always was. Once the idea is established that there is nothing to the supposed authority of the instructors, that their story is empty, their activity indeed appears as merely a method of control. Given that the system was undeniably to their advantage and that they had no disposition to question it, the paradigm of coercion is close enough for it to be said that this arrangement always was unjust, even in the days when it was accepted.

The process of reflective criticism that I have outlined resembles traditional Critical Theory in several respects. Although it does not rely on a theory of moral truth, it does deploy a theory of error; when the question is raised, in given circumstances, whether a given social process is a source of authority for legitimating the social system and its distribution of advantages, there are convincing reasons for giving a negative answer. Moreover, the question is raised in a context in which that answer has practical consequences. The system is not just questioned but contested. The disadvantaged want to know why the power of these others is being exercised over them, and when the question about the source of that authority gets a negative answer, the result is not that the system is in doubt, but that it is unjust.

The use of the Critical Principle shares with the tradition of Critical Theory a concern with power. I said that the critical process of reflection deploys a theory of error. There is certainly no agreement (contrary to other cases we have discussed in earlier chapters) on what substantial properties of inquiry or transmission favour truth in the case of moral claims, or at least of very general moral claims.[21]

On almost any view of the matter, however, if one comes to know that the sole reason one accepts some moral claim is that somebody's power has brought it about that one accepts it, when, further, it is in their interest that one should accept it, one will have no reason to go on accepting it. Not all moral concepts are as closely connected with distributions of power, and distributions of other advantages sustained by power, as justice is. But the Critical Principle schema can be generalized to deal with other moral beliefs as well. Moral beliefs do typically bring with them some kind of normatively sustained restrictions, and to the extent that these beliefs fail the test, the system that inculcates those beliefs may turn out, itself, to be unjust. Injustice can be applied to the possession of beliefs that are not themselves about justice.

The present argument also shares with the tradition of Critical Theory the idea that the interest that the disadvantaged have in this process is emancipation, though it sees that ideal in a particular light. The model of the Ideal Speech Situation understood the absence of *Herrschaft* as the condition under which the truth about justice will emerge. On the present account, the interest of the disadvantaged lies in an aspiration to the most basic sense of freedom, that of not being in the power of another, in particular not in the unrecognized power of another, and the pursuit of truth in this area is concentrated into the aim of destroying representations that have the effect of keeping people in such a situation. Truthfulness emerges from this discussion, I think, with the same kind of political value that was given to it by the best hopes of the Enlightenment. I said earlier in this study that the Enlightenment's relations to the values of truth were double-edged. In the twentieth century we were much reminded of the destructive capacities that the Enlightenment has deployed, with its aspiration to social management as applied scientific truth and its fantasies of reconstructing human and social relations in a radically rationalistic spirit. But those dangerous delusions do not impugn its commitment to honesty and transparency and its rejection of power that falsely presents itself as cognitive authority. We have something to fear from Enlightenment programmes for the advance and application of truth, but a lot to cherish in its concern for truthfulness.

However, we need to remember that it is not necessarily benighted or corrupt to think that even these more benign ideals of the Enlightenment, if less threatening than the others, are equally baseless. It is not foolish to believe that any social and political order which effectively uses power, and which sustains a culture that means something to the people who live in it, must involve opacity, mystification, and large-scale deception. Reasonable people can believe, contrary to the ideals of liberalism, that human beings cannot live together effectively, at least on any culturally ambitious scale, if they understand fully what they are doing. It is not necessarily foolish to believe these things, but they may not be true, and we can still live in the hope (a hope we shall come back to in the next chapter) that they are not.

10

❖   ❖   ❖   ❖   ❖

MAKING SENSE

1. *Narratives*

When we try to make sense of a particular happening, we often tell a story about a sequence of events that led to it. If we do make sense of it (or explain it, or come to understand it), we must take the elements of the story to be true, but that of course is not enough: the sequence of events has to make sense to us, and make sense of the outcome. Such a story is one kind of narrative. It may be a very short and unambitious narrative, which we can call a "mini-narrative," a type that comes in two particularly familiar and significant forms. One form presents an instance of a natural process, and here the mini-narrative explains or makes sense of the outcome by appealing to regularities of nature. It presents the sequence and its outcome as an example of some general type of process, held together by causal relations (though, in recognizing the process, we need not know in detail what the causal relations are).

The other very significant kind of mini-narrative presents a sequence of happenings as held together by an agent's intentions.[1] In some cases, this kind of sequence, though it involves several actions, can easily be described as one action: she bought a house, and that involved these various things she did. In other cases, it may not readily be described as one action, but only as the execution of a plan or design that involves many actions.[2] However, longer-term plans or designs have increasingly complex conditions for their realization, and the longer the haul of the design, the more room there may be for scepticism whether one on-going intention on the part of the agent is what truly makes sense of this sequence of actions, still less a highly determinate plan which he formed at the outset. There is room for the agent to rationalize and redescribe, in order to convince himself and others that there was more foresight, and less improvisation and accident, than there actually was, and others can do the same on his behalf. A significant qualification to this lies in cases where the process is supported, and isolated to some extent from perturbations, by institutional or other normative guarantees (which form part of the machinery of trust). Where a sequence of actions is reliably promised or takes place in an institutional environment which (roughly speaking) is designed to deliver such outcomes, there is a kind of normative analogue to a natural process.

Granted that a mini-narrative is a narrative at all, however short, the process it presents can be decomposed into constituent parts, though, particularly in the case of relatively simple actions or unpunctuated processes such as a lump of ice melting, the parts will not have natural descriptions and will probably possess no everyday interest, except in a case where some constituent of a process is missing, so that doubt is cast on that narrative and its capacity to make sense of what actually happened. In the opposite direction, and much more significantly, mini-narratives can be combined and expanded into longer and, often, very particular and unpredictable stories which also make sense of some outcome, such as a present practice. In many cases, such a story is the only thing that can make sense of it. Why is it that walls in Belfast, in the year 2001, bear the extraordinary legend "Remember 1690"? "Well, . . ." the weary explainer begins.[3] The long and saddening story that follows may make sense of something that seemed at first sight unintelligible.

If the story makes sense of things, this implies that we, the listeners, can make sense of the elements of the story, for instance, of actions that have significantly marked and formed that history. But this does not necessarily mean that we think that those actions make sense: that is to say, that we would regard them as reasonable things for us to do, or that we think the states of mind from which they come, such as a fanatical attachment to one version of the Christian religion, are reasonable. The condition of our understanding is rather this, that it should make sense to us that such actions should make sense to people in those circumstances. Moreover, this variation in what makes sense to people in different circumstances, in particular, different cultural circumstances, does not apply only to what it makes sense for them to do or feel; it extends, and necessarily so, to the level of explanation or understanding as well. To take another example from the powers of religious conviction, it may well be that to neither of us would it make sense to kill ourselves and immolate thousands of other people for political objectives identified with a certain religion: neither of us would do it or conceivably have reason to do it. Perhaps it makes sense to each of us that it could make sense to someone else with a very different formation; indeed, this had better make sense to us, if we are to sustain the hope, however desperately, of making sense of the world we live in. However, we may differ about the terms in which the action makes sense to us. You may make sense of what these men have done only because you have been told that they have been promised rewards in an afterlife. I, on the other hand, do not think that the rewards are either here or there: it is the heroic and self-sacrificial dying itself, as it seems to me, that makes sense to these men, more sense than any life they can otherwise hope to have.

There may be a suspicion that the idea of "making sense" is being used here in a promiscuous way, in particular—and this is a specially nasty offence among some philosophers—because it seemingly runs together fact and value. It does have different implications in different connections, but there is no muddle involved. The basic idea is that it makes sense to a certain person (or group, etc.) *that P.* We can take "P" as the story, and then the idea is that it makes sense (to that person) that things should work out as the story says they worked out—the story may of course mention standing or unchanging factors as well as a sequence of different events. Or "P" may represent an outcome, and the thought then is that it makes sense (to that person) in the light of the story that P should be the case. In this formula, "P" may present someone's action. Thus it can make sense to A that B did a certain thing. There are various different sorts of story in terms of which B's action might make sense; thus, rather unusually, it might come to make sense to A that B did this extraordinary thing because A is told that B had received a sugges-

tion under hypnosis. More usually, B's action will be explained not
by this sort of cause, but by B's own reasons for doing it (this is often
called a "rationalizing explanation" of an action). It now makes sense
to A, for instance, that B suddenly went to Venice, because he is told
that B has an interest in Venetian painting, and he hears a narrative
of how B heard of an opportunity to see certain paintings in Venice
and was able, exceptionally, to take advantage of that opportunity,
and so on.

But if in these terms it makes sense to A that B acted in this way,
it certainly made sense to B himself. Indeed, we can say that B's
recognizing, in a situation of practical decision, that he has a reason
to do a certain thing is a special case of something's making sense
to him as a thing to do.[4] The situation of decision cannot simply be
identified with one in which an agent applies to himself the idea of
what it makes sense to do. For instance, he can apply that idea to
himself retrospectively. He may come to think that he acted unrea-
sonably, but he understands why he did so; in such a case he applies
to himself much the same interpretative and explanatory schemes as
he might apply to someone else. We can say that it makes sense to
him now that he acted in that way, though it would not make sense
to him to act in that way now. Even with regard to the future, an
agent can apply to himself the idea of what it would make sense to
do, without its being a situation of decision: an agent can think about
his future in a predictive or interpretative style that merely leads to
his not being surprised by what he eventually decides to do. But in
the situation of decision, the agent does not merely consider or think
about his beliefs, desires, and so on (though he is not excluded from
doing so); rather, it is from the perspective of those motivational
states that he considers what it makes sense for him to do. He becomes convinced, in the simplest case, that he has sufficient reason
to do a certain thing, and on the strength of that becomes (relatively)
certain that he will do that thing for that reason. This is a special
case of its making sense to him that he will do a certain thing. What
makes it special is not simply that it is a matter of the agent himself
and not someone else, but the fact that in the situation of decision,
the agent's present motivational state does not primarily act as evidence or support for the conviction that it makes sense for him to

act in this way: it is *expressed* in that conviction, just as it is expressed in the action itself.[5]

One way in which an agent's beliefs and desires, in general his motivational states, make sense of his decisions and actions is that they can explain them. But they can explain them only because they are expressed in them, and that is a relation which can hold only between an agent's motivational states and that agent's actions and decisions. When an action presents itself to the agent as the thing to do, his conviction that it makes sense to do it is an expression of his motivational states, and this basic level of its making sense to him underlies the possibility that those motivational states can serve, in an explanatory framework, to make sense of his action to others or retrospectively to himself: a framework, that is to say, in which the states are no longer acting as the springs of action, but simply being recognized as the springs of action.

It is a very basic point that if an agent acts for certain reasons, then those reasons can figure in a subsequent explanation of how he acted.[6] If B acts for certain reasons, others can be in a position to make sense of his action in virtue of those reasons, and so can he. Moreover, one way in which others can come to make sense of the action is by thinking themselves into the position of the agent, while taking on for the purpose of the exercise, so far as they can, his outlook and preconceptions. This form of historical (and, more generally, social) understanding has been properly emphasized by many writers; notably, in English, by the most unjustly neglected of twentieth-century British philosophers, R. G. Collingwood.[7] That this is a basic way of making sense of other people is undeniable. It is important what it does *not* imply. It does not imply that the explainer identifies in his own person with these reasons and would act on such reasons in such circumstances. His identification with the outlook of the agent is temporary and, as it were, feigned, and it does not carry over into his own life, as was suggested by some critics of Collingwood, who supposed that his talk of thinking the same thought as Caesar had on the bank of the Rubicon must mean that the interpreter will be amazed not to find himself on the bank of the Rubicon. (In current jargon, the exercise is conducted "off-line.") Another thing that does not follow is that if there is an explanation or understanding of an action in terms of the agent's reasons, it is a complete or adequate explanation of it. There are, obviously enough, other questions—psychological, cultural, sociological—of why that agent, or any agent, or any agent in that social setting, should act on such reasons. How far those questions are interesting is a matter of the kind of explanation one wants; for instance, of what kind of history one is writing.

Any narrative, short or expansive, is contrasted with a chronicle, which is simply a list of happenings in chronological order. A chronicle is held together by *something*; for instance, they were happenings in a certain place, or which came as news to a certain place, in times when it was not true that everything came as news to every place:

> Here the sun grew dark. And Eorcenberht, king of the inhabitants of Kent, passed away. And Colman with his companions went to his native land. The same year there was a great plague among men . . .
>
> Here Theodore was ordained archbishop.
>
> Here King Egbert gave Reculver to Bass the mass-priest in which to build a minster . . .
>
> Here there was a great mortality of birds.[8]

A chronicle does not try to make sense of anything (they were invented in the first place not to explain or even date events, but to identify years). A list of events that happened at a place could try to do so, if, for instance, it aimed to explain some feature of the place, but a chronicle does not. It does not even try to make sense of each event in terms of the earlier events that it mentions.

In the idea that a narrative, as opposed to a chronicle, tries to make sense of something, there is a distinction that will be important. Consider the story of a person's life that was resolutely inconsequential, such as Diderot's story *Jacques le fataliste*. This may create the impression that one is being told the story of a man's life where the life, and in one way the story, make no sense. This can be correct, inasmuch as the story makes no sense as a whole or, as we may say, makes no overall sense of the life: the patterns of ambition, project, even habit that help to explain long-haul pieces of a person's life are absent from it. The person in the story is largely a victim of chance. However, this does not mean that the story makes no sense of anything. Leaving aside the point that it may make sense of the idea that there could be such a life—in which case it is likely to be an ironical construction, playing against expectations that a life should make some kind of overall sense—the story will make sense of the person's having arrived at each point in the story. If we wonder, in an actual case, why this man should be here now, in such a state, the story will make sense *of that fact*, and in that way the story itself will make sense: the sequence of events up to this point, with all the accidents, coincidences, misunderstandings, and so on, that it involves, is intelligible. What it does not do is make any further overall sense of that sequence of events; it does not represent the person's life in terms of success, or heroic failure, or any such interpretative scheme, but merely as a chapter of accidents. This is still a narrative. Recognizing that the idea is bound to be vague, we may say that a narrative which does this much and no more is a *minimalist* narrative.

The materials of a chronicle are the materials of narratives, and it is tempting to think of a narrative as a selection of elements from a suitably comprehensive chronicle. This model has one advantage and at least two disadvantages. The advantage is that it reminds us that the tests for the truth or credibility of the elements are the same in both cases. Whether the king died in a certain year, or there was a plague, is (allowing for familiar problems of vagueness and so on) a matter of fact, as we may innocently—or by now, I hope, not so innocently—call it. For this to be so, there does not have to be some absolute limit on the extent of a fact, or an absolute demand on its hardness. If it is claimed that some supposed statement of fact in either a chronicle or a narrative is too interpretative or carries too many presuppositions with it—if it were said, for instance, that the king was killed—we can retreat to less contentious statements and work from there. None of this need undermine the model of a narrative as a selection of items from a possible chronicle.

The model, however, does have disadvantages. One is that there is no criterion, independent of some explanatory or narrative interest, of what a "suitably comprehensive chronicle" would contain. The idea of a chronicle containing, even for some given area of space-time, every fact that might go into some narrative is unintelligible. Further, the model may suggest that the narrative selection from this imaginary comprehensive listing will be arbitrary. That contains two ideas, that the facts are there to be picked up or left alone, and that the choice is a matter of taste or prejudice. Both ideas are false. Facts have to be discovered, and the interests that shape the narrative also shape the inquiry that discovers them (which is why the virtues of Accuracy are called upon if the facts that are included are going to be facts at all). This does not mean that the inquiry invents the facts. E. H. Carr unwisely said that a certain event recounted by the historian Kitson Clark as having happened in 1850 was not a historical fact until Kitson Clark (in 1962) put it into his book. That is richly misleading. It is true if it means (in one sense) that the event becomes for the first time part of history; as Richard J. Evans has rightly said, it becomes for the first time historical *evidence*.[9] It is true, too, that the model of "selecting" facts is inadequate, because it suggests that all possible candidates for selection are pre-formed, and this is not a coherent picture; the point at which a given fact becomes evidence for the historian may be (though in many cases it is not) the first time it has been stated, and what statements the historian wants to make or question will be a function of his inquiry.[10] But it is absurd to say that the historian makes something into a fact if this is supposed to deny that a statement about a supposed event in 1850 is true or false in virtue of what happened in 1850. In this most basic sense the facts are not created by the inquiry, and it is hard to believe that anyone (really) thinks otherwise.

Whether particular items are included or rejected by a narrative is not simply a matter of taste. A merely arbitrary or capricious selection of events from a pool or great barn of facts would not make sense of anything to anybody. However, here we begin to see real problems. The model serves to remind us that there can be agreement on facts and disagreement about what makes sense of them to whom. Given some period or sequence of events, very different narratives will make sense of it to different parties, and this may involve not just a difference but a conflict, whether it is a matter of vast public importance, such as the French Revolution or the American Civil War (a case in which it makes an interpretative claim even to call it by that name), or it is tiny in the general scale of things, such as the break-up of a marriage. Perhaps such conflicts between narratives are undecidable and are resolved, if at all, only by fading eventually into the past. Moreover, in which direction they fade, which narrative prevails if either of them does, may be a matter of who has power over or among the later audience for the narrative of these events. This is an area in which it looks as though the deniers, as I have called them, may have a case.

2. *Structures and Explanations*

Mini-narratives make sense of what they narrate simply in virtue of what makes them mini-narratives. Of course, there are philosophical questions about natural processes and intentional patterns of action, about what they are and how we recognize them, but it would certainly be a prejudice to suppose that we cannot recognize them. But once they and other items that might figure in a chronicle are combined into a more ambitious story, it is a real question what it relies on in order to make sense of anything. One question concerns its unity: what in the broadest sense is the story about? Strikingly, two different and very familiar answers are presented by the first words of the two founding narratives of Western literature. *Andra*, the *Odyssey* starts, "the man," and it is the story of a life, or part of a life; *Mênin*, "the anger," the first word of the *Iliad*, points to a set of happenings that had very striking consequences for what is presented as a great enterprise. If we add to these the opening verses of a more self-conscious epic, the *Aeneid*, we get a third traditional subject, the history of a people.

An epic, very obviously, is only one kind of narrative, if any one kind at all. It can encompass a great deal of very various material. Moreover, there are other and more specific patterns of story within it that may be essential to its structure, as the *Odyssey* is a story of home-coming, recovery, and revenge, and the *Iliad* involves a momentous change of mind on the part of Achilles, a change of mind which together with its effects is what makes his total absence from earlier books of the poem into part of the story. Narrative theorists, particularly from a formalist point of view, have written a great deal about types of narrative and asked how many basic kinds of story there may be. I shall not try to follow them. Our question is at a more general level. These structural characteristics of narratives are in some sense rhetorical properties of them: they are what keep listeners or readers involved or concerned, and make them feel at the end that something has gone by which they can grasp. If it is these same characteristics that structure true stories about the past, then those longer narratives that have the status of history and try to make sense of the past will do so in virtue of their rhetorical properties. But how will that stand in relation to the virtues of truthfulness? In particular, will it undo the supposed Thucydidean achievements that I praised in chapter 7? The telling of myths, I said, was a matter of what suited an audience, while telling the truth is not: truth is not audience-relative. But history cannot be a mere chronicle, the barking out of unrelated truths, and if making sense of any substantial part of the past relies on rhetorical powers, truthfulness may seem to be doing less for us than we hoped. Indeed, the term "rhetoric" itself powerfully encourages something that we have encountered several times in the course of this study, the temptation to take some old distinction between the "higher" and the "lower" and then defiantly assert the lower. "Rhetoric" is particularly disposed to set free various suspects from the wrong side of the Platonic divide, carrying with it ideas of manipulation and force, and the implication that there are, almost in the nature of the case, rival speakers (or if not, that is because one has got rid of the others). So, if rhetoric is central to making sense of the past on a larger scale, it may seem that in this connection truthfulness and its virtues have gained us less than we hoped.

We have already come to the practice of history, and I must make plain that in discussing history in terms of narrative, I am not assuming that all history is "narrative history" in a limiting sense of that phrase. There was nothing in the account of narrative in general to rule out the possibility that some explanatory accounts should call on standing structures, or relate items to each other that were coexistent. We can make sense of some features of past societies, and of their relation to the present, in terms of long-standing institutions, practices, or social formations. In the broad sense that concerns us here, this is still a narrative, a selective account of the past, structured sequentially in time, that is designed to make sense of it. Endurance itself is unsurprisingly a temporal phenomenon (the *longue durée* is a *durée*) and it can both explain and need to be explained.

The best-known attempt to incorporate rhetorical categories into the modern theory of history is that of Hayden White.[11] White characterizes various historians and philosophers of history in terms of a complex schematism, presided over by a quartet of rhetorical tropes, Metaphor, Metonymy, Synecdochy, and Irony, which, as well as being exemplified in other fourfold distinctions, work in structuring or "prefiguring" the material that is treated in these stylistically various ways. The details of this formalist schematism, and indeed its use of the tropes, do not seem to me the interesting part of the enterprise; it must be said that the fantastical elaboration of the scheme and its ability to process almost any possibility without much resistance do sometimes make it seem less like a machine than a picture of a machine. Nevertheless, his book raises serious questions and provides some materials that will help in discussing them. It has been criticized for treating history as though it were textually enclosed and had no interest in truth at all. This is a misunderstanding.[12] White recognizes as well as anyone else that history is made of truths; its materials are the same as those of a possible chronicle, and the great nineteenth-century historians whom White studies helped to form the practices by which documents (and, as Collingwood emphasized, archaeological remains) can be put to the question to elicit those truths. But that is where the problem starts, since the truths in any history are at the very least a selection, and indeed that is an under-statement, since they are not simply waiting to be selected. In any text, there is a question of what is left out, above all what is left out and can be claimed to be relevant. There is also a question of what is added, what is inferred to fill the gaps. Over all that, there is the question of what story is being told. It is not a matter of leaving truths or reality or past happenings out of it, of generating a *detached* fiction. As Clemenceau famously said at Versailles to a German who had wondered what future historians would say about all this, "They won't say that Belgium invaded Germany."

With history as with some everyday narrative, every statement in it can be true and it can still tell the wrong story. The problem is not whether truths, and to that extent the virtues of truth, come into it, but how far they take us. It can be put like this: if a narrative is said to make sense of some (extended) period of the past, and this means that it makes the right or correct sense of it, to what extent is this, again, a matter of truth and truthfulness? White's answer to *this* question is "Very little." That answer may be an exaggeration, and I shall suggest that it is, but it is a serious answer to a real question, and it does not imply at all that there is no truth in historical narratives.

It is important in this area not to run together metaphysics and historiography. It is tempting to say that the past "really" or "in itself" is just a sequence of happenings (which is allowed to include actions and natural processes). This picture of an essentially unstructured past presents it as significantly more structured than the early Nietzschean picture, which we encountered in chapter 1, according to which everything is "really" an unconceptualized chaos.[13] In that picture, the "reality" could not be described at all except by a falsification of it. The picture we are now considering, of the past as unstructured, does allow the past to be described, up to a point, in terms of events: concepts can be applied to it. What it does not do, at this level of description, is make sense, except on the small scale of mini-narratives (if mini-narratives are forbidden, it will lose structure altogether). Making sense of it on a larger scale will be a matter of interpretation, and interpretation is up to us. The past will not make sense unless we make sense of it.[14] If we handle it carefully, this account is not too misleading. It does, for instance, pass the test that, if we are supposed to be giving interpretations, there must be some recognizable happenings that we are interpreting—though we have to remember that which happenings need, in a given case, to be interpreted will depend on the interpretation.

However, if we are going to be careful with this account, we need to be especially careful with the idea that it tells us what the past is "really" or "in itself," an idea which can only too easily lead into one or the other of two bad arguments. One of them says that since interpretations are constructs imposed on an unstructured past, they are all equally arbitrary or products of the will. This style of argument is favoured by many deniers, and we shall come to it later. The other bad argument, favoured by many enemies of the deniers, says that since the past is really unstructured, we shall tell the truth about it only if we represent it historically as unstructured. Strictly speaking, of course, this is impossible: we would have to offer simply a chronicle, with arbitrary boundaries and no principle of selection, and there could not be such a thing, let alone one that could pass as history. However, there are various styles of history that claim, roughly speaking, to offer as little structure as possible. They offer a minimalist narrative of some period or set of events, and represent it as making little in the way of overall sense. They may, further, be anxious to bring out the point that there is no overall sense, that history is not much more than one damned thing after another (I think that this is the style that White calls "Ironic"). Such styles of history come in different forms and different degrees of sophistication; I shall not be concerned with their differences but will lump them together under the word "minimalist."

The essential point is that minimalist accounts of the past constitute one style of interpretation among others. Every historical interpretation has to agree that the past contains such things as natural processes and actions, and to that extent it makes small-scale sense— such things make sense in the present, and the past (as chapter 7 reminded us) was someone else's present. This is why there is something to interpret. Moreover, as I have said, every narrative is committed to making *some* sense of what it narrates: it aims, at least, to make us see how things went. An historical style committed to minimalism claims or implies that if you see how things went, there is not much more to be said. It will naturally concentrate on elements of pure contingency and accident, as in the story of Hitler's being appointed to the Chancellorship in 1933 (probably the Nazis' unique chance of gaining power), where it has been convincingly claimed that it crucially depended on a confusion of individual purposes and miscalculations which very easily might have gone otherwise. Of course, there has to be more to the story than those immediate contingencies; it has to be explained why the Nazis had enough seats in the Reichstag for Hitler to be taken seriously, why von

Papen should have had the purposes he had, and so on.[15] Moreover, if the account of these contingencies is convincing, then they had better be recognized by any honest historical account, in whatever style. But there is still a contrast between an historian who claims to find in the Nazi rise to power some more ambitious story, who wants to make overall sense of the catastrophe, and a minimalist historian who does not but presents us, in telling this story, with merely another set of contingencies. The point is that a minimalist style has to hold its own or earn its place against others. The ever deceptive word "really" can suggest that in simply telling us how things went, a minimalist story is merely telling the truth, and that anything else is not just fiction but falsehood. That is the error of what is often called "positivism." The claim that there is no overall or larger-scale sense to be made of the past is itself a larger-scale claim, and it has to be earned, like any of the others. Perhaps it can be earned, but it does not come as a free gift from metaphysics to history. The point is particularly obvious with the self-conscious, Ironic, forms of minimalism, which play against more ambitious styles and want to *make a point* to the effect that while we can tell a story of how things came to a certain state, and an actual path is displayed from earlier to later, there is no further or overall sense to that path. In doing this, they may be doing other, political, things as well. They may suggest that the "reality" of history lies in some class of facts which they prefer, such as the machinations of politicians; they may encourage, in Heine's memorable words, "a convenient soothing fatalism."[16]

We shall come to these further questions, of the point of telling one kind of story over another, in section 4. The immediate question concerns the relations between truthfulness and the formation of the story. The question is not whether historical stories involve interpretation—of course they do. It is not the question whether there are truths about the past—there are only too many. The question is the extent to which the formation of a story can be governed by considerations that have anything to do with truth and truthfulness. A particular application of that question is: Is there anything to be said in the dimension of truth and truthfulness for a minimalist style of interpretation? But before that, we have to ask what in general truth and truthfulness can do for an historical story beyond validating its most basic materials, those that it might share with a chronicle.

There is no sharp line between what historians recover from the record and what they "fill in"; getting data from the record already involves filling in. Explanation is already involved, and further explanatory steps will then be needed to fill in further, to work out why some agent in the past should have done some particular thing, or why some practice that was in place at an earlier time ceased to exist. There has been much discussion of "the nature of historical explanation," but at this level—the level at which history necessarily involves explanation if it is to tell any story at all, however minimalist—the question is surely misconceived. There is no such thing, at this level, as *historical* explanation. There is just explanation. Some of it is explanation applied to happenings or states of affairs in the past, but we explain things in the remoter past in the same ways as we explain things in the present or in the recent past, and those ways depend on the phenomena in question and on the interest of the inquiry. There is also the activity of explaining some present phenomenon *by its history*, such as the graffiti in Belfast. This is narrative explanation in the narrow sense, and on a shorter time-scale and with familiar kinds of materials we engage in it every day. Again, there is explanation *by historians*: applying patterns of explanation to the past may involve the skills that professional historians acquire through their training, in interpreting old documents or ruins or artefacts. Those are in fact skills in explaining *the present*, in the form of the papers, stones, or shards that lie in front of them.

It is the merest truism that there is nothing special about the past as such—it is simply what used to be the present. As we saw in chapter 7, however, the clear recognition of that truism, as it now is, carried significant consequences. As Thucydides saw, the use of general terms to describe happenings in the past has implications for their explanation. To the extent that they are indeed the same sort of happenings, they have similar kinds of explanation. It is equally true that the past, or regions of it, may be special in the sense that what happened then does not happen now. Natural phenomena change, as once there were dinosaurs and there are none now, and the Nile, as Herodotus guessed, earlier had a different course. But we can explain such differences between different times, and it is the same with institutions, customs, and what it makes sense to people to do. In some cases it will be plausible to relate these changes in human life rather directly to an underlying psychology that is expressed differently in different circumstances; in other cases, a much longer story will be needed.

One notable way of misunderstanding the actions of people in the past is to over-rationalize them. In the light of Diderot's view of the mind, which we considered in chapter 8, many historians do seem to overestimate the extent to which people knew what they were doing. In one way, this is no special problem for history, since we all do the same. Moreover, we are usually, like the historian, trying to make sense of people's actions on the basis of very scrappy evidence; we are all in varying degrees "filling in." But historians are typically under special pressure to make sense of what was done, and to do so on the basis of limited evidence that will not get any better, and this can lead to their making past actions out to have been more sensible than they actually were. There is another risk, of misunderstanding the terms in which actions made sense to the agents—in the case of history, this is one kind of anachronism. There is not much to be said about this to the present purpose except that it is a mistake and that knowledge can guard against it. A lot of very interesting history is itself the history of reasons for action, of considerations that at a given time or place could count for or against doing various things. It remains a matter of debate how directly those varying reasons relate to more general types of motivation, and how deep the distinctions between their historical surroundings go. Indeed, as I said earlier, people may differ about the categories in terms of which actions make sense to them. Some people more than others are attached to very reductive explanations, such as accounting for terrorist suicides in terms of the prospects of heavenly rewards.

I believe that knowing enough history should itself guard against heading rapidly toward reductive explanations. The route between grasping the terms in which the world has made sense to some given people, and relating that fact to desires which human beings intelligibly share, may be long, surprising, and stony with contingencies—

even when we include (as we should) among the desires that human beings share the desire that the world should make sense to them in some terms or other. But even those who think that the route from the local to the universal is simpler than I think it is should accept two points. One is that they still need the point of departure: before they set out to explain the terms in which others have made sense of the world, they first have to grasp them. Second, the relation of all this to history is only a special case, and the question arises with any group of people that anyone may seek to understand. I have mentioned earlier in this chapter and elsewhere in this book "different cultural circumstances." I mean this in a sense in which it is indisputable that there are differing cultural circumstances: it is just a fact, for instance, that at certain times and places, and not at most others, something taken as an insult to a man's honour could lead to a ritualized kind of one-on-one combat called "a duel." We can put the questions about explanation that I have just raised by asking how deep the notion of "different cultural circumstances" goes. There is a huge amount to be known about a practice such as duelling and how it worked in fact; some of that knowledge will help one to understand why the practice flourished at some times and places and not at others. We can ask: How much else was intelligibly connected with it and also varied between those various times and places? (These are the kinds of question that it would be good to be able to answer with regard to the virtues of truth themselves.)

For the present discussion, however, the important point is that the procedures that are involved in "filling in" have a relatively unproblematic connection with the truth. "Filling in" calls on various kinds of explanation, and it is a matter for inquiry whether the explanations and the assumptions that go into them hold up. Moreover, there can be nothing here that is a special problem with historical explanation (except, perhaps, a particular shortage of evidence or, with regard to more recent history, an unmanageable surfeit of evidence). Just because at this level there is no distinctively historical explanation, there can be no special problem at this level about truth as an aim. "Filling in" the historical account can be as much a matter of aiming at the truth, and calls as much on the virtues associated with that, as any other kind of inquiry.

To some extent, this extends to "leaving out" as well. If certain facts help to explain a certain phenomenon, at the level we have just been discussing, and the historian leaves them out, he is left with an incomplete or unconvincing explanation, or none at all. Of course there can be disagreements about what counts as an explanation, and sometimes those disagreements go deep into what different historians regard as significant; then the question of leaving things out also goes deeper. A given fact is considered by some historians relevant and important to their whole view of a topic or period. Others think differently. Some of the latter may mention it and say something to put it in what they take to be its place, but some may not mention it at all. Are they less than truthful? We come back to the concerns of chapter 5: they have told no lies, but their account might be thought to be misleading. If it is, who is being misled?

3. *Audiences*

Here we come to a dimension of historical writing that is strikingly missing from Hayden White's account of it. A critic of White has pointed out that, in bringing the rhetorical tradition to bear on the writing of history, he appeals in fact to surprisingly little of that tradition.[17] He reduces it in effect to poetics, the analysis of style or literary effect, but the classical theory of rhetoric treated much more than this. In particular, it covered the means of making a case against actual or possible objections. White's historian is seemingly a solo artist, and his readers are related to him as a receptive audience, but an actual historian is related, not only to other historians, but to an audience with a licence to interrupt. These various readers constitute a community, or more than one, in which the historical writer can have or lack a reputation for trustworthiness. "Would you buy an interpretation from this person?" can become an effective question, and even if in the end you would not buy the interpretation, you might hope to be told quite a lot of what you need in order to accept or reject it. This may well mean that if he knows of facts that support a rival account and he fails to say anything about them, he is being untrustworthy. As with the scientists I discussed in chapter

6,[18] we do not need to ascribe to a trustworthy narrator Platonically pure and high-minded motivations. Certainly, he cannot just be like Adam Smith's baker, since there is a lively and profitable market in bad and tendentious history, but, if things are going well, we might reasonably get some reassurance from his wanting to be a famous historian admired by other historians. However, we shall not get much reassurance from that if things are not going well, and the only historians left to admire him are members of the Party. More generally, there is a question of what kind of community of readers and critics he is addressing.

At this point the question becomes one of the historian's relations to a public. What do those relations demand, not only of the historian, but of the public, and how far are they structured by truthfulness? Truth and truthfulness have seen us some of the way. An historical writer who deliberately or recklessly includes falsehoods is a liar. He is a liar because he is writing in the mode of history, which is now, and has been for a long time, a mode different from fable, a novel, or a patriotic song. It is not simply a matter of correct classification or professional good conduct that the historian should tell the truth, since he comes before the public as one who tells the truth, and he needs its virtues; he is not debarred from singing a patriotic song (or a cosmopolitan one), but he is supposed to do so in the mode of truth. Of course, this leaves us with a question, one that we shall come back to: granted that history is committed to being truthful, why is it *history* that we need?

Among the considerations that shape the disposition of Sincerity, as we saw in chapter 5, is the idea that hearers may have no right to the truth because they want to know too much, but that cannot be the problem between the historian and his audience. The problem is rather the opposite, that the audience may not want to be told various things that they find irrelevant or uninteresting or unhelpful. If the historian leaves out some things which people do not want to hear, but which he thinks important, this is a failure in candour, since he is naturally taken to be saying what he thinks is worth saying. If the things that his particular audience, those who share his own point of view, do not want to hear are things that he knows would embarrass his account, and he fails to mention them, he is again less than trustworthy. But of course the historian may leave things out because he himself merely agrees with the audience that they are unimportant and irrelevant, and, whatever else it may be, that in itself will not be a failure of Sincerity. In itself, it need not be a failure in anything.

Liberal pluralistic societies give a special shape to problems that are inherent in the relations between historians and the public, because they contain more than one audience. There is a diversity of opinions about what is important, and a diversity of writers who share them or contest them, which is why it is quite natural to speak of "conservative" or "left-wing" or "feminist" historians. Some writers themselves present a variety of views. Different accounts will be advanced and defended under the constraints of truthfulness. This will be so among more serious historians, and therefore, one hopes, among professional ones, though one needs to be cautious of the idea that professionalism in itself necessarily brings with it an adequate range of criticism. Professional historians can be not only prejudiced but united in their prejudices. Peter Novick has written, "In the early decades of the twentieth century the most professionally accomplished work on Reconstruction—work hailed by the profession as the most objective, the most balanced, the most fair—was viciously racist; antiracist accounts were for the most part crude and amateurish."[19] Different audiences welcome different interpretations, but at the same time there is enough overlap between the audiences, if the culture is in good shape, for one group to know what may be brought against it by others. The consequent controversies tend on the whole to knock the edges off the distinctive interpretations. Does this process get us, collectively, nearer to the truth? Is it an example of a genuine marketplace of ideas, an approximation to the idealized competition between opinions which I distinguished in the previous chapter from the economic market place *in* ideas?

On some matters, this is surely so. Continued inquiry by critical historians eliminates earlier interpretations, which become, in the face of further information and more searching questions, indefensible. This applies, obviously enough, to particular sets of events: for instance, the sixteenth-century social commotion in England traditionally called "The Pilgrimage of Grace" is by everyone's agreement not simply any of the things earlier accounts took it to be.[20] Even with more extensive phenomena, and even if they have recently been passionately contested for political reasons, controversy can die down and questions be reformulated: this seems to have happened, to some extent, with the argument that raged bitterly in the 1960s and 1970s about the social and psychological effects of American slavery.[21]

The same thing can extend even to certain very large-scale interpretations. Some modes of interpretation come to look antiquated and no longer worth discussing, and this may be not simply because they have fallen out of fashion, but because in the light of the truth they appear hollow and hopeless. One style that is now approaching this condition is the kind of teleological history that represented some nation, or class, or idea as the inevitable and in some sense predestined victor in the historical process. (It must be said that even if few historians now try to spell out such a story, some writers about liberalism, including some philosophers, seem to assume something like it.) One reason for the obsolescence of such stories is that truthful inquiry always shows that there is more ambiguity and contingency in the process than the story can allow. Moreover, there is a large difficulty in principle, that the stories need a mechanism to explain how such a process could be possible. There are indeed, in favourable cases and on a smaller scale, convincing "Invisible Hand" explanations, which show how some seemingly intended or designed outcome can be the product of interactions that involve no such intention or design.[22] Marx aimed to give such explanations of vast historical changes, and the project failed, not so much because the processes were unintelligible, but because the explanations were untrue. In other cases, teleological explanations may get a grip, at least on a small scale, because the actors themselves believed in the teleology—the manifest destiny in question was manifest to the people who collectively contrived its workings. (Marxism itself encountered some famously tricky questions on this point, of how much the eventual victory of the working class would be advanced through the conscious efforts of people who believed in it.) Those explanations are often weak, in particular because such beliefs are just as likely to have perverse effects, but to the extent that they work, they work: there is nothing mysterious in the idea that a consciously shared belief in an outcome can help to bring it about, though it may indeed be mysterious why this should be so in some cases rather than others.

Hayden White listed various extravagant philosophies of history, including those of Spengler and Toynbee, and said, "When it is a matter of choosing among these alternative visions of history, the only grounds for choosing one over another are *moral* or *aesthetic* ones."[23] This shocked many critics, a reaction which strictly speaking may have been out of place, since all he says here is that the criteria for choosing among the items *in this list* are moral or aesthetic, and if you had to choose any of them at all, that might well be true. But elsewhere he suggests that the same applies to historical interpretations in general, and that really is shocking. Portentous long-haul philosophies of history, if they are not merely vacuous, include paradigms of a kind of account that now carries no conviction because it offers no adequate account of how the supposed processes could work, and once that question has been raised, historical accounts that do not answer it are accounts that refuse to answer it, and the canons of truthfulness itself will reject them. Once the question has been raised, there is no respectable route back from confronting it. This is the intellectual irreversibility of Enlightenment. Of course it is only its intellectual irreversibility, and there are only too many ways in which Enlightenment may be reversed in historical fact, given a substantial enough political or natural catastrophe.

White also said that an historian who employs a particular rhetorical mode, say of a mechanistic explanatory kind, "has no authority in a public which is pretheoretically committed to a prefiguration of the historical field" in some other rhetorical mode.[24] If "has no authority" simply meant "will not get much attention or have much effect," this would be not much more than a tautology, but I take it that White meant more than this: that there was no reason, or at least no reason connected with the truth, that this audience should attend to such an historian. This is again wrong: some rhetorical modes offer supposed teleological explanations, and the demand for an account of how the teleological process is supposed to work is an intellectual demand that needs to be met. I said just now that this demand has to be met once the question has been raised, but now I am saying more, that raising such a question—one expression of the arrival of Enlightenment—is from the point of view of truthfulness an improvement. Someone who will not believe in such processes without an explanation of how they work, and who is aware of the many contingencies involved in what are claimed to be inevitable developments, is *better informed* than someone who is not in that position.

Does this mean that, given the processes of critique in a liberal society, it is likely to converge on some version of minimalist history? If so, would this be convergence on the true or correct historical interpretation, so that the minimalist style will have been vindicated over others? The answer to both these questions is no. First of all, as we saw in the previous chapter, liberal society itself is not the idealized marketplace of ideas. The area of critical historical discussion within it is a better approximation to such a place, but there is always a further question (one question I started from in chapter 1) of what authority that area has within the society. Let us assume, though, that it has enough authority (in particular through a perceived truthfulness and resistance to lies) to influence society's opinions about the past. There is still no reason why such critical discussion should converge on a minimalist account. There are other styles of historical interpretation that lie between that style, on the one hand, and long-haul teleological narratives on the other. Even if we rule out manifest destiny stories because they are untruthful, we do not necessarily have to retire into minimalism. This comes out if one considers the kinds of disagreements in historical interpretation that are still very much with us, and how significant those disagreements can be. How peculiar was the Soviet Union?—which means both, how different was it from other twentieth-century authoritarian states, and also, how far was it continuous with the previous history of Russia?[25] What parts were played in the Holocaust by Hitler's personal obsessions and by existing European antisemitism, and, indeed, in what terms can such a question be usefully discussed? What perspectives are provided on systems of subordination by the experiences of the subordinated, as in the case of slavery? How far are those experiences even experiences *of* subordination?—a question that has variously appeared in the discussion, for instance, of the position of women in nineteenth-century bourgeois society. All these questions have at this moment not only a variety of answers but highly contested formulations, and different people tell different stories, fortunately not always or for the most part to different audiences: they are telling them in a society where one aim they have, among others, is to convince the unconvinced. The stories try to make large-scale sense of these periods and institutions and do so in different terms, but each style can, in its best examples, sustain a decent respect for the truth.

There is no one thing that these various stories are "for," other than trying to make sense of the past. There is no one kind of thing that different audiences are seeking when they seek something that makes sense to them. One prominent contemporary example is that of people who think of themselves as a community that has suffered oppression and are looking for ways in which to make sense of it, but that is just one example; moreover, they do not by any means all seek to make sense of it in the same way. Even the few cases I have just mentioned suggest other kinds of interest. Not all interest in the past is directed to the political, even in the broadest sense. At the limit, there is the honourable interest of mere curiosity, but even with that, unless it is terminally mindless fact-acquisition, there is something that makes one story, and one subject of a story, more interesting than another, and this is expressed in what makes sense of those stories: for some, a person's achievement or disappointment; for another, the way in which some remote social system functioned.

Many interpretations and styles of interpretation, then, can be found between false teleological history, on the one hand, and minimalist history on the other. This is a reason why critical exchange in a liberal society will not necessarily converge on history in a minimalist style. Moreover—and this was the second question—even if convergence on such a style happened, this would not show it to be the correct or true interpretation of the past. This is for a reason of very general principle. When we have methods of inquiry that are truth-acquiring (as I put it in chapter 6), then, if inquirers using those methods converge in their beliefs, we have some reason to think that they have converged on the truth. That applies as much in the field of historical inquiry as anywhere else. But a model of convergence on the truth applies only to the extent that we can coherently conceive of what might count as "the truth" about the matter to hand. In general, this requirement is met straightforwardly because what the inquiry is looking for is the answer to a question. I can say that there is a truth of the matter, whether Caesar led his army across the Rubicon, because I mean that there is a true answer to that question. This does not mean that there is such a thing as the truth about Caesar or, come to that, about the Rubicon; there are indefinitely many truths about them, as there are indefinitely many questions that could be asked about them. (That is why, as we saw in section 1 of this chapter, facts are not individuated before any inquiry, though that does not mean that the inquiry creates them out of nothing.) Philosophers of science disagree whether there could be such a thing as "the truth about the universe," but those who think that there could be such a thing certainly do not suppose that there is just one true thing to be said about the universe. They mean something to the effect that there could be a final answer to the question "What are the most basic laws of the universe?" where those most basic laws will have to satisfy some very strong requirements of what they can explain. "Everything," some say, but the success of the project can hardly turn on taking that literally. In the sense in which the scientists are looking for the truth about the universe, they will not have failed because the theory they triumphantly produce cannot explain the Pilgrimage of Grace, Susan's divorce, or Beethoven's Opus 110. Rather, it will have to explain—we cannot put it much better than this—everything that those engaged in the search take it to be the business of cosmology and physics to explain.

In such a sense, there is no such thing as "the truth" about the historical past, though as with the universe or Caesar there are many truths about it. There would be such a thing as "the truth about the past" only if there were one most basic question about the past that was the concern of those inquiring into it, and there is no such question. This means that even if our society came to converge on a minimalist style of interpreting the past, or indeed any other style, this would not mean that it had arrived at the truth about history, because there is no such thing for it to arrive at. This does not mean, to repeat, that there are no truths about the past, and it does not mean that interpretations, whatever they may be, need not be responsive to the demands of truthfulness. It means that while we must demand that interpretations of the past should tell us the truth, in the sense that they should not lie or mislead, what we need them for is not to tell us something called "the truth about the past." We need them to be truthful, and to make sense of the past—to us.

4. Needs

What makes sense of the past to us may not make sense of it to others. This applies to people in the past: we know, historically, that their interpretations of their past differed from our interpretations of both their past and ours. It applies to people in the future. If "the truth about the universe" were discovered, future people would have no reason to change it. The theory that expressed it would be what Crispin Wright has called "superassertible": it would be warranted, and warrant for it would survive any scrutiny of our information and any addition to it.[26] It may be that no-one could ever know that a theory was superassertible, but people who hope for "the truth about the universe" are hoping for a theory that will be. I do not see how anyone could reasonably think that a large-scale interpretation of history might be in this position, or why they should want it to be so. To suppose that future people will need the same things from an interpretation of the past as we do surely implies that life as cultural development will have come to a stop. Moreover, and unlike the case of cosmology, there is no one thing that "we" need from such interpretations now, because in various ways there is no one "we."

In discussions of historiography, someone who accepts these variations in what makes sense to different people is often called a "relativist." Manifestly, there is a relativity—what makes sense to some people is contrasted with what makes sense to others. But it is not a relativity of truth. There is no way in which the king's death could have happened "for" the Anglo-Saxon chronicler and not happened "for" us, or the Germans have invaded Belgium in 1914 "for" some cultures and not for others. The same holds for many small-scale explanations: if the king was murdered, someone killed him, *period*. What is relative is the interest that selectively forms a narrative and puts some part of the past into shape. Some larger-scale patterns of interpretation can themselves fall victim to the truth: I have already suggested that this is so with teleological explanations, and it is so with those that appeal (to the extent that they seriously do so) to supernatural forces. In these cases, the difference between us and them with regard to what makes sense is a matter of the truth, and the "relativist" about interpretation should not deny it. The distinctive claim of the "relativist" about historical interpretation is that one party can differ from another about what makes sense of the past without necessarily thinking that the other party's interpretation is false.

Relativism, of any kind, does its work when it looks as though there is a conflict, and it may be said that there is no work for it to do here, because there does not even seem to be a conflict. There are simply many compatible stories, told from different perspectives, with different emphases, on different scales of detail. This is too simple. First, with the still eagerly contested subjects, such as those from the recent past that I mentioned in the previous section, the different emphases and perspectives make all the difference between someone's accepting or rejecting a story as making sense of what happened. Moreover, even when the matters are less immediately contested, there is very often an implicit conflict in the background, about what kind of consideration makes sense of the past or certain areas of it. There are no doubt some cases in which one can regard two different accounts just as offering pictures on different scales or with different degrees of resolution: one cannot superimpose them or attend to both at once, but one can acknowledge them as equally acceptable representations of the scene. This optical metaphor, however, is basically misleading, because it suggests that the question always concerns how much of what kind of feature you can see. But if one history of a given period emphasizes governmental manipulations, another the circulation of ideas, another economic change, and even if all the claims of fact that they make are compatible with one another, there may well be an implicit conflict about what matters most, what kind of force or change makes most sense of the period.

The use of the term "relativism" also encounters an objection from the opposite direction. Relativism indeed moves in when there appears to be a conflict, but what it aims to do is to remove the conflict, to show that it is only apparent. In the present case, it will be said, a *relativist*, strictly speaking, should insist that one style of interpretation makes sense to one group of people and another to another, so there is no conflict between them, and this is the end of the matter. But with historical interpretation, clearly, this is not how the matter ends. It may be so when we examine interpretations made by people in the past, because the matter they were about is indeed ended. It may be so in the present when nothing turns on it. But as I said in the previous section, people who advance contested inter-pretations are often trying, not just to rally their own group, but to convince the unconvinced. They will not be satisfied with a settle-ment that, in strictly relativist style, offers each party its own history. This is a strong objection, and perhaps it is right that (as usual) the term "relativism" only brings more confusion. But someone who uses it is registering something very important, that the dimensions of disagreement involved are not simply a matter of knowledge or explanation or to be resolved by further historical inquiry. They are matters of the needs of the various parties, and of their relations to people who have other needs. We can be brought to see the needs of other people, and this will alter our own. Moreover, we can be brought to do this, in part, by being told their historical story, which is why it may be worth one group's telling their story to others. But all of this is a matter of the politics, in the broadest sense, of their relations. At the end of the line, the question may be whether one lot of people is going to live with another or not, and that will in-volve the question whether one lot can make sense of the fact that something different makes sense to the other. In less dramatic situa-tions, the same thing applies. People use the word "relativism" here, perhaps, because they have a correct sense that the differences un-derlying these disagreements are basically political, or ethical, or at the very least temperamental.

If we do speak of a relativism of historical interpretation, however, we should not contrast it with "objectivity."[27] This contrast suggests that on a relativist account any narrator is (or might as well be) engaged in misleading people, lying, or special pleading. More subtly, it suggests that even if the narrator is subjectively in good faith, the narration will inevitably be "biassed." The force of this depends on the supposed contrast to "bias." If the contrast is with a supposed story of the past that both makes sense of it on a large scale and is such that no adequately informed and honest person could reject it, the relativist will say that the contrast is irrelevant, since there could not be such a story. If "bias" implies that on the relativist account no story can ever learn from any other story, this is not true. When different stories, with different demands of what makes sense, are told at the same time and in knowledge of one another, they are not insulated from one another, or if they are, this will not be a mere consequence of the relativist account. It will be a political fact, which is constituted by there being two publics that do not speak to each other in ways that make enough shared sense. What will overcome that situation, indeed whether both the parties want it to be overcome, are themselves political questions. "If only they understood the past in the same terms . . . ," a wistful mediator may think. But if they come to do so, that will at least as much be the effect of their reconciliation, never simply its cause: though it may well be helped by each party's recognizing that the other tries to handle its history truthfully.

I have spoken of people's "accepting" or "rejecting" an historical interpretation, but we should resist the voluntarism that is sometimes thrust onto this subject, the idea that we can choose the way in which we see the past. (There are various philosophical errors that underlie this idea, such as the assumption that what is not an object of the understanding, a matter of truth or falsehood, must be a matter of the will, but I shall not take up those issues here.)[28] What makes sense to someone is not, in any connection, a matter of the will; even in a situation of decision, although the agent decides to do the action, he does not decide that the action, or the kind of action, or the considerations that support the action, make sense to him. People can come to see, and come to see quite suddenly, that some course of events or someone's reasons for action make sense to them, but this comes as a discovery. So with historical interpretations: truth is not their ultimate virtue (though they need to be truthful), but in the broader sense that we considered in chapter 8, they are believed or not, and someone who tries to get others to accept an interpretation is trying to *convince* them. He wants them to change their minds, but not as they might, later, change their national anthem; he wants their minds to change. Relatedly, if their minds do change, and this is because the new interpretation better suits their needs, their needs do not figure as a premiss in an argument. It is not like the situation in which someone can say, "I need to lose weight; this will help me lose weight; so I will do this." This applies also to the means of convincing others. One thing that the broader notion of belief has in common with the everyday truth-centred notion is that you cannot get people to believe something by showing them that they need to believe it.

One reaction to our present situation is to think that we no longer need to make sense of the past at all, let alone in terms of what is true rather than mythical. Some "post-modern" theorists have taken something like this stance, but they typically do so on the basis of elaborate readings of the past (in particular, the failures of teleological history). In this book we have sometimes encountered the embarrassments that must go with such a position, and glimpsed the showers of ironical quotation marks that are thrown up by it. The proposition that the world (or some of it) has reached a point where it does not need the past is more significant when it is expressed not by cultural theorists but by those who vote with their feet, by people who would rather think about something else. Those reactions certainly exist, and if they really represented our situation, they would be what mattered: Goethe's Faust expressed the most fundamental truth of political theory when he said *Im Anfang war die Tat*, "In the beginning was the deed."[29] But I do not believe that this is the reality. The need to make sense of the past reasserts itself. It is particularly so when the smooth order of things is disturbed by violence, if only to answer the questions "Why?" "Why us?" "Where from?" Communitarian politics (and, at the limit, renewed tribal wars) are one area in which the need is very much alive, and it appears, too, in the interest in current historical disputes such as those I mentioned. The demand for an explicit and definite story about one's own people or nation is only one form of it, and that particular demand has been more urgent in some places than in others. It is not surprising that historical interpretations, and, more recently, the notion of historical interpretation itself, have been particularly contested in France and in the United States, in both of which, from the late eighteenth century onwards, there has been an on-going project of the nation's trying to give an account of itself. Germans in the last half century have had a special task, which many have pursued with unparalleled determination and honesty, of losing a past without forgetting it. But even in less fraught circumstances than these, the need is there to make sense of one's situation, and that requires an appeal to the past. If it is not to the historical past, then it will be to some kind of myth about it.

But, after all this, why not a myth? Of course, if a story is taken actually to make sense of their actual condition, people cannot *simply* regard it as a fiction, but they could cease to care and cease to look. In relation to the past, Accuracy and its demands could come to be forgotten, and reminders of them ignored or suppressed. A culture of truthfulness, the "sense for facts," would disappear. Should we mind?

It has been the aim of this book to show why there is no one reason for preferring the truth, and to explain why many people much of the time do not even ask for a reason, and rightly so. If the genealogy of truthfulness is vindicatory, it can show why truthfulness has an intrinsic value; why it can be seen as such with a good conscience; why a good conscience is a good thing with which to see it. To say that living in the truth is just a better way to be is a perfectly good answer. But it is not going to impress everyone, and it runs the risk, as answers in that style do, of implying that there are no other answers to the question why, if we are trying to make sense of the past, history is better than myth. Since there are other answers, we can back up a bit and consider what they might be.

An answer to the question will itself have to appeal to a historical story about our situation, about the origins, development, and character of modernity. As with all large-scale historical interpretations, we could not properly convince anyone of this story, or of the need for this story rather than another, without telling it, and if we told it, we would be claiming that it was truthful. Is that a circle? If so, it is the circle of the horizon within which any such speech must occur: one cannot *blast* someone into seeing the point. In any case, we cannot tell that story here but only go to its end or summary, which is: there is no true teleological history of liberalism, because (roughly speaking) there is no true teleological history of anything. In addition, there is only a limited extent to which we can regard the emergence of liberalism as an achievement in improving our knowledge (as everyone except the deniers regards the history of science). Cognitive achievements have indeed been involved, to the extent that earlier legitimations of power depended on conceptions that were false. Enlightenment as critique carried some truthfulness with it. But there is no plausible cognitive account that explains why people in certain parts of the world should recently have grasped the moral rightness of the principles of a liberal society, by which I mean one that aims to combine the rule of law with a liberty more extensive than in most earlier societies, a disposition to toleration, and a commitment to some kinds of equality.

The demand for a cognitive genealogy of liberalism seems particularly pressing because our attachment to its principles is so often represented as a triumph of moral understanding. Much of what is said in favour of liberal society and its principles is, naturally enough, said in the terms that they offer, that is to say, in terms of liberalism's various accounts of itself (the differences between which are the subject of much modern political philosophy). This gives the impression of a self-contained moral vision, which at once raises the question of how it arrived on earth, and makes that question peculiarly hard to answer.[30] However, a lot can also be said in favour of liberal society in terms of its helping people to avoid what every human being everywhere has reason to avoid: those are the considerations that we recalled in chapter 9 as supporting "the liberalism of fear."[31] A critic of liberal societies can point out that they are very imperfect in these respects, have brought about at home and elsewhere their own contributions to humiliation and violence, and are high on hypocrisy, all of which is true. It may be that at other times and places these things have been effectively controlled by other political means. But it is not easy to imagine, let alone find, a radically different alternative that would be possible in the conditions of the modern world and would do better by these universal measures.

Under this account, a liberal society has a definite relation to truthful history; indeed, it has two different relations to it. It helps to make truthful history possible, by arrangements that encourage various accounts and various needs for explanation to encounter one another; new questions can be asked, and the motivations of historical truthfulness can be sustained. Groups who want to tell their own stories have reasons to tell them not just to themselves, and others have reasons to want to hear them. Liberal society, we need to say, *can* do these things. Commercial society in itself does not guarantee them. I have argued that the economic marketplace is not itself an idealized market of ideas, and while it can sometimes be strong on novelty, it is likely to be weak on reaching the truth. But a liberal society has considerable resources to promote historical truth if it wants to, and it uniquely discourages some famous enemies of it, such as a state or religious monopoly—discouraging these things is, after all, its speciality, part of its legacy of Enlightenment.

At the same time, it quite specially needs truthful history. This claim may seem a joke, granted the raft of myth that has sustained liberal societies in the past and still helps to do so. But it is truthful inquiry that has taken those myths to pieces, and we do not have to see this merely as a terminal scene of dialectical self-destruction. Liberalism may have destroyed in some part its distinctive supporting stories about itself—certainly its spirit of critique has soaked them in suspicion—but the resources of the liberalism of fear, which work everywhere, may keep it afloat. A truthful history will remind one of those resources, and of what it costs in terms of quite basic human loss if a mythical order takes over. Here, once more, it is fundamental that there is no conscious road back, that Enlightenment is intellectually irreversible. Even if counter-Enlightenment nostalgia contained more truth than it does (its vast falsehood is a useful thing for truthful history to recall), a return would not be a return to the same place. Attempts to reimpose myths that have been discredited will fail, and many other values will suffer in the process, and this is another truth that truthful history preserves. Of course, if myths are needed and there is no life without them, then they will grow; and surely enough, there are other, and brutal, ways in which Enlightenment can go into reverse. But there is no reason, in truth or in good sense, to insist that it will do so. If one is in a place where things are not too bad, there are no doubt satisfactions in a rueful resignation about the ways of the world, or in proclaiming the end of more or less everything, or in repeating that after Auschwitz there are no songs. But a more hopeful story is likely to serve most of us better.

Some interpretations and styles of interpretation of the past are more hopeful than others. By this I mean a very abstract property indeed: I mean only that they leave room for hope, where hope is contrasted, simply, with despair. Of course, since people value different things, one person's hope may be another's despair. The reactionary historian who with much force and truth shows liberal society in its most empty and self-destructive aspects may bring despair to liberals and hope to reactionaries. One might take this to mean that hopefulness is relative in just the way that "making sense" is, and that a story that makes sense to certain people is a story that conveys hope to those people. But this is too simple. It is not true, sociologically or psychologically, that only hopeful stories make sense to people: they can be in a situation in which, for good or bad reasons, the only story that makes sense to them also makes them despair. The point is, rather, itself a matter of hope: the hope that hopeful but truthful stories can go on making sense, and that while they do, they will be told. Second, what we hope for, like what we fear, is a matter of our identifications. Our hope is that things will go well for us, and who counts as "us" depends on the nature and extent of the danger or risk that things will not go well. In peacetime, the politician hopes much of the time for outcomes that will suit himself or his party and do down the others, but in war he may hope for outcomes that will suit all the parties in his country and do down the enemy (a little truthful history will show how great a simplification this is). Liberals and reactionaries may unite in the hope that a culture will survive containing them both. Many science fiction tales enact the hope that humanity with all its conflicts and differences will survive ("all of us," as they naturally say), and that the aliens will be defeated. One strain in Nietzsche's thought seems to be that final defeat would consist of a state of affairs in which there was no "we" for which an intelligent person could retain any hope. The departure of any such hope, total despair, is nihilism. His own idea was that for an intelligent person hope must demand a world that contained heroically independent, intellectually and artistically creative beings; some forms of human life, such as contentment in a consumer society, the life of the "last man," were worse than nothing. It followed that for Nietzsche the occasion of nihilism lay very near to hand. For most of us, our hopes can reach more widely.

Whether a story is hopeful, then, is a question not just of a group, but of a group picked out in relation to a risk or a threat, and the same is true for despair. It follows that it may be very unobvious whether a story is hopeful, in the relevant sense, or not. Certainly its being hopeful need not imply that it gives good news to our immediate group: our hopes can extend beyond our immediate group. It does not imply that it is cheerful: about many subjects a truthful story that was cheerful could only cause despair. A hopeful story does not need a morally edifying arrangement of the material, which, as in some kinds of imaginative literature, may well arouse reasonable suspicions that it is untruthful. Again, it need not emphasize one kind of explanation over another, for instance, idealistic motives over self-interest; some will draw more hope from the idea that self-interest helped to abolish the slave trade than from an impression that such an important outcome should depend on the triumph of good intentions. In these and many other ways, what makes a style of interpretation hopeful is not the "what" but the "how," and the "how" itself may be vanishingly reticent. The need for an interpretation of the past to be hopeful offers no publication funds to Pollyanna.

Whether a story or a scheme of interpretation is hopeful or not does not provide a *criterion of choice*. As I have said, we cannot choose what will make sense to us. The idea is that the stories we in fact need are, in this very abstract sense, hopeful ones, and that we must hope, further, that this will continue to be so. Who is the object of the hope, the "we" in question, varies with the group to whom the story makes sense and with the risks or dangers that threaten them, but it is one aim of liberal societies to broaden the "we," to bring it about that the truth in narrower stories is audible to more people, and broader stories make sense to narrower groups. Beyond those more immediate aspirations, however, which belong with the familiar concern of liberalism that a tolerant and free society can raise its shared understandings and not degenerate into warring tribes, the ultimate concern is that we, a "we" that extends into the future, can go on telling a truthful enough story that will not leave everyone with despair if they think about it at all. The hope that a truthful story on a large enough scale will not cause despair is already hope.

Doubtless people will continue to make sense of the world in terms that help them to survive in it. But the question is how truthful those terms can be, and how far they can sustain the more ambitious ideals of truthfulness that we possess, together with institutions that both help to make those ideals effective and can themselves be sustained in knowledge of the truth. As Nietzsche served to remind us at the beginning of this inquiry, there are very compelling true accounts of the world that could lead anyone to despair who did not hate humanity. The narrator in *Heart of Darkness* says about Kurtz and his dying words:

> "This is the reason why I affirm that Kurtz was a remarkable man. He had something to say. He said it . . . He had summed up—he had judged. 'The horror!' He was a remarkable man. After all, this was the expression of some sort of belief; it had candour, it had conviction, it had a vibrating note of revolt in its whisper, it had the appalling face of a glimpsed truth . . ."[32]

Conrad, as so often, shows a truth and celebrates the courage of truthfulness. But this truth, the one that Kurtz saw at the last moment of his life, is not one that left to itself could keep anyone alive.

The hope can no longer be that the truth, enough truth, the whole truth, will itself set us free. But it is a lot more than the hope, merely, that the virtues of truth will keep going—in some form or other, they are bound to keep going as long as human beings communicate. The hope is that they will keep going in something like the more courageous, intransigent, and socially effective forms that they have acquired over their history; that some institutions can exist that will both support and express them; that the ways in which future people will come to make sense of things will enable them to see the truth and not be broken by it.

Endnote

❖   ❖   ❖   ❖   ❖

The Vocabulary of Truth: An Example

I said at the end of chapter 3 that there was no history of the concept of truth, though there is of course a history of theories of truth, of ways to find out the truth, of ideas about the true nature of the world, and so on. There is also a history—one with which this book has been concerned—of particular conceptions associated with the virtues of truth. I have tried to explain how there have been various conceptions of Accuracy and of Sincerity, and how it is that conceptions which differ from one another can nevertheless be conceptions of the same quality (one of the qualities schematically identified in the State of Nature story).

Given written documents from a certain place and period, let us say from a particular culture, we can pick out certain words the meanings of which belong to the general field of truth and truthfulness. They will probably include a word that can in certain contexts be translated as "truth" or "true." They may include one that is virtually equivalent to "true," but, more interestingly, they may not. This does not mean that the people who used the language in question did not have the concept of truth—*our* concept of truth, if one insists on putting it that way, though it is no more ours than it is theirs. It is everyone's concept of truth, a concept which, though they may well not reflect on it, they exercise in doing the things that every human group can and must do in using language. However, they may not have one word that stands to these various things as our words "true" and "truth" do. They may have a range of words that stand in various relations to these necessary human activities and purposes, and in coming to understand these words, we shall be able to see what those relations are.

I shall consider an example of this, the language used in writings that survive from archaic Greece, in particular Homer. I shall look at some of the ways in which these archaic expressions are related to the concept of truth and to the basic truth-related practices and qualities that we first encountered in the State of Nature. I do not offer any new philological discoveries; the subject has been extensively researched, and I rely on previous discussion. I have found particularly helpful an article by Thomas Cole (Cole [1983]) which draws clear distinctions and, very significantly, avoids some common confusions about what the questions are that need to be answered.

It is partly because they have asked the wrong question that some scholars have made some very surprising claims about notions of truth in archaic Greece. Marcel Detienne asked, "Does truth occupy the same place in [the thought of archaic Greece] as in our system of thought?" ("La vérité y tient-elle la même place que dans notre système de pensée?") (Detienne [1967], 4). This cannot be right; if this were the question, it would answer itself. If we correctly translate some ancient word as "true" or "vrai," and correctly interpret some ancient Greek writings so that they yield references to "truth" or "la vérité," then the terms in question *must* to a significant extent play the role that "truth" does in our thought. As he violated this quite basic principle in his question, it is not surprising that Detienne gave an incredible answer to it. He claimed that poets were "masters of truth" because they controlled praise and memory, and preserved heroes and their deeds from being forgotten. While these are significant ideas about the role and authority of poets in the archaic world, they cannot be expressed, as Detienne expressed them, by the assertion that ἀληθεία—the word that he translates as "la vérité"—has nothing to do with accordance with the object, nor with other speeches, and is not opposed to "lie"—as he summarizes it, that "there is no 'true' as opposed to 'false'," the only significant opposition being between *Alêtheia* and *Lêthê*. This brings out very clearly the general point: nothing that was *not* opposed to the false could be rightly represented as "the true."

This of course leaves a genuine question, whether the Greek word ἀληθής as it occurs in these writings can be translated as "true." It can—though it is not the only word that can be translated in that way, and, as we shall see, it has some special implications. In accordance with that, it and its abstract noun can refer to the correctness of communications. At *Iliad* 23.360 a judge is stationed at the turning point of the race, ὡς μεμνέῳτο δρόμους καὶ ἀληθείην ἀποείποι: ἀληθεία has further overtones here, but it at least means that the judge will report certain kinds of happenings at the turning point just in case (as philosophers say) they happen. Appropriately to a term meaning "true," ἀληθής sustains oppositions with terms signifying falsehood, notably ψεῦδος and its associates, which, again predictably, can cover both error and deceit. (A point of detail is that the adjective ψευδής does not occur in Homer, unless we accept Aristarchus's reading at *Il.* 4.235.)

It is generally agreed that the etymology of ἀληθής lies in α-privative and the root *lath-*, which is to be found in λήθη and λανθάνω, and covers forgetfulness but also things escaping people's notice or being ignored. Heidegger made a lot of this in terms of *Unverborgenheit*, the unconcealedness of Being, and this seems to have made the idea temporarily unpopular with some scholars as being associated with sectarian philosophical opinions, but it is acceptable in a more everyday sense. Cole takes the point of the idea to lie not in a (relational) property of some circumstances or facts, that they are obvious, but rather in a characteristic of the acquisition and transmission of some particular pieces of information, that they are not subject to error, whether due to forgetting or overlooking relevant items or, generally, absence of due care. It thus comes very close to the range of considerations associated with the quality of Accuracy. However, it is very important that ἀληθεία does not *mean* Accuracy. For one thing, a messenger can have the virtue of Accuracy yet on this occasion be wrong through no fault of his, but ἀληθεία does indeed signify truth. Moreover, ἀληθής is very largely applied, not to people, but to their communications. The idea about their communications is not just that they are correct, but that they are informative and reliable; as Cole puts it, "What is involved is strict (or strict and scrupulous) rendering or reporting—something as exclusive of bluster, invention or irrelevance as it is of omission or understatement" (12).

There are rare exceptions to the rule that ἀληθής does not apply to people: at *Il.* 12.433 it is used of a woman weighing wool, with respect to her accuracy in doing so and not to anything she says. Hesiod, *Theog.* 233, applies it, along with ἀψευδής, to Nereus, a prophetic creature, and in discussion of this passage West (1966) argues that there was a certain continuing resonance for the Greeks of the origins of ἀληθής in a privative attached to the root of λήθη, λανθάνω, and the rest. This fits with the frequent use of such expressions as λέληθεν αὐτοὺς ὅτι . . . , οὐκ ἐλάνθανεν αὐτοὺς ὅτι . . . , for people noticing or failing to notice things. The occurrence of ἀληθείην at *Il.* 23.360, the passage about the race that I have already mentioned, carries this resonance: the judge will keep a close eye on what happens. This does *not* imply that the word does not mean "the truth" here—that is certainly how it should be translated. The point is that it is the word for "truth" favoured in archaic Greek for contexts in which the vigilance and memory of some observer or reporter, his Accuracy, is salient.

The archaic words that come closest to doing just the same all-purpose job as "true" (as ἀληθής itself came to do from the late fifth century onwards) are ἐτεός, ἔτυμος, and ἐτήτυμος (full accounts of the occurrences of these and other terms discussed are given in Levet [1976]; and see also Krischer [1965]). Here the emphasis is simply on correctness, and the terms can apply to the future, as when it is asked at *Il.* 2.300 ἢ ἐτεὸν Κάλχας μαντεύεται ἦε καὶ οὐκί; At *Il.* 10.534 = *Od.* 4.140 the speaker asks himself ψεύσομαι ἦ ἔτυμον ἐρέω; and the question is not whether he will give an adequate account of the matter but simply whether he is mistaken or will state the truth. A word in this family can be applied to a messenger, but principally in contexts where the only issue is whether the message is correct. At *Il.* 22.438 Andromache does not know about Hector's death, οὐ γάρ οἵ τις ἐτήτυμος ἄγγελος ἐλθὼν / ἤγγειλ᾽ . . . , and here the point is not the merits of any messenger, but simply that the truth has not got through to her.

In this connection, it is interesting to go back to *Od.* 19.203, the passage that I mentioned in chapter 4 (see note 19) in which the poet describes Odysseus's lies: Ἴσκε ψεύδεα πολλὰ λέγων ἐτύμοισιν ὁμοῖα. The sense of this, I suggested in the text, is that "he spoke as one who believed those things, and . . . they were things which he made it seem reasonable to suppose were correct." The force of the "resemblance to the truth" (one might recall here the German *wahrscheinlich* or French *vraisemblable*, "probable") is that these things will seem correct *to the listeners*. Suppose—waiving metrical considerations—ἀληθής had appeared in place of ἔτυμος here. I am tempted to think that this would naturally mean something different. There could be no question of resemblance to things that were true and were not subject to forgetfulness or oversight on the part of the listeners. It might mean resemblance to the *sort* of things that are not subject to forgetfulness or oversight on the part of a speaker, but there is no particular point to be made about that. The most natural reading, rather, would be that Odysseus said things like the things that were *actually* not subject to forgetfulness or oversight on his part, that is to say, told a story which, while false, was as near as possible to a true narration, and that of course is not the situation— the story he made up was very distant from the truths that he could actually remember.

There are other archaic words that occur in the field of truth and truthfulness, notably νημερτής, etymologically connected with not missing a target, and ἀτρεκής, which is connected with "straight." Both of these can apply to messages and messengers; the former also to a plan that will be carried out. They import in various ways implications of Accuracy and of Sincerity—that a communication is unerring, and that the speaker has not twisted it. Cole, in a detailed discussion of the relations of these terms to each other and to ἀληθής, says that "*nêmertês* is regularly distinguished from *atrekês* by the greater urgency or importance of the information to be communicated, *atrekês* from *alêthês* by the greater accessibility of the information and its greater ease of transmission. *Atrekês* assumes as a matter of course that the speaker is in full command of what is to be communicated . . . and in the standard formula ἀλλ' ἄγε μοι τόδε εἰπὲ καὶ ἀτρεκέως κατάλεξον it does little more than contribute a certain epic elevation to humdrum inquiries" (15).

In relation to the method of this book, three general points emerge from investigations into the archaic vocabulary. One is that there is a variety of terms that imply truth and can, in some contexts, simply be translated as "true," and there is no term that does just what "true" does. Second, these terms (and there are others that I have not mentioned) carry overtones or resonances all of which are clearly related to the basic demands on human communication outlined in the State of Nature story. Third, the richness and complexity of the archaic truth vocabulary does not mean that the concept of truth, as we would recognize it, is absent. Indeed, it is only in the light of its presence, the fact that people in this culture stated things as true, questioned whether they were true, passed them on as true, and so on, that we can understand what this rich vocabulary means.

Cole offers an interesting line of thought on the question why at the end of the fifth century ἀλήθεια won out against its "equally emphatic, equally expressive rivals" as the general term for "truth." He connects the development with the rise of written communication:

> Unlike *akribeia* (cf Arist. *Rhet.* 1413b8–9), *alêtheia* never came to be felt as a characteristic excellence of written discourse, but it had been associated, from the beginning, with qualities of care, precision, order and coherence that are more readily available and more easily verified in written than in oral discourse . . . ,

and he notes,

> The first prose writer in which this identification [of *etymon* with *alêthes*] is complete is Thucydides; and it may be more than mere coincidence that he is also the first writer to combine investigation of *alêtheia* with a style and manner of presentation that makes complete use of a certain range of possibilities inherent in written rather than oral discourse. (27)

If this is right, the development I described in chapter 7 involved a change in the vocabulary of truth itself.

Just because the various implications of this vocabulary are connected with the basic structures that appear in the State of Nature, it is predictable that from the earliest times truth and truthfulness were linked—for instance, by some of the vocabulary applying equally to people and to their communications. It has been a major theme of this book that the specific filling or determination of the virtues of truth, particularly of Sincerity, has been culturally various, and this is notable with regard to the archaic world, where being a skilful and resourceful liar was, with certain important qualifications, an admired characteristic. What exactly those qualifications were, and where deceit was unacceptable, are interesting and complex questions, which I have not tried to explore. In chapter 5 I said that in the world of Odysseus the distinction that made a difference with regard to deceit, as to many other things, was that between friends and enemies, and this is right so far as it goes, but it leaves many questions unanswered, such as who counts as an enemy and when. Indeed, at one point Achilles seems prepared to regard someone as an enemy just because he is a liar: in a grand declaration to Odysseus, he says something that Odysseus would certainly never have said himself, "More hateful to me [ἐχθρός, an enemy] than the gates of Hades is the man who hides one thing in his heart and says another" (*Il*. 9.312–13).

Walcot (1977) notes that admiration of the skilful liar is common in peasant societies, and cites evidence that makes this intelligible. Odysseus's own skill in lying, however, does unnervingly take on a life of its own. Walcot discusses as a possible example of peasant "teasing" the scene in the last book of the *Odyssey* in which, even though the suitors have already been defeated and there is no point in the pretence, Odysseus persists in lying to his father and does not reveal who he is until the old man has collapsed in distress. It reminds us that unravelling the structure of Sincerity in that world (as in any other) requires one to understand many things besides the demands of communicating information—for instance, the local sense of humour.

Notes

❖ ❖ ❖ ❖ ❖

ABBREVIATIONS

DK   H. Diels and W. Kranz, *Die Fragmente der Vorsokratiker*, 6th ed., 3 vols. (Berlin: Weidmann, 1951–1952).

FGH   F. Jacoby et al., *Die Fragmente der griechischen Historiker* (Leiden: Brill, 1950–1963).

M-W   R. Merkelbach and M. L. West, *Fragmenta Hesiodea* (Oxford: Clarendon Press, 1967).

PWK   Pauly-Wissowa-Kroll, *Realencyclopädie der classischen Altertumswissenschaft* (Munich and Stuttgart: A. Druckenmüller, 1957–1990).

THE EPIGRAPHS

J'ai toujours honoré ceux qui défendent la grammaire ou la logique. On se rend compte cinquante ans après qu'ils ont conjuré de grands périls.

        —*A la recherche du temps perdu*, Pléiade edition (Paris: Gallimard, 1989),
        4:376–77 [from *Le temps retrouvé*]

Mangel an historischem Sinn ist der Erbfehler aller Philosophen ... Demnach ist das *historische Philosophieren* von jetzt ab nötig und mit ihm die Tugend der Bescheidung.

        —*Menschliches, Allzumenschliches*, I. 2

CHAPTER ONE
The Problem

1. This criticism is developed by Thomas Nagel, in Nagel (1997). I have discussed Nagel's arguments, and the question of how far they can take us, in Williams (1998).

2. For an account of this, see Appleby, Hunt, and Jacob (1994), chapters 3 and 4; Novick (1988).

3. Among well-known figures contributing to this enterprise are Bruno Latour and Sandra Harding. Chapters 5 and 6 of Haack (1998) offer a very crisp and effective critique, with some richly revealing quotations. See also her shrewd remark: "[T]he revolutionary scientism encountered in contemporary philosophy often manifests a peculiar affinity with the anti-scientific attitudes which, as I conjecture, are prompted by resentment, as scientism is prompted by envy, of the sciences" (201).

4. Most famously in Horkheimer and Adorno (1969) (first edition 1944).

5. In Rorty (1989) and elsewhere.

6. Susan Haack is a sturdy opponent of the "deniers," and her collection of essays, Haack (1998), makes many effective points against them (cf. note 3 above). However, their positions are usually traced simply to such things as exaggeration, desire for fame, and the neglect of elementary distinctions. As a self-styled "old-fashioned prig," she can be heard saying, rather too often, that she can't see what the fuss is about.

7. For what counts as "having a value" in this connection, see in particular chapter 4, section 1, and chapter 5, section 1.

8. Mamet (1993). The play was first staged on May 1, 1992, by the Back Bay Theater Company in association with the American Repertory Theater. In 1994 it was made into a movie, directed by Mamet himself.

9. In particular, in chapter 3, section 2, where I consider the idea of a "plain" truth.

10. *The Will to Power*, 481. He did not publish this remark: *The Will to Power* is a compilation from his Nachlass, put together by his sister.

11. Silverman (1975), xi; quoted by Barnes (1994), 134.

12. Barthes (1976), 23; quoted by Josipovici (1999), 15.

13. Josipovici (1999), 24.

14. The title of a collection of readings, Allison (1985). There are many books about Nietzsche that offer this kind of interpretation, and many about other subjects that assume it.

15. *The Gay Science*, 284; *The Antichrist*, 50.

16. *Beyond Good and Evil*, 177; *The Gay Science*, 344: in the passage that follows, as in the title of the book, "science" translates "Wissenschaft," which goes much wider than natural science and includes the humanities.

17. *Genealogy*, III. 26.

18. *The Gay Science*, 121; cf. *Beyond Good and Evil*, 11.

19. *Human, All Too Human*, 517; *The Gay Science*, 76, 110.

20. *The Will to Power*, 5; cf. *Beyond Good and Evil*, 10.

21. *Ecce Homo*, preface, 3. A very similar passage occurs in the Nachlass (*The Will to Power*, 1041). In both places the "measure of value" is offered as a way of reading the history of philosophy.

22. *The Antichrist*, 59. For a famous—rather too famous—remark contrary to this emphasis, see above, section 2, and note 10.

23. The essay, which was published only posthumously, is translated in Breazeale (1979). The quotation is at 84.

24. This is well argued by Clark (1990).

25. The idea surfaces again in *The Gay Science*, 110, 121, and it survives into the Nachlass, e.g. *The Will to Power*, 521.

26. *The Will to Power*, 567.

27. In the famous words of Democritus, one of the first to hold such a view: "By convention sweet, bitter, hot, cold, colour; but in reality atoms and the void" (frag. 9 DK).

28. MacIntyre (1990), chapter 2; and see also chapter 9. A genealogy in his sense cannot be what I call "vindicatory": see below, chapter 2, section 5.

CHAPTER TWO
Genealogy

1. Michel Foucault, "Nietzsche, Genealogy, History," translated by Donald Bouchard and Sherry Simon, in Boucher (1977), 139–64.

2. Hume, *A Treatise of Human Nature*, Book 3, Part 2, Section 2; Craig (1990).

3. See James (1984).

4. Gilligan (1982).

5. I have in mind here the crudely reductionist ideas that were particularly associated with this word by the work of E. O. Wilson and others, as in Wilson (1975) and Wilson (1978). As will be seen below, I do not deny the relevance of evolutionary biology to cultural studies.

6. The editors of a well-known collection, Barkow, Cosmides, and Tooby (1992), in their introduction, reject reductionism but call for "vertical integration" of the sciences. They say that this is "simply [a] different name" (13, note 1) for consistency or compatibility, but they cannot really mean this. Two sciences could be consistent if they were about two totally disjunct subject matters and not integrated at all. It is because these writers mean something stronger than consistency that they think that social scientists who do not care about biology are indifferent to consistency. In the

same volume, Tooby and Cosmides, in "The Psychological Foundations of Culture," direct a great deal of rhetoric against what they call "the Standard Social Scientific Method": their attack simply equates a method (or rather a class of methods: any that ignore evolutionary psychology) with a theory (blank-slate empiricism).

7. Dawkins (1976), 206; "meme" is a catchy abbreviation of "mimeme." The "idea of God" is mentioned as a meme on 207. A similar idea of a unit of cultural inheritance is advanced in Cloak (1975). (I owe this reference to W. G. Runciman.)

8. Durham (1991), 204.

9. This is emphasized by W. G. Runciman, an advocate of the evolutionary approach, in Runciman (1998).

10. Nozick (1974), 7, referring to Hempel (1965), 335.

11. A classical example of such hypothetical scenarios is their use in explaining selection for "altruism": see Hamilton (1964), Trivers (1971).

12. Nozick (1974), 19, 18.

13. Ibid., 9. For a discussion of Nozick's work in this connection, see my (1996).

14. "[P]hilosophers may, if they please, extend their reasoning to the suppos'd *state of nature*; provided they allow it to be a mere philosophical fiction, which never had, and never cou'd have any reality." *A Treatise of Human Nature*, Book 3, Part 2, Section 2. There are many important questions about Hume's model that I leave aside, such as the exact relation of the artificial to the natural virtues, and the role of "uncompounding" the forces of the understanding and the affections.

15. It is not the same as a reason for collective action: that is possible without the influence of the artificial, or indeed any other, virtues and can arise from self-interest operating directly on a shared objective, as when (to adapt an example of Hume's) we all row together to get each of us away from the manifestly sinking ship.

16. There are some deliberative and intentionalist elements in Hume's own account, but they are relatively superficial: the way in which he deploys the idea of "convention" leaves enough room for the artificial virtues simply to emerge, under the admittedly very stringent conditions that hold in his story.

17. Brandom (2000), 363. His emphases.

18. In particular, the proto-contract theory offered by Glaukon and Adeimantus in Book 2, which may seem to us virtually the opposite of the exploitation theory which Thrasymachus gives in Book 1, is treated by

everyone in the discussion as merely another version of it. I have suggested reasons for this in "Plato against the Immoralist," in Höffe (1997).

19. This term has been used in significantly different, though related, ways. David Wiggins (see various papers in Wiggins [1991]) has used the phrase "vindicatory explanation" for an explanation of the belief that P (in particular, of convergence on the belief that P) which involves its being true that P. My use of it here, and also in Williams (2000a), is broader. The question is whether a genealogical explanation of an outlook or set of values is such, when it comes to be understood, as to strengthen or weaken one's confidence in them. This question significantly applies to real, historical, genealogies as well as to fictional ones.

20. *Zur Genealogie der Moral* (1887). The title is often translated as *The Genealogy of Morals*, but see the bibliography. Nietzsche himself refers to the *"pudenda origo,"* the shameful origin, of our moral ideas at *Daybreak*, 102. In the sense of "genealogy" in which MacIntyre discusses it in MacIntyre (1990), a genealogy is necessarily subversive. This is connected with the point that it is not supposed to adopt any discursive or theoretical position of its own, and stands only in an oppositional relation to something else. For this outlook and MacIntyre's discussion of it, see the end of chapter 1.

21. What I have elsewhere called "the morality system," as opposed to ethical ideas more generally: see Williams (1985), especially chapter 10. As Raymond Geuss has pointed out in an interesting discussion, Geuss (1999), Nietzsche himself remarks that the history of a set of valuations does not directly bear on its value (*The Gay Science*, 345; *The Will to Power*, 254). But Geuss rightly adds that people's beliefs about its history can affect their attitude to a set of values, and this has wider impact than perhaps he allows. Particularly with regard to the morality system, it is important to people's respect for it and hence to their confidence in it that it should not have the kind of origin that Nietzsche says it has.

22. *The Genealogy of Morality*, I. 7. I say a little more about how Nietzsche's story might be understood in Williams (2000b), an article on which the present chapter is partly based.

23. I argue for the broader conception in Williams (2000a). It is significant that Wittgenstein, who took as seriously as anyone could the question of what philosophy might now be, but stuck firmly to a conception of it as quite separate from other intellectual enterprises, came to the conclusion that philosophy could not offer any explanations at all.

CHAPTER THREE
The State of Nature: A Rough Guide

1. See Peacocke (1999), section 3.5, where he discusses the application of Wittgenstein's remark "The explanation by means of *identity* does not work here" (*Philosophical Investigations*, 350). Space and time are taken together here, but differences between the cases will be relevant to the development of ideas that transcend the local: see section 3 below.

2. Important consequences of this are noted by Craig (1990).

3. The first, in the next chapter; the second, in chapter 8.

4. This itself may be thought to beg some questions: whether Accuracy really aims at truth, as opposed to agreement; whether Sincerity should be explained in terms of truth, since it is concerned simply with expressing beliefs, true or false. These worries will be addressed in chapters 5 and 6.

5. There is an over-simplification here. For many cases, including the one I go on to discuss, it will not be necessary that the meaning of *T* itself must be picked up in this way, but rather that *T* should belong to a type of sentence some examples of which will have to be so learned. The simplification avoids a range of complications and does not affect the principle of the argument.

6. The phrase "explicit concept" is meant to register, very crudely, the point that there are more primitive, non-linguistic, abilities that imply possession of some notion of the past: cf. J. Campbell (1994) and literature cited there.

7. Act 2, scene 2.

8. Pragmatic conditions of assertion were explored by H. P. Grice, who called them *conversational implicatures*. This idea will be important when we come to the ethics of assertion: see below, chapter 5, sections 4–6.

9. Davidson's work, in this respect like Quine's, has concentrated on the situation of radical translation: that is to say, one in which an observer who knows one language is confronted with people using another which he has to translate into his own. It would be a mistake (a mistake which Davidson does not make) to suppose that a child's task in learning language for the first time was just that task. There are important similarities: notably the one on which I concentrate, that, for many sentences, if their meaning is to be learned, they have to be uttered in situations in which they are true.

10. For some difficulties in the notion of the supernatural, see my (1993), chapter 6.

11. The "principle of charity" has been much discussed in relation to Davidson's work. For reasons related to those given in the text, it has been suggested that a "principle of humanity" would be more appropriate: see Grandy (1973), in particular "it is better to attribute to [the speaker] an explicable falsehood than a mysterious truth" (445).

12. In using this phrase, I am of course referring to the everyday ideas of time that we apply to historical events and generally to happenings on a human scale. No issues of relativity theory come into the discussion.

13. In speaking, here and elsewhere, of *individuals'* having such interests against the community, I use this only as a shorthand. I do not want to imply that it is necessarily a matter of single people, or that the problem is just one of egoism: the same problems arise with a collection of competitive families or other groups. In virtue of these same conflicts of interest, it is very rough indeed to say, as has just been said, that it is generally in the interest of the community that each person should possess Accuracy. As soon as we get to issues of differential power, it is a real question whether it may not be in the interest of one group that other groups should not be too good at discovering the truth. These issues will come up in chapter 9.

14. For instance, "Solidarity and Objectivity," "Pragmatism, Davidson and Truth" (especially 128, 140–41), and other papers in Rorty (1991); "Is Truth a Goal of Inquiry?" "Hilary Putnam and the Relativist Menace" (especially 53–54), and other papers in Rorty (1998). Rorty's position is an illustration of a famous and deep joke ascribed to Sydney Morgenbesser: "Of course pragmatism is true; the trouble is that it doesn't work."

15. See below, chapter 6, section 2.

16. Nietzsche, *The Antichrist*, 50: quoted in full in chapter 1, section 2, above.

17. One book that claims to be a history of the concept of truth and is explicitly a history of philosophy is R. Campbell (1992). The point that the concept of truth is universally familiar is illustrated by a discussion of archaic terms for truth in the "Endnote" below.

CHAPTER FOUR
Truth, Assertion, and Belief

1. Davidson (1996), 265.

2. Tarski (1956). There is an immense literature on this subject. See, for instance, the papers collected in Platts (1980); Soames (1984).

3. Karl Popper held this view: see Popper (1959, 1963). For a version that is supposed to be as near as possible to triviality but still interesting, see Searle (1998).

4. For this objection, see, e.g., Davidson (1990). The problem for a correspondence theory presents itself in two stages. The first lies in the difficulty of individuating facts for any purpose; as Stephen Neale has put it, "The task for a friend of facts is to put together a theory according to which facts are not so fine-grained that they are sentence-like and not so coarse-grained that they collapse into one" (Neale [1995], 816). The second point, emphasized in the text, is that a correspondence theory approaches this task under the specific constraint of honouring supposed intuitions about what particular fact makes a particular sentence true on a particular occasion.

5. The term is used by Horwich (1990, 1998), who allows truth to be a property, but an entirely uninteresting one. More radical versions are often called "deflationary." The "performatory" version of such a theory goes back to Ramsey: see "Facts and Propositions," in Ramsey (1990). Quine (1970, 1990) has emphasized the role of "true" as a disquotational device. For an important discussion of the issues, see Wright (1992); and for criticism, see in particular Davidson (1996) and Wiggins (1980, 2001).

6. Paul Horwich argued to this effect in Horwich (1990), but in Horwich (1998) he agrees that no particular attitude to the value of truth follows from his theory, adding that if there is a problem about truth's being an intrinsic good, it lies in the notion of an intrinsic good, not in the idea of truth (62).

7. The quantification "For some P . . ." ranges over propositions as objects, and an open sentence "Φ(P)" will be appropriately closed by replacing "P" with a name; but in ". . . believe that P if P," etc., "P" stands proxy for a sentence. See Davidson (2001), 39–40, Wiggins (2001).

8. Jane Heal has argued, in Heal (1987/88), that in setting a value on truth, we must set a value on having some relation to it, e.g., believing it; so if we set an intrinsic value on truth, we must want to believe any truth just because it is true; so we must want to believe every truth, which is absurd. This takes "intrinsic," as opposed to "instrumental," to imply "as such" or "for its own sake" in a sense that excludes all other determinants of the interest. This is unreasonable. "He loves music as such" or ". . . for its own sake" does not imply that there is no music he does not want to hear.

9. From "Words," Auden (1976), 473.

10. Such ideas are emphasized and developed in Brandom (1994): see in particular 16–17 and chapter 3. There is an argument to the effect that it is false or vacuous to say that we, our assertions, or our inquiries "aim at truth." It is based on the idea that, although in the abstract we seem to be able to distinguish between the situation of its being true that P and that of our merely believing that P is true, in any particular case we cannot effectively make this distinction, because our belief that the first situation obtains is no more than an instance of the second situation. This style of argument is not the concern here; I shall come to it in chapter 6, section 2.

11. As Michael Dummett pointed out a long time ago: see "Truth" (1959), reprinted in Dummett (1978).

12. Timothy Williamson (1996) raises these questions; for comment on his specific proposal, see below, section 3.

13. There is no question here of variable or relative *content*, which could lead to different truth values in different circumstances; the content of a given assertion is assumed to be determinate with regard to meaning and reference, including that secured by indexicals.

14. Dummett (1978), preface, xvii. His emphases.

15. Dummett does not actually state an additional assumption he makes, that when it is discovered in a finite time that the speaker was not right in what he said, he is still around to withdraw his statement.

16. Lewis (1983), 167. Related problems come up with "saying." Jennifer Hornsby assimilates "Sue says something to Helen in uttering a sentence which means that P" to "Sue says that P to Helen," and this must be too rapid, since "saying that" is a variant on "asserting that" (Hornsby [2000], 91 ff.). For a reason why such formulations might seem attractive, see below, section 2 and note 20.

17. Searle (1969), 44. Searle's example was directed against a more complex proposal of Grice's, designed to explain utterer's meaning; for Grice's (even more complex) response, see Grice (1989), 100 ff.

18. Searle (1969), 65.

19. *Odyssey* 19.203. The formula occurs also at Hesiod *Theogony* 27: for discussion, see West (1966) on the passage. For the force of the word translated as "true," *etumos*, see the "Endnote."

20. Williamson (1996), 511. A similar point might charitably be associated with Lewis's and Hornsby's formulations criticized above, section 2 and note 16.

21. Cf. Grice (1989), 123. Grice's proposal is more complicated than this, because he invokes the more complex kind of intention that is the basis of his theory of meaning.

22. An illuminating discussion of this area is Hampshire (1959), chapter 2.

23. Williamson (1996): he cites Unger (1975) and Slote (1979). He does not mean that it is a demand uniquely on assertions that they should express knowledge—obviously other speech-acts (e.g., swearing that P is true) are subject to the same requirement. He means that assertions are characterized by the exact requirement to express knowledge, no less and no more (e.g., they are not required to express certainty). His claim is not, of course, that someone makes an assertion only if he *observes* the norm; the point is that one who makes an assertion is *subject* to the norm, just as someone can break the rules of a game only if he is playing it. In what follows I argue that it is less than clear what it is for assertions to be "subject to" this norm, and that there is no need to invoke it in explaining what assertions are.

24. See Williamson (1996), 509, 520 ff. These analogies seem to offer the best guidance to what he takes the consequences of breaking the norm to be.

25. It is worth noting that this does not have a parallel in the case of commands. If the captain shouts, "Hard to port," and this command is passed on down a chain of speakers to the helmsman, the chain does not consist of people *giving that command*. The captain commands the helmsman to turn the ship, but no-one on the way commands the next man to do that. No-one but the captain has the authority to give the order, and no-one but the helmsman can carry it out.

26. J. L. Austin made suggestions about parallels between "I know" and "I promise" which are to a similar effect: see "Other Minds," in Austin (1961), 66 ff.

27. I have argued that belief is not subject to choice in "Deciding to Believe," in Williams (1973).

28. Questions connected with this formulation were discussed in chapter 3, section 2. "Confronted with" of course implies conditions on the speaker, that his senses are in good order, his eyes are open, and so on: these are part of the conditions on what it is to get to know about the world by observation, which must be pre-reflectively assumed in the State of Nature.

29. A searching elaboration of the connections between truth conditions and capacities, particularly conceptual capacities, is Peacocke (1999).

30. Michael Dummett has written, "We have opposed throughout the view of assertion as the expression of an interior act of judgment; judgment, rather, is the interiorization of the external act of assertion" (Dummett

[1973], 362). Leaving aside the word "rather," I do not think that there is an opposition between the two views.

31. Not entirely so, even among language-users; apart from inarticulate beliefs in adults, needed to explain their orientation to the world, we may recall the beliefs of language-learners, mentioned above, section 2. Some other animals have beliefs, the content of which we identify in terms of our explanations of their behaviour. The same is true of the beliefs that we ascribe to other human beings; the vital difference is that the content we ascribe to others' beliefs must match to a significant degree the content of the beliefs that they ascribe to themselves.

32. For an account and discussion of Pascal's argument, see Hacking (1972).

CHAPTER FIVE
Sincerity: Lying and Other Styles of Deceit

1. This idea, which is well criticized by Harry Frankfurt in Frankfurt (1992), is stock-in-trade with some versions of Utilitarianism. It is not invoked by the Kantian type of argument which appeals to *ideal* consequences: "What would it be like if everyone did it (all the time)?" is not relevantly met by "Enough of them won't."

2. I shall assume that shared observance of certain norms can constitute the existence of *a language*, something that transcends idiolects. The matter is controversial: see Chomsky (1995), Wiggins (1997).

3. *The Wealth of Nations*, Book 1, Chapter 2, para. 2: Campbell, Skinner, and Todd (1976), 26–27.

4. All these various expectations rely on signs that the trusted party has one or another kind of motivation. On this, see Bacharach and Gambetta (2001), to which I am indebted. For a more detailed discussion of what is involved in trust, see "Formal Structures and Social Reality," reprinted in Williams (1995), and other essays in the volume where that paper first appeared, Gambetta (1988). That paper, like the present discussion, makes use of some elementary game-theoretical formulations. I hope it will be obvious that this does not commit one to any assumptions in favour of exclusively egoistic motivations: see note 3 to the reprinted version of the paper (Williams [1995], 122).

5. As imagined, for instance, in some Western movies. More generally, Westerns at their best constitute a powerful anthology of political philosophy. Clint Eastwood's remarkable *Unforgiven*, for instance, raises the ques-

tion: Does the monopoly of violence with which the Gene Hackman character secures peace in a particular town give him authority over that town?

6. That is to say, in terms of game theory, they are playing the Assurance Game rather than the Prisoners' Dilemma, but we make the realistic assumption that they have imperfect information about each other's preference schedule.

7. This dualistic opposition is, of course, notably Platonist: it corresponds, for instance, to the two sides in the battle between the Gods and the Giants, *Sophist* 246A. For genealogy as transcending such oppositions, see above, chapter 2.

8. I have pressed this criticism in various places, e.g. Williams (1985), chapter 6.

9. See Gauthier (1986).

10. In the terms of chapter 2, the genealogy is vindicatory: see above, chapter 2, section 5.

11. I concentrate on history, but of course local determinations of trustworthiness may be investigated by other methods, such as those of social anthropology. Some relevant material is discussed in Barnes (1994).

12. *OED* s.v. I.1.a: e.g., Shakespeare, *Cymbeline* 5.5.107, "Briefly dye their ioyes, That place them on the truth of Gyrles, and Boyes." The sense is now perhaps most familiar from the archaic phrase "plighting one's troth." The transition to the modern sense had occurred by the fourteenth century. It has been suggested that the change is associated with the spread of literacy—the correctness of texts replacing reliability of the personal word (Green [1999])—but there are serious chronological difficulties: see Saul (1999), a review of Green. In any case, words that mean something like "true" in its modern sense are, unsurprisingly, to be found in pre-literate societies: for an example, see the "Endnote."

13. This is "head sense 1" in Empson's "dictionary entry" for the word in chapter 10 of *The Structure of Complex Words* (Empson [1952], 204). Chapter 9 of the book assembles evidence for the use of "honest" and "honesty" since the middle of the sixteenth century; chapter 11 is Empson's classic study of "honest" in *Othello*.

14. As we shall see in more detail in the next chapter, and as Nietzsche vividly reminded us: see above, chapter 1, section 3.

15. As with trustworthiness in general, we must also be able, to some acceptable level, to recognize these people, and deceivers work to make this difficult. Bacharach and Gambetta (2001) refer to "[t]he ceaseless semiotic warfare between mimics [i.e., potential deceivers] on the one hand and their trustworthy models . . . on the other" (176).

16. I do not know of a history with exactly this purpose. There are histories of the casuistry of lying, e.g. Zagorin (1990). Jonsen and Toulmin (1988) is a general history of casuistry, with an informative section on equivocation, to which I am indebted: see below, note 30. The appendix to Bok (1978) contains a selection of texts. However, with the exception of MacIntyre's brief but suggestive treatment, on which I comment in note 25 below, historical accounts of deception have perhaps tended not to address directly the question of what conceptions of speech and trustworthiness are involved, and how they relate to other contemporary values.

17. I think that this is what is intended by Sissela Bok (Bok [1978], 15), but her formulation, "an intentionally deceptive message in the form of a statement," goes too wide, unless "in the form of" does a heroic amount of work: it would fit the assertion by the speaker who opened the mail. Interesting material about lying and socialization is reviewed in Barnes (1994), chapter 8.

18. See Grice (1989), chapters 1–7, 15, and 17. Conversational implicatures are, for Grice, a sub-class of non-conventional implicatures (26), but these further distinctions are not relevant here, and I shall mostly refer to them just as "implicatures."

19. There has been much discussion about what counts as part of the content (contributing to the truth-conditions) of a sentence, and about what tests are appropriate to deciding this. Grice himself claimed that the idea of temporal succession in, e.g., "She gave him the key and he opened the door" was an implicature, the truth-condition being confined to truth-functional conjunction. This has been denied (e.g., Carston [1988]), in part on the ground that the sentence can receive the denial "No: he opened the door and then she gave him the key." But this argument overlooks the point that negation can be applied to *any* dimension of an utterance, even pronunciation: "No, it isn't a *tomahto*, it's a *tomayto*." (I owe this observation to the late David Lewis.)

20. Chapter 4, section 2.

21. For a contrary view of metaphors, that they are suggestive falsehoods or, indeed, suggestive literal truths ("no man is an island"), see "What Metaphors Mean," in Davidson (2001). I am grateful to Michael Dummett for the example in the text, and for emphasizing the significance of the fact that we have the word "literally."

22. Grice (1989), 26, 28. This material comes from "Logic and Conversation," originally given as the William James Lectures at Harvard in 1967. In some later material written in 1987, recognizing problems connected with the frequent absence of co-operation in conversation, Grice suggested

that the rules of implicature might be connected with "the rationality or irrationality of conversational conduct" as abstracted from special conversational interests (369), but he did not develop this. It has been suggested by Sperber and Wilson (e.g., [1995]) that the distinctions Grice noted can all be explained in terms of their relevance theory. Notions of relevance are obviously involved in many cases—the mail-opening example turns on the withholding of information clearly relevant to the hearer's understanding of the situation—but their notion of relevance, at least, is not adequate to explaining the phenomena.

23. There is a huge literature on this question, which is of course particularly relevant to medical ethics. A sympathetic, exceptionally careful, and finally devastating discussion of the doctrine of double effect itself is McIntyre (2001).

24. Jonathan Bennett has insisted on this point in Bennett (1995) and elsewhere. Bennett and others infer from such cases that the distinction between bringing things about and letting them happen is *never* relevant, or is not relevant "in itself." This does not follow. As we shall see in the present case, there are some special circumstances in which the distinction between lying and other forms of deceit does make a difference, and when this is so, it is precisely *that* distinction which matters.

25. MacIntyre (1995) gives a helpful account of this tradition, to which I am indebted. Our conclusions partly overlap, though he is considerably more impressed by the supposed moral consequences of what an assertion is than I am.

26. *Summa Theologiae* IIa IIae, Q 69, 1 and 2 ; English translation, Gilby (1975), 117–19. Aquinas's view is even stronger than it sounds here, since, for him, the intention to deceive is not included in the definition of a lie, which covers any intentional assertion of a falsehood. Augustine, who shares the moral distinction, gives the standard account of a lie (cf. note 17 above): Bok (1978), 32–33, and passages quoted in translation, 250–55.

27. *On a Supposed Right to Lie from Philanthropy*, in Gregor (1996), 611–15. The essay was written in reply to Benjamin Constant.

28. Geach (1977), 114. MacIntyre (1995), 336.

29. *The Metaphysics of Morals*, Ak. 6, 429: Gregor (1996), 552. It is important that Kant thinks of lying as a violation of a duty to oneself, not to the hearer; contrast the view of Constant, which is taken up in section 6 below. Kant's outlook is discussed further below.

30. I owe this example, and also the reference below to Garnet's treatise, to Jonsen and Toulmin (1988), 205, 208, who give references and further relevant material.

31. The idea that one's relation to God is essentially involved comes out explicitly in the treatment that Grotius gives to the somewhat similar case (mentioned in section 6 below) of breaking a promise made to extortioners such as pirates. He repudiates Cicero's opinion (*De officiis* 3.29.107) that it is perfectly legitimate to do so: "Even if no right [of delivery] lies with the person, the relationship is with God [*cum Deo negotium est*]," *De iure belli et pacis* 2.13.15, sections 1–2.

32. *The Metaphysics of Morals*, Ak. 6, 429: Gregor (1996), 552. Particularly in discussing "duties to oneself," Kant tends to fall back on traditional teleological notions: the same is true of his attitude to suicide, and his ferocious condemnations of masturbation.

33. "aliud lingua promptum, aliud pectore inclusum gerere": Sallust *Catiline* 10.5. Kant's citation of it is in the passage referred to in note 32 above.

34. Emended by T. R. Harrison from a mangled version in Barnes (1994), 32.

35. The idea of some such default position has been defended by Tyler Burge, who argues for the principle "A person is entitled to accept as true something that is presented as true and that is intelligible to him, unless there are stronger reasons not to do so" (Burge [1993], 467). This may seem contrary to what I have claimed in the text, but I am not sure that it is. It depends on what count as "stronger reasons": knowing nothing at all about one's interlocutor might be one. Burge admits that the principle (which is a norm of justification, not an empirical premiss) can be variously applicable in actual life; in the two cases that he cites as illustrating its force, language-learning and familiar institutional arrangements, I would endorse it too. He makes some further suggestive remarks about its connection with rationality; I am simply not clear whether they are consistent with the account of assertions and knowledge given in chapter 4, section 3, above.

36. Cavell (1979), 298, stresses the continuity between promises and other ways of making a commitment. He points out that promises and other such "rituals" come into it when "it is important to be explicit."

37. Cf. Hume's characteristically well-judged provocation: "[I]nterest is the *first* obligation to the performance of promises" (*Treatise* Book 3, Part 2, Section 5, his emphasis).

38. *The Theory of the Moral Sentiments*, Raphael and MacFie (1976), 332. Cited by Scanlon (1998), 324.

39. I have discussed motivations of this kind in Williams (1993), especially chapter 4 and endnote 1.

40. I touch on some political implications of this point in chapter 9.

41. In thinking that when lying (and also promise-breaking) are wrong, the wrong is to the other party, and not to some practice or institution, I agree with Scanlon (1998), chapter 7, to which I am indebted.

42. This is too simple, but it would be cumbrous to spell out a wider range of cases. One obvious addition is that of someone such as a spy who lies to his friends from motives of another and concealed loyalty which has no claim on their sympathies.

Chapter Six
Accuracy: A Sense of Reality

1. See Hacking (1983).

2. The general significance of this point is emphasized by Richard Moran in Moran (2001).

3. In the passage from *The Gay Science* quoted in chapter 1, section 3, above.

4. In thinking that the idea is coherent and centrally important, I agree with the position of Alvin Goldman in Goldman (1999), which he calls "veritism." Of course, some "methods of inquiry" may be so bad at acquiring the truth that one might say that they were not methods of inquiry at all; but this is a quite general point about methods of doing anything and has no special interest.

5. See in particular "Is Truth a Goal of Inquiry? Donald Davidson versus Crispin Wright," in Rorty (1998). Among various aims of inquiry, "convincing as many audiences as possible" is mentioned on 38. Unless "convincing" is supposed to have something to do with truth, it is not clear why the number of converts should be particularly picked out as an objective of inquiry, or indeed an objective at all.

It may be that there is another reason behind the denial that inquiry aims at the truth—an idea that if it aimed at truth at all, it would have to aim at *the* truth, in a sense which implied that there must be one unitary truth, at least about a given subject matter. For the mistake in this, see chapter 10 below, end of section 3.

6. Davidson thinks that there is enough in the indistinguishability argument for us to agree that it is "pointless" to say that truth is a goal, or something to be pursued ("Truth Rehabilitated," in Brandom [2000b]). I think that this allows the argument more than it deserves.

7. For criticism of the symmetry assumption, see Williams (1978), appendix 3.

8. It is fair to recall here the frivolity shown by politicized academic critics of "the truth" and related categories, who were mentioned in chapter 1, section 2. If the categories that they despise really do no work except to disguise elementary social forces, why should they with their academic conversation expect to remain in business?

9. On the related question of oracles and fatalism, see Williams (1993), 136 ff.

10. For a discussion of this formula and its relation to wanting to know whether P, see Williams (1978), 37 ff.

11. This is why the philosophical search for certainty assumes very special aims and conditions, as Descartes himself clearly realized: Williams (1978), chapter 2, particularly 61 ff.

12. For an important discussion of various phenomena of this kind, see Pears (1984).

13. Throughout this discussion, I take the idea that some states of affairs are dependent on my will in the everyday and (I hope) uncontentious sense that there are some states of affairs that I can bring about. Metaphysical issues about the freedom of the will are not in question.

14. There is more than one way in which a belief can be "dependent on" a wish. I examine a very basic, perhaps the most basic, form of wishful thinking in section 4 of chapter 8 below.

15. For suggestions on these lines, see Wright (1992). The idea has been pressed in a strong form in connection with moral beliefs by Harman (1977).

16. Max Weber's famous lecture *Wissenschaft als Beruf*, given in 1918, though dated in some of its assumptions, remains immensely instructive: translated as "Science as a Vocation," in Gerth and Wright Mills (1991). On the word "Science" here, see above, chapter 1, note 16.

17. Watson (1968). For a more sober account of the heroic years of molecular biology, see Judson (1979).

18. For a notably patient, but finally negative, assessment of such programmes, see Jardine (1991).

19. This relates to what I have elsewhere (Williams [1978]) called "the absolute conception of reality." It remains controversial whether the idea of an absolute conception is coherent; though some criticisms miss the mark by mistaking it for a representation which uses no concepts at all: see Williams (2000a). For a perceptive analysis of the issues (together with some striking metaphysical suggestions), see Moore (1997).

20. The *Republic* most strongly conveys the first sense. Contrary to many interpretations, the second is very much present in the *Symposium*.

21. Levi (1985), 42–43 (I have slightly altered the translation). See also 52–53, where (alongside the reference to mountaineering mentioned below) Levi says that he later found his needs better met by physics than by chemistry, with its confusion of alternative recipes, and its suspect origins with the alchemists and "their Levantine swindles typical of charlatans or magicians." I owe the reference to Levi in this connection to Cora Diamond's helpful paper Diamond (1993), though I may read his text rather differently.

22. Though if your civilization is at an end, acrostics may be a more seemly reaction than incoherent metaphysical despair, as Auden points out in "The Epigoni": "To their lasting honour, the stuff they wrote / Can safely be spanked in a scholar's footnote": Auden (1976), 460.

23. This is related to the distinction between what has been called "social" and "non-social" intelligence (Cheney and Seyfarth [1990]), which turns on the capacity of an animal to modify its behaviour as a function of the expected reactions of other individuals, a capacity which underlies flexible social life. It also delivers the possibility of genuine deceit as opposed to mimicry: another term for "social" as applied to intelligence is "Machiavellian" (Byrne and Whiten [1988]).

24. *The Antichrist*, 59.

25. Rorty (1989), chapter 8.

CHAPTER SEVEN
What Was Wrong with Minos?

1. "Of the Populousness of Ancient Nations," in *Essays: Moral, Political and Literary* (1741); Miller (1985), 422. Kant agreed with him.

2. Fewer still, perhaps none, would agree with Collingwood's remarkable judgement that Herodotus was the inventor of scientific history and Thucydides was not a historian at all: Collingwood (1946), part 1.

3. Geoffrey de Ste Croix. See Ste Croix (1977), 130–48.

4. See Edmunds (1975); Parry (1981); Hunter (1982); Macleod (1983).

5. Yeats: Egan (1978); Nietzsche, *The Twilight of the Idols*, "What I Owe to the Ancients," section 2, and *Daybreak*, 168. See further Williams (1993), 161–64 with note 59.

6. Cornford (1907).

7. Thomas (1988), 56. This type of situation is called by Goody (1977) "restricted literacy." For a discussion of Herodotus in relation to anthropological questions about orality and literacy, see Murray (1987). For the

general issues, see also Goody and Watt (1963): particular reference to myth and history at 321–26.

8. See above, chapter 3, section 3.

9. Lateiner (1989), 17, 63, 118. At 63 he refers us to 2.15.3, but in that passage the expression ἀνθρώπων γένος quite certainly means "the human race." The temporal translation has a long history: see below, note 19.

10. At 2.142 he reckons three generations to a century, but his use is not consistent: see Mitchel (1956).

11. 2.164.1. Powell (1938) distinguishes a further meaning, "nationality," but it is clear that the phrases cited (at 1.35.1, 2.134.3) mean simply "by birth."

12. So 3.23.4, τὴν τοῦ ἡλίου λεγομένην τράπεζαν, for some precious metal object among the Ethiopians, where the expression represents what they call it (as, much more frequently, with καλεόμενος); 6.127.1 Ἀμύριος τοῦ σοφοῦ λεγομένου, presumably meaning his nickname or soubriquet, rather than what he was, rightly or wrongly, said to be. At 2.145.1 and 156.4, however, τῶν ὀκτὼ τῶν πρώτων λεγομένων θεῶν means "of what are said [by the Egyptians] to be the first eight gods."

13. Hes. frag. 144 M-W, from ps-Plato *Minos* 320D.

14. PWK XV–2:1926.

15. τὸ . . . παλαιὸν, 1.171.2; τώρχαῖον, 1.173.1; the Trojan War, 7.171.

16. Lateiner (1989), 16–17.

17. Notably 2.29, on his investigation of Egypt, and often. It has been claimed (Immerwahr [1966], 6) that Herodotus was capable of claiming that his sources were oral when they were written: 2.73 "they say," for the account of the phoenix, which comes from Hecataeus and contains quotations (*FGH* 1, F324B). There is much disagreement about Herodotus's sources, his own claims to have seen things himself, and in general his reliability: for a summary, see Dewald and Marincola (1987), sections 3 and 4.

18. Indeed, Shimron (1973), followed by Vandiver (1991), Moles (1993), and others, has claimed that this is marked by the words that Herodotus uses about Polycrates in the passage we are considering, πρῶτος τῶν ἡμεῖς ἴδμεν. The formula τῶν ἡμεῖς ἴδμεν, "of whom/what we know," is said to refer to persons and events in the period starting with Croesus, roughly 550 B.C.; the idea is that Herodotus really only bothers, at least on questions of this kind, with what has happened in "our times," that is to say, the time of the last three generations or so. He uses the expression of Croesus himself at 1.6.2: he was "the first of the barbarians of whom we know who subdued some of the Greeks." In the previous chapter Herodotus has said

that he will not pronounce on certain events before the Trojan War about which the Persians and the Phoenicians differ; and there his point is that he does not know about them, whereas he does know about Croesus. However, Herodotus does not use the formula consistently in this way. Perhaps the most famous occurrence of it is in the description of Xerxes' expedition against Greece: "Among expeditions of which we know, this was by far the greatest, so that others counted as nothing in comparison, neither Darius's against the Scythians, nor the Scythians' which provoked that, nor, from what is said about it, the Greeks' against Troy, nor, before the Trojan War . . ." (7.20.2): these very ancient expeditions, like the others, are *included* in those "of which we know." When we look back from this to our passage, we see that "Polycrates was the first of whom we know . . . apart from (πάρεξ) Minos . . ." means ". . . of whom we know, if we do not count . . . ," rather than "of whom we know, that is to say, not counting . . ." Indeed the qualification we are discussing, "but of the human race . . . ," would make even less sense if Herodotus had already excluded anyone earlier than Polycrates from the comparison.

19. Legrand (1932), 39; cited by Hunter (1982), 19. Finley (1965), 294. The terms *spatium mythologicum* and *spatium historicum* are sometimes used to mark distinctions of this kind; Hunter notes various uses of these expressions.

20. Vidal-Nacquet (1960).

21. ". . . du temps qu'on appelle le temps des hommes," Vidal-Nacquet (1960), 67. Jacqueline de Romilly had earlier and untypically made the same mistake: Romilly (1956), 275.

22. Hunter (1982), 74.

23. Herodotus (2.100) says that the Egyptian priests read out to him the names of 330 kings from a papyrus roll. Hartog (1980) argues that Herodotus is ambivalent about the value of written records, as compared with oral testimony.

24. What counts as a conflict that needs reconciliation? Appeal is naturally made to what is to be expected in the world of the story, as we do with what we call fiction—how gods generally behave, for instance. This is different from a critique based on explanatory principles that apply to the everyday world, such as are used by Thucydides (see below) and, with regard to the coherence of myths, by Hecataeus.

25. Veyne (1986), 28. It is not altogether a good question, a point that he recognizes himself. Elsewhere in his book (e.g., 11), he substitutes another inquiry, which implies an extravagant relativism about truth, or worse: "It creates an odd effect at first, to suppose that nothing is true or false, but

one quickly gets used to it. And for good reason: the value of truth is useless ... 'truth' is the name we give to those options that we will not let go. We could have retorted [to the Nazis] that they were wrong, but what would be the point? They were not on the same wavelength as us" (137). The many interesting ideas in the book are independent of this rhetoric.

26. Cf. Thomas (1988), 62: "Standing between orality and literacy meant that Herodotus possessed and employed the skills of both mentalities, and the disparity between them is readily apparent in *The Histories*." However, Thomas says further, "Like Herodotus, Thucydides notes a distinction between present and past but, unlike Herodotus, he treats the two as distinct entities" (63): this could be taken to mean almost the opposite of what I am claiming.

27. How and Wells (1912), 295.

28. It is worth remarking that Thucydides' move depends on identification of the seas mentioned in the Minos stories as real seas, known to the story-tellers and to him: but it is an important characteristic of many myths, as of many present-day fictions, that they are told about real places.

29. There is no reason to ascribe so much to Hecataeus, though he seems to have taken a more sharply critical line than Herodotus; at the opening of his *Genealogies*, he said, "I Hecataeus will say what I think to be the truth (ὥς μοι δοκεῖ ἀληθέα εἶναι): the tales of the Greeks are many and ridiculous" (*FGH* I.1.fr1). About Herodotus, Momigliano (1990) moderately said that "the burning fire of incredulity was absent in him." The various attempts to rehabilitate Herodotus in this respect stress his frequent refusal to assert things he does not know, but credulity can be shown by what one is prepared even to entertain. Hecataeus is often thought to have influenced the tone of Book 2.

30. Of course, the exact temporal ordering of happenings is constrained by vagueness: historical events do not happen at instants. But this is not a point about history; in understanding what an event of a certain kind is, whenever it happens, we understand this. (It should be added, perhaps, that in thinking about historical time, we are considering things only on a terrestrial scale; no issues about relativistic frames of reference are relevant.)

I assume that historical time is, in the implied sense, linear, but I do not take this to be the same sense as that in which "linear" is contrasted, in many discussions of Greek ideas, with "cyclical" time. That distinction concerns the content of (happenings in) time, not its structure: if there are "cycles," then each is a distinct item in a succession of cycles. A fragment of Eudemus *Physics*, cited by Simplicius (DK⁶ 58 [45], B 34) seems to offer the good argument that "eternal recurrence" in a strict sense (which he ascribes to the Pythagoreans) would be not recurrence at all but just one temporal cycle. (Contrary to Vidal-Nacquet's [1960] reading of this fragment, εὔλογον does not qualify χρόνον: it means "it is reasonable to suppose . . .")

31. This is the point I made in chapter 3 by saying that there is no history of the concept of truth: see chapter 3, section 4, above, with note 17. Paul Veyne writes, "We agree with Michel Foucault: the history of ideas properly starts when one historicizes the philosophical idea of truth" (Veyne [1986], 39). A great deal turns here on the force of "philosophical." In fact, much of Foucault's work addresses epistemological issues, of what at different times counts as establishing truth in different fields.

32. As in the proems to each of Hesiod's poems: *Works and Days* 10, "And I, Perses, would tell of true things [ἐτήτυμα]"; *Theogony* 27–28, "we [the Muses] know how to speak many false things [ψεύδεα] which are like true things [ἐτύμοισιν], but we know, when we will, how to utter true things [ἀληθέα]." On the phrase in *Theogony* 27, see above, chapter 4, section 2, with note 19; and on the words for "true" in archaic Greek, see the "Endnote."

33. This has been disputed: Connor (1984), 66 note 37.

34. And of any similar events that occur in the future. I agree with those who take this to mean the future relative to Thucydides, not the future relative to his future readers: he is not offering his history as a predictive handbook.

35. There are many different classifications of stories in oral cultures: Murray (1987) gives references. He also points out that Herodotus himself uses μῦθος only twice (2.23, 2.45), to designate "*logoi* which Herodotus believes to be ridiculous as well as false" (100).

36. There are boring counter-examples ("You will be pleased to hear this . . ."); and there is a different sense in which truth can be audience-relative, in the case of indexical sentences. I hope it is clear why such cases are irrelevant to the argument.

37. Politicians after Pericles, 2.65.10; on the contrast πρὸς ἡδονήν . . . πρὸς ὀργήν, see Connor (1984), 60 note 24. Nicias, 7.8.2, cited by Thomas (1988), 65, who remarks, "The thoughts attributed to Nicias are surely those of the historian."

38. Finley (1965).

39. Political power as based on economic resources and, in particular, sea power, as Jacqueline de Romilly has emphasized; she points out that (influenced no doubt by the case of Athens) he repeatedly mentions the

conjunction of these two factors in the "Archaeology," for instance in relation to Minos (Romilly [1956], 263). De Romilly also points out how the insistence on such explanations affects the substance of the text: "La première des originalités du texte—et non la moindre—est en effet de renouveler la matière même de l'histoire" (241). For constancy and variation, cf. 3.82, the account of στάσις: such events will always happen ἕως ἂν ἡ αὐτὴ φύσις ἀνθρώπων ᾖ, but their particular form will be determined by the circumstances.

40. A matter on which Nietzsche, unless he mysteriously made a mistake, plays a trick on his reader: *Beyond Good and Evil*, 230.

41. There are of course half-way states of mind. It is said that listeners and viewers write in to the authors of soap operas to express distress if a character is going to die, and to ask that she be spared.

42. In China such conceptions may be much older: equally, the history of literacy was different.

43. In a somewhat different connection, cf. Thucydides' comment on Nicias: "rather too given to divination and such things" (7.50.4).

44. A few writers seem to think that the whole idea of sequential time in history is a Western hegemonic imposition which should be abandoned. But, as a critic has remarked, a writer who claims that "historical time is a thing of the past" may have overlooked a few ironies. See Evans (1997), 141–42, for references and comment.

CHAPTER EIGHT
From Sincerity to Authenticity

1. I shall attempt no more than a very partial, philosophically directed, reading of two writers. The history in question certainly has something to do with Christian traditions of self-inquiry, and it is tempting to speculate that the rise of ideas of authenticity—besides its connection with the weakening of fixed social identities, mentioned in the text—was shaped by the Protestant rejection of auricular confession. The priest could absolve me on the basis of what he took to be my best efforts at sincerity, and reassure me that I had done enough. When I was alone before a silent God, it might well seem that only an absolute sincerity would do, a total confrontation with myself.

2. In Book 10 of the *Confessions* Rousseau says that Diderot "will always be my old friend," but remarks in later writings about him and "the Holbach clique" suggest that he ceased to feel this. (References to Rousseau

will be given to the Pléiade edition by volume and page number: in this case, 1:536. All the translations in this chapter are my own.) Diderot, in a letter to Sophie Volland of December 20, 1765 (France [1972], 152), written after the break, says that it would give him great pleasure to have a visit from Rousseau; but it did not happen, and, so far as is known, they never met again.

3. Joyce (1942), 228.

4. Starobinski (1971). It has been translated as Goldhammer (1988).

5. Starobinski (1971), 32.

6. 1:276, 278.

7. A passage rejected from the *Confessions*: Starobinski (1971), 218.

8. Beaudry (1991), 82; Kelly (1987), 85 note 15. Rousseau himself particularly emphasizes, as reasons for wanting to explain himself, the incident of the ribbon (see below, section 2) and also his decision to give away his children to the Foundling Hospital, for which he was particularly criticized.

9. The first of four letters to M. Le Président de Malesherbes, January 4, 1762: 1:1133.

10. *Confessions* Book 10, 1:516.

11. *Rêveries*, fourth Promenade, 1:1024; sixth Promenade, 1:1051; third Promenade, 1:1017. Painting himself in profile: fourth Promenade, 1:1036; Montaigne: 1:1150, and cf. 1:516.

12. Fourth Promenade, 1:1025.

13. 1:84–7. The point about the "mirror image" is remarked by Lejeune (1975).

14. However Wollheim (1999), 165, surprisingly seems to take what Rousseau says at face value.

15. Quoted in Cranston (1997), 160.

16. De Man (1983), 111–12.

17. Reported in Diderot's letter cited above, note 2.

18. Part 4, letter 6: 2:424. One must not forget, certainly, that this is Wolmar, who is a passionless rationalist and turns out, to the great distress of his wife, Julie, to be an unbeliever. Nevertheless, he is agreed to be very virtuous, even if he does "carry in the depths of his heart the terrifying calm of the wicked" (Part 5, letter 5: 2:588).

19. Notably in Book 12 of the *Confessions*, 1:639–40; and cf. the end of the book, 1:656, where he tells of what he said to some people to whom he had read the *Confessions*, and mentions the total silence with which they received it.

20. Eighth Promenade, 1:1078.

21. An extreme version is Talmon (1952).

22. See his article on Rousseau in Furet and Ozouf (1988), to which I am indebted. The quotation is at 884.

23. Trilling (1972), 93. This book did a lot, a long time ago, to stimulate my interest in these questions, and I am sure that there are many others who have had a similar experience.

24. For a strong version of this interpretation, see Ferrara (1993), chapter 5.

25. Part 3, letter 18: 2:355–56.

26. Trilling (1972), 93–94.

27. I take the term "neo-conservative" in this connection from Ferrara (1993), a study of Rousseau's thought in relation to modernity, which offers an account of such critiques, associated in particular with Daniel Bell, David Riesman, Richard Sennett, and Christopher Lasch. The remark mentioned below about hypocrisy's being thought worse than egocentricity comes from Riesman (1980), 21; quoted by Ferrara, 13. A similar confusion of criticisms is applied to the supposed legacy of Rousseau in Bloom (1979). The point that authenticity is genuinely an ideal, and not just a cover for consumerist whimsy, is well emphasized by Charles Taylor in Taylor (1992).

28. It is worth noting that Voltaire was spectacularly odious toward Rousseau, particularly with regard to *La nouvelle Héloïse*, which he described as "stupid, bourgeois, impudent, boring," and he did his best to get it suppressed. Cranston (1991), e.g. 263, 278.

29. For the nature of the enterprise, see Darnton (1979).

30. P 395. References to Diderot are to the Pléiade edition, given by "P" followed by the page number. The translations are my own, but I am indebted to Tancock (1966). For convenience I give references to that translation, marked "T" with the page number: here T 33.

31. Trilling points out that he is still eclipsed by his uncle: the portrait on the cover of the Penguin translation is (or at least was, when the book was first published) of the great Rameau (Trilling [1972], 29).

32. P 422, T 64–65.

33. P 426, T 69.

34. P 434–35, T 79.

35. P 462, T 111.

36. Anderson (1990), 252.

37. Sections 522 ff., in Miller (1977), 317 ff.

38. Trilling (1972), 47. Chapter 2 of Trilling's book offers an interesting account of Hegel's relations to Diderot's text, and to Goethe.

39. *Daybreak*, 119.

40. P 885, T 164. The *Conversation* is the first part of a work consisting of three scenes. Tancock's translation puts all the three pieces under the title *D'Alembert's Dream*; to be exact, it is just the second that is called *La rêve de d'Alembert*.

41. Above, chapter 4, section 2.

42. There is a good deal in common between what I suggest here and the views of Alan Gibbard in Gibbard (1990), 74–75; except that he seems to imply that a "norm of consistency," involved in interchange with others, is something added to a disposition of spontaneous avowal. As I have approached the matter, spontaneous avowal is already in the business of aiming at the truth, and so already committed to norms of consistency.

43. *Confessions* Book 9, 1:455 ff. Cranston (1991), 47. For an account of the break in the context of Diderot's life, see Furbank (1992), especially 151–64, 175–79.

44. Roth (2001), 108.

45. A phrase I have used elsewhere in connection with the closely related topic of moral luck: Williams (1981), 27.

Chapter Nine
Truthfulness, Liberalism, and Critique

1. I shall consider some questions about the relations between a sense of community and, specifically, truthful history in chapter 10.

2. See "The Liberalism of Fear," reprinted in Shklar (1998), a posthumous collection of papers.

3. The issue is helpfully discussed by Timothy Garton Ash: see "Trials, Purges and History Lessons," in Garton Ash (2001).

4. But see Bok (1978) and (1984).

5. *Abrams v. United States*, 250 U.S. (1919), J. Holmes dissenting. The quotation is at 630.

6. For an economic argument, see Goldman (1999), chapter 7.

7. For this and related concerns about the impact of the media, see Sunstein (2001).

8. See, for instance, Schauer (1982), chapter 2; Post (1995). I am indebted to Robert Post, particularly for discussion of First Amendment issues.

9. There is of course an interpretation of "tyranny" under which the market system is precisely its ally and instrument, by helping to conceal

the real interests of the people. This was advanced by the Frankfurt School, but it is difficult to detach it from strongly ideological interpretations of the people's interests.

10. Meiklejohn (1960): the quotation is at 26. Current advocates include Sunstein (see above, note 7) and Owen Fiss: see Fiss (1996).

11. Post (1993) makes this criticism.

12. Rawls (1971), section 15. Other proposals include resources (Ronald Dworkin) and capabilities (Amartya Sen): see Dworkin (2000) and Sen (1992). The focus of liberal discussions of these matters has been primarily on equality, and the question has correspondingly tended to take the form "equality of what?"; but the general question of a currency of social assessment comes before that.

13. Walzer (1983).

14. It is thus not being used as the Critical Theory tradition, in particular Habermas, uses *Herrschaft*. On this, see Geuss (1981), 16–17; and on *Herrschaft* and the Ideal Speech Situation, see below, section 5.

15. There is a large literature on this question. See in particular Cohen (1978) and Elster (1985).

16. Habermas has in fact modified or moved away from some aspects of the theory, such as the "transcendental" idea mentioned below. I have not tried to give a detailed account of his views, in particular of how they have changed. The aim is simply to contrast the version of a Critical Theory Test offered here with the abstract and foundationalist character of Habermas's original model.

17. Geuss (1981), 65 ff., who gives references.

18. This idea has been sustained in a strong form by Karl-Otto Apel. See, for instance, the final chapter of Apel (1980).

19. See chapter 5, section 5, above. Habermas's own version of the idea comes very close to Kant's Categorical Imperative itself.

20. Plato himself, some of the time, recognized this point: see Williams (1993), 154–58.

21. My use of "very general" here is a (not very accurate) way of signalling an important qualification. I have argued elsewhere that claims which use "thick" ethical concepts (those that have a rich and moderately determinate empirical content) can have fairly straightforward truth-conditions and can be the object of moral knowledge. Equally, we can often explain why people are mistaken about their application. The problem is that different societies or individuals need not agree on what "thick" concepts to use (compare the recent history of "chastity"). With "thin" concepts such as "good" and "right," all individuals and societies use some versions of

them, but there is much less agreement about their application, and the statement in the text applies. See Williams (1985), chapter 8, and "Truth in Ethics," in Hooker (1996).

CHAPTER TEN
Making Sense

1. The contrast is with "natural process"; there is no suggestion that acting on intentions does not involve causality.

2. On plans, see Bratman (1987).

3. The importance of such "narrative explanations" has been emphasized over many years by William Dray: see Dray (1957).

4. Alan Gibbard, in Gibbard (1990), uses "makes sense" as his basic normative operator. I shall not take up the question of how my informal use of the expression relates to his theory.

5. This does not exclude the possibility that a decision to act at a later time can allow for changes in the agent's motivational state between now and the time of action. To allow for them is itself an expression of (other) elements in his present motivational state.

6. This point, and other questions of what makes sense to whom and how, are of course relevant to discussions of "internal" and "external" reasons. For perspectives on this, see now Millgram (2001).

7. Particularly in Collingwood (1946), he does, to put it mildly, sometimes give the unfortunate impression that only intentional actions can be historically understood, and that this is the only way of understanding them. What he does not think, as has often been supposed, is that "thinking the agent's thought" is a recipe for historical understanding: it is a description of its success. On this see Gardiner (1996).

8. The Anglo-Saxon Chronicles, the Winchester MS (A), years 664–671: Swanton (2000), 34. "Here" means "In this year." The "chronicle" in the text is an ideal type, accurately represented by such early examples. There are writings called "Chronicles" which have a connected theme, and indeed the Anglo-Saxon Chronicles themselves came to include increasing amounts of extended narrative.

9. Evans (1997), 76 with notes, gives references. The real trouble with Kitson Clark's "fact" is that it looks as though the event in question may not have happened.

10. For problems about the individuation of facts, see chapter 4 above, section 1, with note 4.

11. White (1973). I take this book as a forceful example of a certain kind of theory; I have not addressed later writings by White in which he has somewhat modified his views.

12. White's text does seem to have encouraged this idea, and not just in prejudiced readers. It is presumably because he says very little about the use of evidence. Richard J. Evans writes, "White's argument rested on the idea that it did not matter whether the history we used to further our present concerns was true or not" (Evans [1997], 139), which seems to me a misleading account of the passage he refers to (at 238, however, he admits that "White accepts the possibility of proving historical truth at the level of the individual fact"). Another acute and careful critic who has the same impression is Momigliano in his (1981).

13. See above, chapter 1, section 3.

14. The idea is starkly expressed in the title of a book by a philosopher and essayist who was murdered by Nazi supporters in 1933, Theodor Lessing: *Geschichte als Sinngebung des Sinnlosen* (1919).

15. See Turner (1996).

16. Quoted by White (1973), 139.

17. Nancy S. Struever, "Topics in History," in Kellner et al. (1980).

18. See above, chapter 6, section 4.

19. Novick (1988), 14.

20. See most recently Hoyle (2001), informatively reviewed by Collinson (2001).

21. Documented in chapter 14 of Novick (1988), significantly called "Every Group Its Own Historian."

22. They were mentioned in section 4 of chapter 2.

23. White (1973), 433; his emphases.

24. Ibid., 430.

25. Malia (1999) engages deeply and controversially with these questions.

26. Wright (1992), 44 ff.

27. Novick's informative and otherwise helpful book unfortunately uses this contrast.

28. What is wrong is not just the "either/or" assumption but the notion of the will itself. It is a familiar point that a metaphysical conception of the will as self-determination or self-creation has something wrong with it, but the trouble may be more radical, in the sense that our inherited everyday conception of decision has too much of that metaphysics associated with it. Some archaic formulae to describe arriving at a practical conclusion are instructive: cf. chapter 2 of my (1993).

29. *Faust*, Part 1, 1237.

30. We encountered this in the form of the "contingency" of our outlook in chapter 2, section 1. I have tried to say some more elsewhere (Williams [2000a]) on why it is not in itself unnerving.

31. See above, chapter 9, section 1, with note 2. In the paper referred to there, Shklar, borrowing a distinction from Emerson, associated the liberalism of fear with "the party of memory" as opposed to "the party of hope." My claim in these pages—and Shklar would in fact have agreed—is that those titles can apply to the same party. It is all a question of what, and how much, you hope for.

32. Conrad (1946), 151.

Bibliography

❖   ❖   ❖   ❖   ❖

Allison, David B., ed. 1985. *The New Nietzsche.* Cambridge: MIT Press.

Anderson, Wilma. 1990. *Diderot's Dream.* Baltimore: Johns Hopkins University Press.

Apel, Karl-Otto. 1980. *Towards a Transformation of Philosophy.* London: Routledge and Kegan Paul.

Appleby, Joyce, Lynn Hunt, and Margaret Jacob. 1994. *Telling the Truth about History.* New York: Norton.

Auden, W. H. 1976. *Collected Poems.* London: Faber and Faber.

Austin, J. L. 1961. *Philosophical Papers.* Edited by J. O. Urmson and G. J. Warnock. Oxford: Clarendon Press.

Bacharach, M., and D. Gambetta. 2001. "Trust in Signs." In *Trust and Social Structure,* edited by Karen Cook. New York: Russell Sage Foundation.

Barkow, Jerome H., Leda Cosmides, and John Tooby. 1992. *The Adapted Mind.* New York and Oxford: Oxford University Press.

Barnes, J. A. 1994. *A Pack of Lies: Towards a Sociology of Lying.* Cambridge: Cambridge University Press.

Barthes, Roland. 1976. *S/Z.* Paris: Editions de Seuil.

Beaudry, Catherine A. 1991. *The Role of the Reader in Rousseau's Confessions.* New York: Peter Lang.

Bennett, Jonathan. 1995. *The Act Itself.* Oxford: Clarendon Press.

Bloom, Allan. 1979. Introduction to Jean-Jacques Rousseau, *Émile; or, On Education,* translated by Allan Bloom. New York: Basic Books.

Bok, Sissela. 1978. *Lying: Moral Choice in Public and Private Life.* New York: Pantheon.

———. 1984. *Secrets.* Oxford: Oxford University Press.

Boucher, Donald, ed. 1977. *Language, Counter-Memory, Practise.* Ithaca, N.Y.: Cornell University Press.

Brandom, Robert. 1994. *Making It Explicit.* Cambridge: Harvard University Press.

———. 2000a. "Facts, Norms, and Normative Facts: A Reply to Habermas." *European Journal of Philosophy* 8:356–74.

Brandom, Robert, ed. 2000b. *Rorty and His Critics*. Oxford: Basil Blackwell.

Bratman, Michael. 1987. *Intentions, Plans, and Practical Reason*. Cambridge: Harvard University Press.

Breazeale, Daniel, ed. and trans. 1979. *Philosophy and Truth: Selections from Nietzsche's Notebooks of the Early 1870's*. Atlantic Highlands, N.J.: Humanities Press International.

Burge, Tyler. 1993. "Content Preservation." *Philosophical Review* 102:457–88.

Byrne, Richard W., and Andrew Whiten, eds. 1988. *Machiavellian Intelligence: Social Expertise and the Evolution of Intellect in Monkeys, Apes, and Humans*. Oxford: Clarendon Press.

Campbell, John. 1994. *Past, Space and Self*. Cambridge: MIT Press.

Campbell, R. H., A. S. Skinner, and W. B. Todd, eds. 1976. *Adam Smith: An Inquiry into the Nature and Causes of the Wealth of Nations*. Oxford: Clarendon Press.

Campbell, Richard. 1992. *Truth and Historicity*. Oxford: Clarendon Press.

Canary, R. H., and Henry Kozicki, eds. 1978. *The Writing of History: Literary Form and Historical Understanding*. Madison: University of Wisconsin Press.

Carston, Robyn. 1988. "Implicature, Explicature, and Truth-Theoretic Semantics." In *Mental Representations*, edited by Ruth M. Kempson. Cambridge: Cambridge University Press.

Cavell, Stanley. 1979. *The Claim of Reason*. Oxford: Oxford University Press.

Cheney, Dorothy L., and Robert M. Seyfarth. 1990. *How Monkeys See the World: Inside the Mind of Another Species*. Chicago: University of Chicago Press.

Chomsky, Noam. 1995. "Language and Nature." *Mind* 104:1–61.

Clark, Maudemarie. 1990. *Nietzsche on Truth and Philosophy*. Cambridge: Cambridge University Press.

Cloak, F. T. 1975. "Is a Cultural Ethology Possible?" *Human Ecology* 3:161–82.

Cohen, G. A. 1978. *Karl Marx's Theory of History*. Oxford: Clarendon Press, 1978.

Cole, Thomas. 1983. "Archaic Truth." *Quaderni Urbinati di Cultura Classica* 13:7–28.

Colli, Giorgio, and Mazzino Montinari, eds. 1988. *Nietzsche: Sämtliche Werke: kritische Studienausgabe*. Munich: Deutsche Taschenbuch Verlag.

Collingwood, R. G. 1946. *The Idea of History*. Edited by T. M. Knox. Oxford: Clarendon Press. [A revised edition, edited by W. Jan van der Dussen, appeared in 1993.]

Collinson, Patrick. 2001. "What News?" *London Review of Books* 23 (November 1): 19–22. [A review of Hoyle (2001).]

Connor, W. Robert. 1984. *Thucydides*. Princeton: Princeton University Press.

Conrad, Joseph. 1946. *Youth. Heart of Darkness. The End of the Tether*. London: J. M. Dent and Sons.

Cornford, F. M. 1907. *Thucydides Mythistoricus*. London: Arnold.

Craig, E. J. 1990. *Knowledge and the State of Nature*. Oxford: Clarendon Press.

Cranston, Maurice. 1991. *The Noble Savage: Rousseau 1754–62*. Chicago: University of Chicago Press.

———. 1997. *The Solitary Self: Jean-Jacques Rousseau in Exile and Adversity*. Chicago: University of Chicago Press.

Darnton, Robert. 1979. *The Business of Enlightenment*. Cambridge: Harvard University Press, Belknap Press.

Davidson, Donald. 1990. "The Structure and Content of Truth." *Journal of Philosophy* 87:279–328.

———. 1996. "The Folly of Trying to Define Truth." *Journal of Philosophy* 93:6:263–78.

———. 2001. *Inquiries into Truth and Interpretation*. 2d ed. Oxford: Clarendon Press.

Dawkins, Richard. 1976. *The Selfish Gene*. Oxford: Oxford University Press.

De Man, Paul. 1983. *Blindness and Insight: Essays in the Rhetoric of Contemporary Criticism*. 2d ed. London: Methuen.

Detienne, Marcel. 1967. *Les maîtres de la vérité dans la grèce archaïque*. Paris: Maspero.

Dewald, Carolyn, and John Marincola. 1987. "A Selective Introduction to Herodotean Studies." *Arethusa* 20:9–40.

Diamond, Cora. 1993. "Truth: Defenders, Debunkers, Despisers." In Toker (1993).

Diderot, Denis. *Letters to Sophie Volland*. See France (1972).

———. *Oeuvres*. Bibliothèque de la Pléiade. Paris: Gallimard, 1951.

Dray, William H. 1957. *Laws and Explanation in History*. Oxford: Clarendon Press.

Dummett, Michael. 1973. *Frege's Philosophy of Language*. New York: Harper & Row.

———. 1978. *Truth and Other Enigmas*. London: Duckworth.

Durham, William H. 1991. *Coevolution: Genes, Culture, and Human Diversity*. Stanford: Stanford University Press.

Dworkin, Ronald. 2000. *Sovereign Virtue*. Cambridge: Harvard University Press.

Edmunds, Lowell. 1975. *Cause and Chance in Thucydides*. Cambridge: Harvard University Press.

Egan, Kieran. 1978. "Thucydides, Tragedian." In Canary and Kozicki (1978).

Elster, Jon. 1985. *Making Sense of Marx*. Cambridge: Cambridge University Press.

Empson, William. 1952. *The Structure of Complex Words*. London: Chatto and Windus.

Evans, Richard J. 1997. *In Defence of History*. London: Granta Books.

Ferrara, Alessandro. 1993. *Modernity and Authenticity*. Albany: SUNY Press.

Finley, M. I. 1965. "Myth, Memory and History." *History and Theory* 4:281–302.

Fiss, Owen M. 1996. *Liberalism Divided: Freedom of Speech and the Many Uses of State Power*. Boulder, Colo.: Westview.

France, Peter. 1972. *Diderot's Letters to Sophie Volland*. Selected and translated by Peter France. London: Oxford University Press.

Frankfurt, H. 1992. "The Faintest Passion." *Proceedings and Addresses of the APA* 66.3:5–16.

Frye, Northrop. 1957. *The Anatomy of Criticism: Four Essays*. Princeton: Princeton University Press.

Furbank, P. N. 1992. *Diderot: A Critical Biography*. London: Secker & Warburg.

Furet, François, and Mona Ozouf. 1988. *Dictionnaire critique de la Révolution française*. Paris: Flammarion.

Gambetta, Diego, ed. 1988. *Trust: Making and Breaking Co-operative Relations*. Oxford: Blackwell.

Gardiner, Patrick. 1996. "Interpretation in History: Collingwood and Historical Understanding." In *Verstehen and Humane Understanding* (Royal Institute of Philosophy Supplement 41), edited by Anthony O'Hear. Cambridge: Cambridge University Press.

Garton Ash, Timothy. 2001. *History of the Present: Essays, Sketches and Despatches from Europe in the 1990s*. Rev. ed. New York: Vintage.

Gauthier, David. 1986. *Morality by Agreement*. Oxford: Oxford University Press.

Geach, P. T. 1977. *The Virtues*. The Stanton Lectures, 1973–74. Cambridge: Cambridge University Press.

Gerth, H. H., and C. Wright Mills, ed. and trans. 1991. *From Max Weber: Essays in Sociology*. 2d ed. London: Routledge.

Geuss, Raymond. 1981. *The Idea of a Critical Theory*. Cambridge: Cambridge University Press.

———. 1999. "Nietzsche and Genealogy." In *Morality, Culture, and History*. Cambridge: Cambridge University Press.

Gibbard, Allan. 1990. *Wise Choices, Apt Feelings*. Cambridge: Harvard University Press.

Gilby, Thomas, ed. and trans. 1975. *Thomas Aquinas, Summa Theologiae*. Vol. 38. Cambridge: Blackfriars.

Gill, Christopher, and T. P. Wiseman. 1993. *Lies and Fiction in the Ancient World*. Exeter: University of Exeter Press.

Gilligan, Carol. 1982. *In a Different Voice: Psychological Theory and Women's Development*. Cambridge: Harvard University Press.

Goldhammer, Arthur. 1988. *Jean-Jacques Rousseau: Transparency and Obstruction*. Chicago: University of Chicago Press. [A translation of Starobinski (1971).]

Goldman, Alvin I. 1999. *Knowledge in a Social World*. Oxford: Oxford University Press.

Goody, Jack. 1977. *The Domestication of the Savage Mind*. Cambridge: Cambridge University Press.

Goody, Jack, and I. P. Watt. 1963. "The Consequences of Literacy." *Comparative Studies in History and Society* 5:304–45.

Grandy, Richard. 1973. "Reference, Meaning and Belief." *Journal of Philosophy* 70:439–52.

Green, Richard Firth. 1999. *A Crisis of Truth: Literature and Law in Ricardian England*. Philadelphia: University of Pennsylvania Press.

Gregor, Mary J., ed. and trans. 1996. *Immanuel Kant, Practical Philosophy*. Cambridge: Cambridge University Press.

Grice, Paul. 1989. *Studies in the Way of Words*. Cambridge: Harvard University Press.

Haack, Susan. 1998. *Confessions of a Passionate Moderate*. Chicago: University of Chicago Press.

Hacking, Ian. 1972. "The Logic of Pascal's Wager." *American Philosophical Quarterly* 9:186–92. Reprinted in Jordan (1984).

Hacking, Ian. (1983): *Representing and Intervening*. Cambridge: Cambridge University Press.

Hahn, Lewis E., ed. 1998. *The Philosophy of P. F. Strawson*. Chicago: Open Court.

Hamilton, W. D. 1964. "The Genetical Evolution of Social Behaviour." I and II. *Journal of Theoretical Biology* 7:1–52.

Hampshire, Stuart. 1959. *Thought and Action*. London: Chatto & Windus.

Harcourt, Edward, ed. 2000. *Morality, Reflection and Ideology*. Oxford: Oxford University Press.

Harman, Gilbert. 1977. *The Nature of Morality: An Introduction to Ethics*. New York: Oxford University Press.

Hartog, F. 1980. *Le miroir d'Hérodote*. Paris: Gallimard. Translated by Janet Lloyd as *The Mirror of Herodotus*. Berkeley and Los Angeles: University of California Press, 1988.

Heal, Jane. 1987/88. "The Disinterested Search for Truth." *Proceedings of the Aristotelian Society* 88:97–108.

Hempel, C. G. 1965. *Aspects of Scientific Explanation*. New York: The Free Press.

Höffe, Otfried, ed. 1997. *Platons Politeia*. Berlin: Akademie Verlag.

Hooker, Brad, ed. 1996. *Truth in Ethics*. Oxford: Blackwell.

Horkheimer, Max, and Theodor W. Adorno. 1969. *Dialektik der Aufklärung*. Frankfurt am Main: S. Fischer. Translated by John Cumming as *Dialectic of Enlightenment*. New York: Herder and Herder, 1972.

Hornsby, Jennifer, 2000. "Feminism in Philosophy of Language: Communicative Speech Acts." In *The Cambridge Companion to Feminism in Philosophy*, edited by Miranda Fricker and Jennifer Hornsby. Cambridge: Cambridge University Press.

Horwich, Paul. 1990. *Truth*. Oxford: Basil Blackwell.

———. 1998. *Truth*. 2d ed. Oxford: Clarendon Press.

How, W. W., and J. Wells. 1912. *A Commentary on Herodotus*. Oxford: Clarendon Press.

Hoyle, R. W. 2001. *The Pilgrimage of Grace and the Politics of the 1530s*. Oxford: Oxford University Press.

Hume, David. *A Treatise of Human Nature*. Edited by L. A. Selby-Bigge. Oxford: Clarendon Press, 1888.

Hunter, Virginia. 1982. *Past and Process in Herodotus and Thucydides*. Princeton: Princeton University Press.

Immerwahr, Henry R. 1966. *Form and Thought in Herodotus*. Cleveland: Western Reserve University Press.

James, Susan. 1984. *The Content of Social Explanation*. Cambridge: Cambridge University Press.

Jardine, Nicholas. 1991. *The Scenes of Inquiry: On the Reality of Questions in the Sciences*. Oxford: Clarendon Press.

Jonsen, Albert R., and Stephen Toulmin. 1988. *The Abuse of Casuistry*. Berkeley and Los Angeles: University of California Press.

Jordan, J., ed. 1984. *Gambling on God: Essays on Pascal's Wager*. Lanham: Rowman & Littlefield.

Josipovici, Gabriel. 1999. *On Trust: Art and the Temptations of Suspicion*. New Haven and London: Yale University Press.

Joyce, James. 1942. *A Portrait of the Artist as a Young Man* (1916). Travellers' Library edition. London: Jonathan Cape.

Judson, Horace. 1979. *The Eighth Day of Creation*. New York: Simon and Schuster.

Kant, Immanuel. *Practical Philosophy*. See Gregor (1996).

Kellner, Hans, et al. 1980. "*Metahistory*: Six Critiques." *History and Theory* Beiheft 19.

Kelly, Christopher. 1987. *Rousseau's Exemplary Life*. Ithaca, N.Y.: Cornell University Press.

Krischer, Tilman. 1965. "ΕΤΥΜΟΣ und ΑΛΗΘΗΣ." *Philologus* 109:161–74.

Lateiner, Donald. 1989. *The Historical Method of Herodotus*. Toronto: University of Toronto Press.

Lazar, Ariela. 1999. "Deceiving Oneself or Self-Deceived? On the Formation of Beliefs 'Under the Influence.'" *Mind* 108:265–90.

Legrand, Ph.-E. 1932. *Hérodote: Introduction*. Paris: Les Belles Lettres.

Lejeune, Philippe. 1975. *Le pacte autobiographique*. Paris: Editions du Seuil.

Levet, J. P. 1976. *Le Vrai et le Faux dans la pensée grecque archaique: étude de vocabulaire*. Paris: Les Belles Lettres.

Levi, Primo. 1985. *The Periodic Table*. Translated by Raymond Rosenthal from *Il sistema periodico*. Turin: Einaudi, 1975.

Lewis, David. 1983. *Philosophical Papers*. Vol. 1. Oxford: Oxford University Press.

MacIntyre, Alasdair. 1990. *Three Rival Versions of Moral Enquiry*. London: Duckworth.

———. 1995. "Truthfulness, Lies, and Moral Philosophers: What Can We Learn from Mill and Kant?" In *Tanner Lectures on Human Values*, vol. 16. Salt Lake City: University of Utah Press.

Macleod, C. 1983. "Thucydides and Tragedy." In *Collected Essays*. Oxford: Clarendon Press.

Malachowski, Adam, ed. 1990. *Reading Rorty*. Oxford: Blackwell.

Malia, Martin. 1999. *Russia under Western Eyes*. Cambridge: Harvard University Press, Belknap Press.

Mamet, David. 1993. *Oleanna*. New York: Vintage Books.

McIntyre, Alison. 2001. "Doing Away with Double Effect." *Ethics* 111:219–55.

Meiklejohn, Alexander. 1960. *Political Freedom: The Constitutional Power of the People*. New York: Harper.

Miller, A. V., trans. 1977. *Hegel's Phenomenology of Spirit*. Oxford: Clarendon Press.

Miller, Eugene F., ed. 1985. *Hume's Essays*. Indianapolis: Liberty Classics.

Millgram, Elijah, ed. 2001. *Varieties of Practical Reasoning*. Cambridge: MIT Press.

Mitchel, F. 1956. "Herodotus' Use of Genealogical Chronology." *Phoenix* 10:48–69.

Moles, J. L. 1993. "Truth and Untruth in Herodotus and Thucydides." In Gill and Wiseman (1993).

Momigliano, Arnaldo. 1981. "The Rhetoric of History and the History of Rhetoric: On Hayden White's Tropes." *Comparative Criticism* 3:259–69.

———. 1990. *The Classical Foundations of Modern Historiography*. Berkeley and Los Angeles: University of California Press.

Moore, A. W. 1997. *Points of View*. Oxford: Clarendon Press.

Moran, Richard. 2001. *Authority and Estrangement*. Princeton: Princeton University Press.

Murray, Oswyn. 1987. "Herodotus and Oral History." In Sancisi-Weerdenburg and Kuhrt (1987).

Nagel, Thomas. 1997. *The Last Word*. Oxford: Oxford University Press.

Neale, Stephen. 1995. "The Philosophical Significance of Gödel's Slingshot." *Mind* 104:761–825.

Nietzsche, F. See Colli and Montinari 1988.

———. *On Truth and Lies in a Nonmoral Sense*. See Breazeale (1979).

———. *Human, All Too Human*. Translated by Gary Handwerk. Stanford: Stanford University Press, 1995.

———. *Daybreak*. Translated by R. J. Hollingdale. Cambridge: Cambridge University Press, 1982.

———. *The Gay Science*. Translated by Josefine Nauckhoff. Cambridge: Cambridge University Press, 2001.

———. *On the Genealogy of Morality*. Translated by Carol Diethe. Cambridge: Cambridge University Press, 1994.

———. *Thus Spake Zarathustra*. Translated by Walter Kaufmann. New York: Viking, 1954.

———. *Beyond Good and Evil*. Translated by Walter Kaufmann. New York: Vintage Books, 1966.

———. *The Twilight of the Idols* and *The Antichrist*. Translated by R. J. Hollingdale. Harmondsworth: Penguin, 1968.

———. *Ecce Homo*. Translated by Walter Kaufmann. New York: Vintage Books, 1969.

———. *The Will to Power*. Translated by Walter Kaufmann and R. J. Hollingdale. London: Weidenfeld and Nicholson, 1967.

Novick, Peter. 1988. *That Noble Dream: The "Objectivity Question" and the American Historical Profession*. Cambridge: Cambridge University Press.

Nozick, Robert. 1974. *Anarchy, State, and Utopia*. New York: Basic Books; Oxford: Oxford University Press, 1976.

Orwell, George. 1949. *Nineteen Eighty-Four*. London: Secker and Warburg.

Parry, Adam Milman. 1981. *Logos and Ergon in Thucydides*. New York: Arno Press. [A Harvard dissertation submitted in 1957.]

Peacocke, C. 1999. *Being Known*. Oxford: Oxford University Press.

Pears, David. 1984. *Motivated Irrationality*. Oxford: Clarendon Press.

Platts, M., ed. 1980. *Reference, Truth and Reality*. London: Routledge and Kegan Paul.

Popper, Karl. 1959. *The Logic of Scientific Discovery*. London: Hutchinson.

———. 1963. *Conjectures and Refutations: The Growth of Scientific Knowledge*. London: Routledge and Kegan Paul.

Post, Robert. 1993. "Meiklejohn's Mistake: Individual Autonomy and the Reform of Public Discourse." 64 *University of Colorado Law Review*, 1109–37.

———. 1995. "Social Practices: Recuperating First Amendment Doctrine." 47 *Stanford Law Review*, 1249–81.

Powell, J. E. 1938. *A Lexicon to Herodotus*. Cambridge: Cambridge University Press.

Quine, W. V. 1970. *Philosophy of Logic*. Englewood Cliffs, N.J.: Prentice Hall.

———. 1990. *The Pursuit of Truth*. Cambridge: Harvard University Press.

Ramsey, F. P. 1990. *Philosophical Papers*. Edited by D. H. Mellor. Cambridge: Cambridge University Press.

Raphael, D. D., and A. L. MacFie, eds. 1976. *Adam Smith: The Theory of the Moral Sentiments*. Oxford: Oxford University Press.

Rawls, John. 1971. *A Theory of Justice*. Cambridge: Harvard University Press.

Riesman, David. 1980. "Egocentrism: Is the American Character Changing?" *Encounter*, September–October.

Romilly, Jacqueline de. 1956. *Histoire et raison chez Thucydide*. Paris: Les Belles Lettres.

Rorty, Richard. 1989. *Contingency, Irony and Solidarity*. Cambridge: Cambridge University Press.

———. 1991. *Objectivity, Relativism and Truth*. Vol. 1 of *Philosophical Papers*. Cambridge: Cambridge University Press.

———. 1998. *Truth and Progress*. Vol. 3 of *Philosophical Papers*. Cambridge: Cambridge University Press.

Roth, Philip. 2001. *The Human Stain*. London: Vintage.

Rousseau, Jean-Jacques. *Oeuvres complètes*. Vols. 1 and 2. Bibliothèque de la Pléiade. Paris: Gallimard, 1959, 1964.

Runciman, W. G. 1998. *The Social Animal*. London: HarperCollins.

Sancisi-Weerdenburg, Heleen, and Amélie Kuhrt, eds. 1987. *Achaemenid History II: The Greek Sources*. Leyden: Nederlands Instituut voor het Nabije Oosten.

Saul, Nigel. 1999. "From Trothe to Truth." *Times Literary Supplement*, July 2. [A review of Green (1999).]

Scanlon, T. M. 1998. *What We Owe to Each Other*. Cambridge: Harvard University Press.

Schantz, R., ed. 2001. *What Is Truth?* Berlin and New York: de Gruyter.

Schauer, Frederick. 1982. *Free Speech: A Philosophical Enquiry*. Cambridge: Cambridge University Press.

Searle, J. R. 1969. *Speech Acts*. Cambridge: Cambridge University Press.

———. 1998. "Truth: A Reconstruction of Strawson's Views." In Hahn (1998).

Sen, Amartya. 1992. *Inequality Reexamined*. Cambridge: Harvard University Press.

Shimron, B. 1973. Πρῶτος τῶν ἡμεῖς ἴδμεν. *Eranos* 71.

Shklar, Judith. 1998. *Political Thought and Political Thinkers*. Edited by Stanley Hoffman. Chicago: University of Chicago Press.

Silverman, David. 1975. *Reading Castaneda: A Prologue to the Social Sciences*. London: Routledge and Kegan Paul.

Slote, M. A. 1979. "Assertion and Belief." In *Papers on Language and Logic*, edited by J. Dancy. Keele: Keele University Library.

Soames, Scott. 1984. "What Is a Theory of Truth?" *Journal of Philosophy* 81:411–29.

Sperber, Dan, and Deirdre Wilson. 1995. *Relevance: Communication and Cognition*. 2d ed. Oxford: Basil Blackwell.

Starobinski, Jean. 1971. *Jean-Jacques Rousseau: la transparence et l'obstacle*. Paris: Gallimard.

Ste Croix, G.E.M. de. 1977. "Herodotus." *Greece and Rome*, 2d ser., 24:130–48.

Sunstein, Cass R. 2001. *Republic.com*. Princeton: Princeton University Press.

Swanton, Michael, ed. and trans. 2000. *The Anglo-Saxon Chronicles*. Rev. ed. London: Phoenex Press.

Talmon, J. L. 1952. *The Origins of Totalitarian Democracy*. London: Secker and Warburg.

Tancock, Leonard, trans. 1966. Denis Diderot, *Rameau's Nephew* and *d'Alembert's Dream*. Harmondsworth: Penguin.

Tarski, A. 1956. "The Concept of Truth in Formalized Languages." In *Logic, Semantics, Metamathematics*, edited by J. H. Woodger. Oxford: Oxford University Press.

Taylor, Charles. 1992. *The Ethics of Authenticity*. Cambridge: Harvard University Press.

Thomas, Carol G. 1988. "Between Literacy and Orality: Herodotus' Historiography." *Mediterranean Historical Review* 3:54–70.

Toker, Leona, ed. 1993. *Commitment in Reflection*. Hamden: Garland.

Trilling, Lionel. 1972. *Sincerity and Authenticity*. Cambridge: Harvard University Press.

Trivers, R. L. 1971. "The Evolution of Reciprocal Altruism." *Quarterly Review of Biology* 46:35–57.

Turner, Henry Ashby. 1996. *Hitler's Thirty Days to Power*. London: Bloomsbury.

Unger, P. 1975. *Ignorance*. Oxford: Oxford University Press.

van Straaten, Z., ed. 1980. *Philosophical Subjects*. Oxford: Oxford University Press.

Vandiver, Elizabeth. 1991. *Heroes in Herodotus: The Interaction of Myth and History*. Frankfurt am Main: Peter Lang.

Veyne, Paul. 1986. *Les Grecs ont-ils cru à leurs mythes?* Paris: Editions de Seuil. Translated as *Did the Greeks Believe in Their Myths?* Chicago: University of Chicago Press, 1988.

Vidal-Nacquet, P. 1960. "Temps des dieux et temps des hommes." *Revue de l'histoire des religions* 157. Reprinted in *Le chasseur noir*. Paris: Maspero, 1981. Translated as *The Black Hunter*. Baltimore: Johns Hopkins University Press, 1986.

Walcot, Peter. 1977. "Odysseus and the Art of Lying." *Ancient Society* 8:1–19.

Walzer, Michael. 1983. *Spheres of Justice*. New York: Basic Books.

Watson, James. 1968. *The Double Helix*. London: Weidenfeld and Nicolson.

West, M. L. 1966. *Hesiod,* Theogony. Oxford: Clarendon Press.

White, Hayden. 1973. *Metahistory: The Historical Imagination in Nineteenth Century Europe*. Baltimore and London: John Hopkins University Press.

Wiggins, David. 1980. "What Would Be a Substantial Theory of Truth?" In van Straaten (1980).

———. 1991. *Needs, Values, Truth*. 2d ed. Oxford: Blackwell.

———. 1997. "Languages as Objects." *Philosophy* 72:499–524.

———. 2001. "Marks of Truth: A Normative cum Substantive View." In Schantz (2001).

Williams, Bernard. 1973. *Problems of the Self*. Cambridge: Cambridge University Press.

———. 1978. *Descartes: The Project of Pure Enquiry*. Harmondsworth: Penguin.

———. 1981. *Moral Luck*. Cambridge: Cambridge University Press.

———. 1985. *Ethics and the Limits of Philosophy*. Cambridge: Harvard University Press.

———. 1993. *Shame and Necessity*. Berkeley and Los Angeles: University of California Press.

———. 1995. *Making Sense of Humanity*. Cambridge University Press.

———. 1996. "Dallo stato di natura alla genealogia." *Studi Perugini 2*.

———. 1998. "The Last Word in Philosophy." *New York Review of Books* 45:18. [A review of Nagel (1997).]

———. 2000a. "Philosophy as a Humanistic Discipline." *Philosophy* 75:477–96.

———. 2000b. "Naturalism and Genealogy." In Harcourt (2000).

Williamson, Timothy. 1996. "Knowing and Asserting." *Philosophical Review* 105:489–523.

Wilson, E. O. 1975. *Sociobiology: The New Synthesis*. Cambridge: Harvard University Press, Belknap Press.

———. 1978. *On Human Nature*. Cambridge: Harvard University Press.

Wollheim, Richard. 1999. *On the Emotions*. New Haven: Yale University Press.

Wright, Crispin. 1992. *Truth and Objectivity*. Cambridge: Harvard University Press.

Zagorin, P. 1990. *Ways of Lying: Dissimulation, Persecution and Conformity in Early Modern Europe*. Cambridge: Harvard University Press.

Acknowledgements

❖   ❖   ❖   ❖   ❖

Among the very many people who have given me help in writing this book, I should like to express my thanks particularly to the following, some of whom have commented on it in manuscript: John Burrow, Donald Davidson, Ronald Dworkin, Raymond Geuss, Stephen Greenblatt, Ariela Lazar, Jonathan Lear, Adrian Moore, Richard Moran, Alexander Nehamas, Derek Parfit, Christopher Peacocke, Robert Post, T. M. Scanlon, Samuel Scheffler, Barry Stroud, David Wiggins, and Patricia Williams.

I am grateful to Casey Perin and to Kirstie Laird for research assistance.

I have been given the opportunity to spend time at several institutions in the course of which I have worked on and presented some of the material. In particular, I am (like many other scholars) indebted to the extraordinary hospitality of the Wissenchaftskolleg zu Berlin, and to the co-operation of its then Rector, Wolf Lepenies, and members of its staff in assisting my idiosyncratic schedule in 1996–97. I am grateful for the opportunity to give the Christian Gauss Seminar in Criticism at Princeton in 1992; for periods spent as a visitor to the Institute of Humanities at the University of Michigan, 1994, as Jeannette K. Watson Professor in the Humanities, Syracuse University, also in 1994, and as the Cardinal Mercier Professor at the Hoger Instituut voor Wijsbegeerte, Leuven, in 1998; and for a visit to the Institut für die Wissenschaften vom Menschen in Vienna, in 1997.

I am grateful for invitations to give the Woodbridge Lectures at Columbia University and the Clark Lectures at Trinity College, Cambridge, both in 1993; the Sara H. Schaffner Lectures at the University of Chicago in 1995; and the fifty-fourth Werner Heisenberg Lecture at the Carl Friedrich von Siemens Foundation in Munich, 1996. I have also presented some of the material in lectures or seminars in Oxford, Berkeley, and Göttingen; at the Royal Institute of Philosophy, London; at the Southern Association for Ancient Philosophy; and at the "B" Club in Cambridge. I am indebted to those who took part in discussion on these occasions.

Some of the occasions I have mentioned issued in publications which overlap with material in this book. The most substantial of these is the book of the lectures that I gave at the IWM in Vienna: *Der Wert der Wahrheit*, translated by Joachim Schulte (Vienna: Passagen Verlag, 1998). This book, which has not appeared in English, contains earlier versions of parts of chapters 1, 3, and 6, and a substantial part of chapter 9. Chapter 7 has appeared, in slightly different versions, under the title "Did Thucydides Invent Historical Time?" in the *Jahrbuch* of the Wissenschaftskolleg zu Berlin, and also in *Representations* 19 (2001). Some material in chapter 8 appeared in "The Politics of Trust," in *The Geography of Identity*, edited by Patricia Yaeger (Ann Arbor: University of Michigan Press, 1996). Another version of the Heisenberg Lecture given in Munich was presented to a conference in Oxford in 1996, and is close to chapter 2; it is published as "Naturalism and Genealogy" in Harcourt (2000). Other publications that anticipate in various degrees parts of the present book are: "Les vertus de la vérité," translated by Catherine Audard, in *Le respect*, edited by Catherine Audard (Paris: Editions Autrement, 1993); "Truth, Politics and Self-Deception," *Social Research* 63 (1996); and my introduction to Nietzsche's *The Gay Science*, translated by Josefine Nauchkhoff (Cambridge: Cambridge University Press, 2001).

Index

❖   ❖   ❖   ❖   ❖